Australian & New Zealand Edition

Leadership

FOR

DUMMIES®

T0348246

Australian & New Zealand Edition

Leadership

FOR

DUMMIES®

by Kris Cole

WILEY

Wiley Publishing Australia Pty Ltd

Leadership For Dummies®

Australian & New Zealand Edition
published by
Wiley Publishing Australia Pty Ltd
42 McDougall Street
Milton, Qld 4064
www.dummies.com

Copyright © 2008 Wiley Publishing Australia Pty Ltd

The moral rights of the author have been asserted.

National Library of Australia
Cataloguing-in-Publication data

Author:	Cole, Kris.
Title:	Leadership For Dummies / author, Kris Cole.
Edition:	Australian and New Zealand ed.
ISBN:	978 073 140787 3 (pbk.)
Series:	For Dummies.
Notes:	Includes index.
Subjects:	Leadership.
Dewey Number:	658.4092

About the Author

Kris Cole, industrial psychologist and manufacturing technologist, is one of Australia's best-known trainers in the areas of leadership, management, communication and productivity. She has worked with leading organisations around the world helping people lead, communicate and work more effectively with their followers, colleagues and customers, and juggle their priorities to achieve their goals and flourish.

Kris is also Australia's No. 1 best-selling business author, with books published in seven languages. Her other books cover topics including making time work for you, workplace relations, business administration and supervision, call centre communication, a survival guide for supervisors and how to succeed at job interviews.

Kris can be contacted through her Web site, www.bax.com.au, where you can find interactive topics on business and management.

Dedication

This book is dedicated to my ancient cat, Benya, whose warm, purring body on my lap made writing 20 books (including second and third editions and overseas editions of those books) that little bit more enjoyable.

Author's Acknowledgements

Thank you to the many wonderful leaders with whom I've worked and from whom I've learned, and to all the fantastic leaders I've trained and learned from. Yours is one of the most demanding and essential roles in any organisation, whatever the size, sector or industry, and I take my hat off to you.

The wonderful team at John Wiley has been great to work worth. Thank you for being lots of fun and thoroughly professional. Thank you especially to Acquisitions Editor Charlotte Duff and Editor Carolyn Beaumont for guiding me patiently through the project.

While I'm on a roll, I would also like to heap praise upon the head of my fabulous hubby, Don, who puts up with me with grace and good humour. I take my hat off to you, too!

Publisher's Acknowledgements

We're proud of this book; please send us your comments through our Dummies online registration form located at www.dummies.com/register/.

Some of the people who helped bring this book to market include the following:

Acquisitions, Editorial and Media Development

Project Editor: Carolyn Beaumont

Acquisitions Editor: Charlotte Duff

Technical Reviewer: Jim Hayward

Editorial Manager: Gabrielle Packman

Production

Layout and Graphics: Wiley Composition Services, Wiley Art Studio

Cartoons: Glenn Lumsden

Indexer: Karen Gillen

Contents at a Glance

Table of Contents

Introduction

Congratulations on taking a big step to successful leadership by choosing to read *Leadership For Dummies*, a guide to everything you need to know to become a successful leader — or to become a better leader than you already are.

Whether you're an aspiring leader, a new leader or a seasoned leader, you probably know that quality leadership is critical to an organisation's effectiveness and to its success. Without good leaders, no organisation can achieve its objectives or come close to achieving its vision.

Leaders set the pace and build an organisation's identity. Leaders show the way. Leaders inspire, energise and make their followers feel valued and appreciated for their contributions. Leaders help people find, develop and refine their talents.

Over the past 30 years, I've worked with a variety of organisations, large and small, in a variety of sectors and industries, in many parts of the world. What I know for certain is that even when you have the best followers, the best buildings, the best technology, the best equipment and the best procedures, poor leadership can spoil every plan. Nothing is more valuable to an organisation than a successful leader.

But what is a successful leader? Many different types of effective leaders exist and every leader is different from every other leader. Successful leaders perform many of the same tasks and share the same skills and characteristics, but add their own special twists. The best leaders put their own signatures on the qualities of leadership.

About This Book

Leadership is personal. If you want to be a successful leader, you need to build a strong and flexible set of leadership muscles that define you as a leader. *Leadership For Dummies* helps you to do that.

When you put into practice the principles and techniques I explain in this book, you can earn the title of 'leader'. Your followers can look to you for encouragement and guidance and draw strength from you. Other leaders can respect you and find they can follow your lead as well. By using *Leadership For Dummies*, you can make a worthwhile and significant contribution to your organisation and to your followers, not just today and tomorrow, but as a contribution that lasts well into the future.

Although I've written what is now referred to as 'the definitive textbook on management and leadership', I'm not really into fancy theories and fancy words. I'm into what works. I'm into common sense and sound, tried-and-tested principles and approaches to leadership. I'm also into Step 1, Step 2, Step 3 simple procedures that work for you and save you from reinventing the wheel.

Rest assured, the advice and information in *Leadership For Dummies* is backed up by sound leadership theory and solid, current, cutting-edge research. But I spare you the theory and the research and the fiddly notations, which are a bit of a yawn. If you want to read the more technical stuff, then I include all the official language that you're likely to hear or might want to use as you go about your day-to-day leading. (If you aren't into that style of jargon, then I tell you the facts of leadership in plain English too.) Words that you need to know the meaning of are in italics with their definitions close by.

How to Use This Book

You may be an aspiring leader or you may recently have made the leap from being a skilled follower to a novice leader. If that's the case, consider this book to be a crash course in leadership to kick-start you on your way and guide you down the road to success. You may want to read the book through from cover to cover and mark the chapters or sections that cover information of the most immediate relevance to your situation. Then you can go back and pinpoint the most valuable tips.

If you're an experienced leader looking for a few quick hits of inspiration or answers to a few questions or dilemmas, or if you want to beef up one or two specific topics in your kitbag of skills and knowledge, you can find solutions in these pages. You can dip into sections or chapters and find what you need when you need it. The extended Table of Contents and the Index at the back of the book are designed to point you to the right places.

Whatever your leadership experience or your seniority as a leader, the type of organisation you lead in or even the number of followers you lead, *Leadership For Dummies* gives you a comprehensive overview of what you need to know and what you need to do to be a successful leader. The book even explains how to lead a virtual team of followers you seldom or never meet face-to-face; and how to lead the other types of non-traditional followers and teams that are springing up everywhere.

Long after you've read what interests you at the moment, I hope you keep this book close by you as a reference. *Leadership For Dummies* is designed for you to use as a refresher and for ideas and encouragement as you continue on your leadership journey, and for a handy just-in-time reference when you're chasing information on a specific leadership topic.

How This Book is Organised

This book is organised into six parts, each covering an important aspect of leadership. Chapters within the parts explain a topic in detail. Here's a quick overview of what you can find in each part.

Part I: What it Takes to Be a Leader

Part I gives you a rundown on what it takes to be a successful leader and reviews the skills that leaders need to master. I explain the different types or styles of leadership you need to get to know and how to decide which style to use when. I also explain the different roles of leaders — or the 'hats' you need to wear with flair. Then I explain how to develop your leadership skills and how to look, sound and act like a leader.

Part II: Leadership Is Personal

Leadership begins inside, and Part II shows you how to be a successful leader from the inside out. You discover your purpose as a leader and your most important areas of responsibility and accountability. I give you tips to boost your confidence and explain how to navigate the 'traps for new leaders'. You find out how to use your organisation's values, vision and mission and develop a team purpose that energises and inspires your followers and helps them concentrate on shared goals so that everyone is working in the same direction. You find out how to develop plans that work, how to use your limited time to best effect and how to communicate as a leader to individual followers and to groups. Finally, I explain the ins and outs of power politics and networking so that you develop and nurture the 'right' contacts and build a reputation that supports your leadership aspirations now and in the future.

Part III: The Science and Art of Leadership

Leadership may be personal but a strong body of science stands behind the art of leadership. Part III explains the nitty gritty of leadership: How to manage people's expectations; how to make your own expectations clear to others; and how to work well with people who have personalities and working styles different from yours. As well, I look at what to do when you're led by a poor leader. This part includes advice on how to bring out the best in your followers; how to keep improving the way the job is done; how to solve pesky problems and big problems; and how to make sound leadership decisions. I explain how to assign work and how to delegate your own work to others and I clue you in on what you need to know about making meetings work.

Part IV: Building and Leading a Winning Team

Leaders can't succeed if their teams don't succeed. I begin this part by describing how to introduce and lead change in this era of unrelenting change and then I turn to teams. I explain how to find the right followers for your team and how to understand what's going on inside the team you're leading. You find out how to build the strength of your team's 'muscles' and how to keep those muscles in peak condition. Then I explain how to lead the new types of teams and followers you may find yourself leading in the future.

Part V: When the Going Gets Tough

Leadership isn't a bed of roses. In fact, leaders often face challenging and difficult situations, need to deliver unpleasant news and need to hold difficult conversations. That's when your mettle is really tested. Part V shows you how to lead followers who don't follow and what to do with followers who don't perform. You also find out how to avoid falling into deep waters and what to do when you find yourself in trouble.

Part VI: The Part of Tens

The final two chapters are a potpourri of ideas that you can dip into when you have a few moments or need some inspiration. These ideas are inspired by the best leaders I've known and worked with over the years and who distil the mix of skills and experience that makes them successful. You find out the ten qualities that characterise successful leaders and the good news is that you can learn, develop and perfect each of these ten traits. You also find out the ten moves you can make that can have the biggest impact on making you a successful leader.

Icons Used in This Book

To guide you and draw your attention to important points in *Leadership For Dummies*, you can search out helpful icons scattered through this book. The icons aim to help you pinpoint information that may help you now or in the future if you want to dip back in to check some information.

This icon highlights information that's particularly handy to remember. I think all the advice in this book is worth remembering but these juicy bits really stand out.

Some readers like to delve into the technical terminology and believe me, leadership has its share. If you want to know the lingo, then this icon can point you at the smart jargon and the heady information that you may want to use (and understand) when talking the language of leadership.

This icon targets handy hints that can help make your leadership successful.

Heed the cautions that come with this icon. You can save time and trouble by avoiding difficult and dangerous situations, thanks to the advice you find here.

Part I
What it Takes to Be a Leader

Glenn Lumsden

*'Leading by example sounds like a lot of hard work ...
couldn't I just rule by fear and loathing like Grandpa?'*

In this part . . .

This part gives you the grounding you need to become a successful leader. You find out what leadership is and what it isn't. I take you through the realities of leadership and show you that the ways you lead people can change, depending on the situation and your followers. As well, I outline the characteristics of a leader and explain the different leadership styles and the different leadership roles — or 'hats', which you need to wear comfortably, with confidence and a touch of panache. Finally, I help you identify your personal path to success.

Chapter 1

What Leaders Are and What Leaders Aren't

Can you imagine a world without leaders? Who would help you achieve the goals you want to achieve? Who would provide the energy you need when your spirits flag or when you feel overwhelmed? Who would stand up and speak out in a crisis? Who would organise people to focus on a goal and work together to achieve it? Who would give you something to strive for and help you grow to improve your skills?

Leaders are needed in all walks of life. Rock groups and orchestras need leaders. So do museums, sports teams, cafés, clubs, pubs and hotels. Volunteer groups, science labs, countries and major corporations need leaders. Leadership is everywhere and leaders come in all shapes and sizes. Some are tall, some are short, some are geeks, some are athletes. Some leaders are formally appointed; many are not — some people just naturally go to these 'unofficial' leaders with ideas and questions and ask for advice and assistance because of the way these people show personal leadership qualities or expertise.

On the surface, various leaders may seem to be different, but what these leaders do is essentially the same. An amazing 18,890 books on leadership are available on Amazon.com, all purporting to know the secrets of leadership.

But leadership has no secrets. There aren't any magic tonics, mysterious rituals or special skills known to only 18,890 authors who are prepared to share them. What is important about leadership — and what I share with you in this book based on my work in the field — is a lot of common sense, as well as tested principles of leadership that are divided into general approaches or specific strategies that can make you a successful leader.

Defining Leadership

A fun activity for leadership-training programs is to ask people attending for their definition of leadership. A leader on one program said:

> 'Leadership isn't about *making* people work; it's about *letting* people work.'

Another person said:

> 'A leader is not a teller but a guide.'

Here's another definition of leadership that I like:

> 'Leadership is getting things done through others.'

If you take two organisations, which are absolutely identical in every way — in products, technology, buildings, systems, equipment and so on — the organisation with better leaders performs better, every time. Leadership is essential to getting results because leaders — not plant, equipment and technology — establish and communicate a vision and set goals worth working towards. Leaders focus their followers' efforts, harness their energies and help them flourish.

Japanese people have a saying that leadership is like air — necessary for life, but impossible to see or touch. Leadership is an elusive quality that inspires, persuades and shows followers the way. Leadership is strengthened by invisible but powerful qualities and skills, such as integrity and courage, a sense of fair play, self-mastery, clear thinking and honesty. (I examine these aspects of leadership in Chapters 2, 3 and 4.) Leadership is also a state of mind. Leaders need to *want* to lead and to *feel* like leaders.

Confucius taught that talent, virtue, behaviour, character, conduct, education and ability — not birth or blood — make a person worthy to lead. He also taught that leaders should exist only for the welfare of those they are leading; and leaders who abuse their power lose their mandate to lead. That's a powerful leadership state of mind and one paralleled in recent corporate history, which has seen a number of leaders of failed corporations deposed and even jailed.

My childhood leaders

When I was 7 years old, I delivered newspapers for a living. I hopped on my bike and rode all over the neighbourhood while everyone else was still in bed. I didn't have a leader and I only had to lead myself. When I was 9 years old, I started hanging out at the apple stand next door. Mr McGregor owned the orchard and sold apples by the bushel and homemade apple cider by the gallon from his roadside stand. After a while, I was put 'in charge' of the stand — the 'displays', the 'point-of-sale' material and, eventually, the cash box. Looking back, Mr McGregor was a leader in that he showed me what to do, gave me assignments and held me accountable for carrying them out properly, and gradually increased my 'responsibilities'. I'm sure he always kept an eagle eye out, watching my progress and making sure I was okay because that's what leaders do too.

When I was 15, I got a 'real' job, waitressing at Parker's Restaurant. I worked there for seven years, through high school and university. The chef was named Bill and I didn't know it then, but he and Ma Parker were both extraordinary leaders who had the 'front of house' and

kitchen staff working together like an Olympic relay team. If I brought a plate back into the kitchen that wasn't practically licked clean, Bill immediately asked why: Didn't the customer like the food? Bill taught me a lot about the importance of happy customers. He also tried to teach me about food presentation, but I never was very good at it, which only goes to show the importance of knowing your strengths and developing them, rather than trying to be someone you're not (see Chapter 3 for more on being true to your particular talents).

Ma Parker was a leader, too. She made clear what she wanted in no uncertain terms. Boy was she strict! I loved her, though. Every night after the restaurant closed and the staff finished cleaning up, I'd go to her for my pay. She'd sit me down and say a few words about how hard I'd worked, and occasionally she'd mention some task I hadn't managed quite up to her standards ('Next time, Kris ...'). She'd tell me when she next wanted me in, and what extra duties I'd be doing (usually in the kitchen). Then she'd slip a few extra dollars into my pay envelope, with a wink and another thankyou for my hard work.

Recognising Leaders

Throughout history, leaders have been commanders and controllers. That style of leadership worked when kings, emperors and generals led conquering armies and ruled the earth.

As the world and ways of working became more complex, a bit of 'humanism' was introduced to the roles of commanding and controlling. However, not until the 1990s, and the advent of the global knowledge economy, did people truly realise that behaving like a dictator just doesn't suit modern life and times.

The leader whose behaviour is opposite to that of an aggressive dictator doesn't have much luck either. I call these 'do nothing' leaders — the types that are about as useful as a limp ruler. Other types of poor leaders exist too — some toxic, while others hold back their followers in less poisonous ways (see Chapter 9 for more on poor leadership). Inadequate leaders do triple damage by

- ✔ Costing their organisations a lot of money when they have to replace followers who leave in droves
- ✔ Failing to lead and inspire
- ✔ Preventing — simply by being there — someone else from fulfilling that essential leadership role more effectively

Today's successful leaders involve their followers in projects, support their followers and coach and inspire their followers. Today's leaders aren't automatically granted respect and loyalty because of their titles; they must earn respect and loyalty. Today's leaders introduce more change to their teams in one year than leaders used to introduce in their entire careers. Modern leaders need to be more flexible, more able to cope with uncertainty, more strategic in their thinking and far, far, more skilled than leaders of the past (for more on styles of leadership, see Chapter 2).

Leading isn't what it used to be

Today's world is different from yesterday's world and today's followers are similarly different. Australian and New Zealand leaders are leading in a new world economy, a changing society and an uncertain and unpredictable environment and depending on ever-more powerful technology to get the job done. Australian and New Zealand followers are demanding more flexibility and more involvement and they are a more diverse group of people than ever before. Followers are becoming older and include more women, as well as more people from minority groups and more people with disabilities. The types of employees are also more varied and include part-time workers, job sharers, virtual employees, telecommuters, casual, contract and temporary workers and so on. (Chapters 16 and 17 have more on who makes up the teams of followers.)

Leading or managing?

I'm not going to get hung up about this subject so I'll say it here and leave it: Leading and managing are different skills. Basically, you can manage processes and systems. But when you want to get the best performances out of people, you need to lead them.

- ✔ Managers control and administrate.
- ✔ Leaders create and innovate.
- ✔ Managers keep things running smoothly by marshalling resources, planning, programming and progressing work.
- ✔ Leaders initiate changes to systems and processes to enhance their followers' performances. Leaders set visions, inspire, enthuse and get into their followers' hearts and minds.

Table 1-1 shows other differences in the ways managers and leaders deal with followers.

Table 1-1	Leading versus Managing
Leaders	*Managers*
Coach	Inspect
Encourage	Direct
Inspire people	Organise people
Lead by example	Rely on authority
Show	Tell
Support	Monitor

Finding the Source of Your Leadership Strength

If all this information sounds daunting, take heart. Leading well is much easier after you build up a strong set of leadership 'muscles', beginning with your core muscles — your values. Knowing and acting in line with your values is the first step to leadership strength. The second step to leadership strength is developing the mindsets leaders need (I cover both of these steps in Chapter 3).

Leaders are self-disciplined and self-controlled beings. Leaders consistently act with integrity and honesty. Their self-respect and respect for others support them in voicing their ideas and opinions clearly — and support them when they have to deliver 'hard messages' tactfully, considerately and kindly.

The qualities (muscles) that strengthen your primary leadership skills are

- Being engaged in and enjoying what you're doing
- Focusing on what matters most
- Mastering yourself
- Setting high standards and challenging goals
- Staying true to your values
- Taking the initiative and acting, rather than reacting

These muscles give you confidence, calm your nerves and help you look, sound and act like a leader (for more on building your mental muscles, see Chapters 3 and 4). With these qualities, you can respond suitably — not react unthinkingly — and behave with integrity. These muscles attract strong followers, and other effective leaders, to you. The way you lead your followers pivots on the way you use your leadership muscles.

Understanding Yourself and Others

Leadership is a journey of discovery, much of it about yourself, and the better you understand yourself, the better you can lead. Self-awareness is an essential requirement of successful leadership. True leaders understand their motivations, feelings, beliefs, values, attitudes and views about the world around them and acknowledge them as the underlying cause of their actions. Successful leaders share similar mental attitudes and beliefs about themselves, others and the world around them, which gives them the inner clout they need, especially in tricky situations and when the going gets tough. (See Chapter 3 for more tips on leaders' values and mindsets; Chapter 18 for how to deal with difficult followers; and Chapter 20 for what to do when circumstances seem to conspire against you.)

Leaders recognise their personal biases and limitations and use this understanding to improve their thinking and planning. They know their motives and make sure they don't act out of spite, to 'get even', to be hurtful or purely in their own self-interest. They pursue feedback that may reveal errors in their judgements or approach and make needed adjustments.

(See Chapter 19 for more about recognising your biases and motives and Chapter 20 to find out about using feedback to improve your leadership.)

Leaders are aware of their own strengths and shortcomings and know what works best for them. Leaders know, for instance, whether variety or routine works best for them, whether details or the big-picture overview works best for them, and whether they feel more comfortable in a large or small, formal or informal organisation.

Leaders know it isn't 'all about me' and use their self-understanding to understand others. When you can apply that skill, you can decide which followers to invite onto your team, which followers to assign to particular duties, how to work well with your own leader and other leaders in your organisation, and how to sell your ideas persuasively. (Chapter 3 has more information on understanding yourself and working well with others.)

Leaders understand that people do what they do to achieve a goal that they consciously or unconsciously want to achieve — either from habit or to act in line with their deep-seated beliefs and values. This knowledge helps leaders to deal with people fairly and with compassion, and quashes the tendency to make a judgement on that person's methods.

Playing the Role of Leader

Lest you think leadership sounds a bit 'Pollyanna-ish' — optimistic about everyone and every situation — I can tell you that leaders can be tough when they need to be and they know when that time has arrived. (See Chapters 18, 19 and 20 for what to do when the going gets tough.) Leaders understand power — how to get it and how to use it — and they have the sense to connect with people who can help them and who they can help in return with advice, assistance and support (Chapter 8 has more on this). Building supportive networks also makes leading a little less lonely than it otherwise may be.

Leadership isn't a title. Leadership is about

- ✔ Acting and making plans happen
- ✔ Being a resource for your followers
- ✔ Being someone with whom your leader and other leaders can bounce around ideas
- ✔ Being someone your leader and other leaders can call on for advice

> ✔ Finding out what information and resources your followers need and finding ways to get that information and resources
>
> ✔ Taking care of the task at hand, your team and your individual followers (see Chapter 15 for more on how leaders look after the task, the team and their individual followers)

To be a leader, you need to focus, and stay focused, on what matters most. That's why every good leader I work with can reel off, without hesitation, their seven (or so) most important key result areas, their areas of accountability and responsibility, and which important measures of success to track to make sure they're on course. The best leaders also know why they, personally, are leading, and they can articulate those reasons in a single, clear sentence. (See Chapters 4 and 6 for more on finding your purpose as a leader and setting priorities.)

Because their days are hectic and their time is at a premium, leaders are organised and efficient. They have a solid grip on the way they use time so it doesn't whoosh by, leaving too few results in its wake. (Chapter 6 has more information on how to become more organised and efficient.)

More than anything else, though, successful leaders communicate — frequently and clearly. These leaders set the pace and set the example. I believe these qualities are the essence of leadership. (Chapter 7 is packed with information about how leaders communicate and Chapter 14 explains how to apply that information to leading change.)

Pinpointing Leadership Skills

You won't find a mould that churns out leaders. Every leader is different, every follower is different and every situation calling for leadership is different. However, leaders do share a package of mindsets, attributes, knowledge and skills that combine to influence followers to achieve meaningful, worthwhile goals.

In fact, true leaders have a huge swag full of highly developed and polished skills that keep them on track, attract followers to them and keep their followers on track, too. Leaders have skills that help determine what track to take and how to make that track attractive to their followers. Leaders also have skills to help their followers successfully navigate the bumps and holes along their chosen tracks. I think of the vast array of skills that leaders need as skills of the heart, skills of the hands and skills of the mind. Each of these sets of skills overlaps and intertwines with the others.

Listening to your heart

Imagining a good leader who lacks people skills is an impossibility for me. I've known many a manager who lacks people skills — but never a successful leader who lacks them. *People skills* help leaders inspire followers and bring out their potential. People skills, such as communicating effectively, help leaders build strong teams and help leaders work effectively with a wide range of people and followers. The ability to give and gather good information, persuade people, choose words with care and turn arguments into agreements, all depend on skills of the heart.

Skills of the heart enable leaders to see themselves as others see them. Equally importantly, skills of the heart enable leaders to see followers as the followers see themselves. This enables leaders to understand where people are coming from and, as a result, communicate effectively with them.

Skills of the heart also help leaders with everyday leadership tasks — assigning work and delegating effectively, participating, leading meetings efficiently and so on. (Chapters 12 and 13 fill you in on assigning work and leading meetings.) Heart skills also help leaders build helpful networks so they can draw on assistance from others to help reach their goals. Skills of the heart even help leaders to use their powers wisely and well. (Chapter 8 explains how to build and benefit from networks and how to build and use your leadership power.)

Applying hands-on skills

Leadership isn't all about charisma and communication. To lead effectively, you also need hands-on leadership skills. You need to know how to identify suitable followers, train, coach and develop them and bring out their best qualities. You need to know how to plan and resolve problems, reach sensible and workable decisions and deal with disruptive followers and followers who aren't performing. Planning and leading meetings need hands-on skills — that is, skills of the hands as well as the heart.

Leaders also need to know how to get through fast-paced days with a sense of equanimity and calmness by managing their time, dealing with interruptions, staying focused on their priorities, organising themselves and staying on top of their many duties and responsibilities. (Chapter 6 describes how to keep your cool and get your important duties done.)

The specific technical skills that leaders need depend on who they're leading and where they're leading. A sound understanding of the nature of what their followers do — whether or not the leader is an expert in that field — the systems their followers use and the procedures they follow, gives leaders a measure of credibility and authority. This knowledge allows leaders to establish meaningful measures of success and to monitor the outputs of their followers.

The 21st-century leader must also have solid information and communication technology skills. These skills enable leaders to find, organise and use information, and to collaborate effectively with people from a distance.

Using your mind skills

You don't have to be a genius to be a leader, not by any means. But you do need thinking skills to help you think through situations and problems clearly. Leaders who can't get to the heart of a problem and fix it properly, who can't anticipate future problems and act to prevent them, and who can't recognise possible ramifications of actions and decisions aren't leaders for long. (Chapter 11 takes you through the straightforward steps that help you to approach problems and decisions systematically and analytically.)

Leaders need to be able to coordinate and keep an eye on the varied activities of their followers and step back to see the overall project — where their organisation and team are headed, and how each part of the organisation fits into the other parts and into the community, country and, often, the world. Leaders need to make sure their followers understand the organisation's goals too. These conceptual skills let leaders offer a vision that energises and inspires followers, gets them moving in the same direction and allows them to keep calm when all around them are losing their cool. (Chapter 5 looks at the bigger picture of your organisation's values, vision and strategy and how to use that big picture to enthuse and energise your team.)

Chapter 2

Leading — with the Right Style and the Right 'Hat'

In This Chapter

▶ Checking out the four main ways to lead

▶ Figuring out when to use which style of leadership

▶ Choosing the right leadership 'hat' to wear

Sadly, not all leaders are good leaders. Some are tyrants, some abuse their position of trust, some are control freaks and others are so 'laid back' they don't really lead at all.

Some leaders are able to transform entire organisations by gaining their followers' trust and confidence, and giving them an exciting vision and a clear (if sometimes difficult) path to follow to reach it. These leaders are the rare ones you hear about in the media. Most work long hours and devote themselves to the success of their organisations, often at the expense of their personal lives.

But rather than concentrate on the bad leaders or the rare few fascinating and transformational leaders at the top of big companies, this chapter describes the good, solid, everyday leaders that don't rely on their personal magnetism and charisma to pull rabbits out of hats. In this chapter, you find out how capable leaders lead and what strengths they offer their followers and their organisations, which is where good leadership — the kind that is vital to every group's success — begins. Here I introduce you to the four main ways to lead that you, as a leader, need to master. And I explain how you decide which of the four ways to use when. You also discover in this chapter the various roles leaders play, or the 'hats' leaders can wear and the skills you need to wear each hat successfully.

Working Out the Leadership Style to Use

You have four main styles of leadership to choose from, but your aim isn't to choose just one style and stick to it. Instead, your best bet is to master each of the four leadership styles and then figure out which of the four styles best suits

- The goals you want to achieve
- The organisation in which you're a leader
- The people you're leading

You also need to be comfortable leading in the style you choose. If you feel uncomfortable with the leadership style that the situation you're leading in requires, then your leadership becomes more stressful than successful.

Leading from the front — a nose-to-the-grindstone leader

A leader who leads from the front firmly concentrates on the task at hand and makes sure everyone follows the rules and does their jobs in the prescribed way. This directive kind of leader

- Plans and schedules work
- Plays a major role in solving work-related problems
- Provides plenty of training to make sure people know what to do and how to do it
- Sets objectives for people to work towards
- Stays close to followers and keeps a watchful eye open to offer help if help is needed

Leaders who lead from the front are known as *autocratic* leaders and *authoritarian* leaders but this incorrectly implies that 'follow-me' leaders are 'harsh' or 'nasty'. Effective nose-to-the-grindstone leaders are always civil and respectful towards followers. However, these leaders concentrate on the task first.

Nose-to-the-grindstone leadership suits routine, repetitive jobs where 'one best way' really is the right way. This style also works well with these types of followers:

- ✔ Inexperienced
- ✔ Non skilled
- ✔ Semi skilled
- ✔ Unmotivated

Nose-to-the-grindstone leadership also works well in situations with large numbers of followers. If those circumstances apply to you, your followers and their jobs, you can be confident in your choice to lead from the front.

Here are some other scenarios where you may choose to lead from the front:

- ✔ In an emergency situation (such as when time is tight or when a crisis is looming) when people expect someone to take the reins
- ✔ In times of major change (such as an organisation restructuring or a merger) when people look for strong leadership
- ✔ When you inherit a team that doesn't work well together

If you're a bit of a control freak, your natural inclination is likely to be to march to the front when leadership is needed. That approach isn't always the best way to lead. You need to be able to drop a style of leadership and pick up a style more suited to the situation and the followers' needs when required.

Leading from the centre — a join-with-me leader

Join-with-me leaders, who have faith in their followers and believe their followers are trying to do their best, lead from the centre. These leaders

- ✔ Agree on goals with followers, discuss and develop plans with followers, and coach followers so that their contributions keep improving
- ✔ Explain why the task needs to be done and, when the work needs to be done in a certain way, show their followers (patiently, of course) how to do the work
- ✔ Keep followers involved in what's happening and invite and consider followers' opinions and suggestions

Three degrees of centre

A rugby team may have only one centre but when it comes to leading, three centres are called into play:

✔ You can bring in a bit of leading from the front and mix it with a bit of leading from the front of centre when your followers aren't fully trained or experienced. Then tell your followers why something needs to be done, or done in a certain way. (The term for this is — wait for it — *explaining*.)

✔ You can lead from the very centre and sit down with your followers, explain the situation, listen to their thoughts, questions and ideas, consider what you hear and then make the final decision yourself. (The term for this is *consulting*.)

✔ Or you can move towards leading from the back. When you lead from the back of centre, you thrash out a decision or problem with your followers and, together, figure out the best approach. (The term for this is *participating*.)

When you're leading from the centre, you pull in the reins a bit while people are learning — and you gradually loosen the reins as your followers build experience and confidence. You skilfully vary the amount of overseeing, training and coaching support you offer, depending on each follower's level of skill and experience. The task at hand and your followers are uppermost in your thoughts. (The terms for those who lead from the centre are *democratic* leaders and *participative* leaders.)

You can choose to lead from the centre when you're

✔ Working with motivated followers who like to be involved and who have relevant experience and expertise to offer

✔ Working with small, highly skilled teams undertaking complex or flexible tasks in a dynamic and rapidly changing work environment or marketplace

Leading from the centre doesn't work so well in situations where

✔ Jobs are very straightforward, routine and easy to learn

✔ Jobs are done in one best way and you need to make sure your followers follow the correct procedure

✔ People really aren't interested in becoming involved

Consider leading from the front in these three situations (refer to the previous section on leading from the front).

The leadership sands of time

Over the decades, leadership has taken on the following roles.

- ✔ **1960s:** Command and control was at the forefront.

- ✔ **1970s:** A few women were let into the hallowed halls of power, and sensitivity to people's feelings became more important.

- ✔ **1980s:** 'Hero' leaders ransacked and 'de-layered' companies. Leadership was also about coming to grips with 'new-fangled technology', such as faxes and computers.

- ✔ **1990s:** Leaders set about the task of winning back trust (after the savage 'downsizing'

of companies) and persuading followers to work towards a common goal.

- ✔ **2000s:** This is an era of change and of conceptual goals, such as adding vision, value, ethics and integrity to the workplace; and loosening the reins to encourage more creative input from followers.

So what of the future? The 2010s is expected to be about leading change and bringing out the best qualities in ever-more diverse teams of followers, including remote followers who leaders seldom or never meet in person.

Leading from the back — an over-to-you leader

Leaders who lead from the back don't take command because they don't need to — their followers know what they're doing and can be relied on to achieve their goals. Sometimes over-to-you leadership is called *laissez-faire leadership*, often translated as '*do nothing*' *leadership*. However, this isn't the type of leading from the back I'm talking about. The type of over-to-you leadership that works is called *free rein leadership*.

Leaders who lead from the back focus on their followers more than the task. These leaders

- ✔ Begin by making sure their followers know clearly what each person's job is and what results each person needs to achieve

- ✔ Enable followers to suggest their own targets, work plans and schedules

- ✔ Offer general directions or guidance or enable followers to decide how to tackle jobs

- ✔ Provide or assist followers to obtain what they need to do their jobs (such as time, information, equipment and so on)

- ✔ Stand back and enable followers to do their work without interference

- ✔ Support followers when they need assistance but never 'hover' over followers while they work

You can breathe a sigh of relief and take a 'back seat' when your plans are going well and your followers are

✔ Clear about what's expected of them and how to deliver it; and you don't need to constantly tell them what to do

✔ Committed to deliver results

✔ Cooperating well

✔ Motivated and taking responsibility

When a crisis or a major change or uncertainty looms, shift your leadership style from over-to-you leadership to leading from the front. When tasks require followers to use established methods and face goals that must be met regularly, leading from the back probably isn't the best way to lead. And when you're wrong about your followers' skills and motivation, and you discover they need more guidance than a back-seat driver offers, then the followers are likely to flounder and fail — and, as their leader, so are you.

Leading from underneath — a supportive leader

Whether leading from the front, the centre or the back, the best leaders see themselves as people who serve their organisation and their followers. They understand that leadership is about building trust, behaving with integrity and honesty and engaging the hearts and minds of their followers in order to produce results of lasting value. These leaders are coaches who smooth the path so their followers can progress more easily and are precisely the sorts of leaders most needed in our age of 'mean and lean' organisations and skills shortages.

Leaders who lead from underneath care about their followers and, in return, their followers care about them. Supportive leaders

✔ Are stewards of the future and can be counted on to behave honourably

✔ Have strong leadership 'muscles', based on their own personal values and a strong sense of 'right' and 'wrong'

✔ Provide a strong and energising vision for followers to follow and on which to concentrate their efforts

To successfully lead from underneath, you need to

- ✔ Be able to see 'the big picture' and the implications of actions and decisions
- ✔ Be willing to work in the best interests of those around you and see your role as helping people succeed
- ✔ Have a genuine desire to help your organisation and your followers become the best achievers they can be

Whether you're leading from the front, centre or back, you can probably achieve the best results by thinking in terms of serving others, as well as your organisation and yourself. In fact, the word for this type of leader is *servant leader*. (See Chapters 15 and 16 for more information on how to use each of the four leadership styles to build a strong team.)

It's moments like these ...

Moments like these ... mostly appear when we're relaxed and even daydreaming.

In olde Syracuse, King Hieron asked the Greek mathematician Archimedes to figure out whether the gold crown he'd had made really was pure gold or whether its maker had cheated him by adding silver.

Archimedes was stumped. Inspiration finally struck while he was in the bath. He noticed how the water level rose as he settled in and he realised that the crown would displace less water if it were pure gold than if it contained silver, a less dense metal.

Rumour has it that Archimedes was so pleased with his clever solution that he sprang out of the bath and ran naked through the streets shouting '*Eureka!*' (Greek for 'I've found it!').

It's true. Eureka really is a Greek word, which makes it kind of appropriate, at least for you Victorian readers, with the Eureka Stockade in your state's history and Melbourne with its large Greek-speaking population.

Aussie digressions aside, great ideas favour the prepared mind — but only when it's a relaxed mind. Leaders need to make the time to 'veg out' — not occasionally, but regularly. The next time you need inspiration, chill out. Step back, relax and let your subconscious mind take over for a while — just like Archimedes in the bathtub. (Try not to run naked through the streets like Archimedes when the solution pops into your mind.)

Arthur knows best

The most common reward for an unselfish act is the personal satisfaction it brings. But material rewards are known to follow people who help others, too.

In the legend of King Arthur, Arthur was an early example of a supportive person whose unselfish act in serving another brought him a kingdom.

In the story of King Arthur, the former king dies and a successor needs to be chosen to rule the kingdom. But who is to be the successor?

To find the new king, a sword is magically embedded into a rock with only its handle showing. Only he who is to be crowned king is able to withdraw the sword.

Many try but no-one can remove the sword. Until . . .

One day, Arthur, a humble peasant farmer, is assisting a knight in a contest. The knight he serves loses his sword and Arthur goes in search of another for his master to use. Keen not to delay the joust, he runs to the sword in the stone, grasps the sword's handle and smoothly pulls the blade from the rock. When the people realise what Arthur has done, they proclaim him the new king.

Choosing the Right Leadership Style for the Situation

Knowing which leadership approach to use — and when — is the tricky part. As a leader, you can focus on the task first (nose-to-the-grindstone), on people first (over-to-you) or on both, more or less equally (join-with-me).

Because a successful leader in one situation can be a failed leader in another, figuring out where to lead from, in each situation you're leading in, is important. Think about the task at hand, your followers and what leadership style is likely to work best. And you need to be both comfortable and competent in your choice.

When deciding which leadership style to use, consider the make-up of the task at hand in these terms:

✔ **Complexity:** Think about how complex or ambiguous the task is. When established procedures need to be followed, lead from the front or centre, depending on how skilled your followers are. When a lot of leeway is allowed with the way people can work, move back.

- ✔ **Importance:** Think about how critical the task is or how big a potential disaster it can be if the work is done poorly or incorrectly. The more critical the task is, the more you need to lead from the front.

- ✔ **Time constraints:** The tighter the time frame, the more you need to lead from the front.

When deciding which leadership style to use, consider the followers you're leading in these ways:

- ✔ **Autonomy:** Think about how much independence your followers want. When followers value their independence, lead from the centre. When followers are less skilled, lead from the front or the front of centre. When followers are very skilled, lead from the back.

- ✔ **Confidence:** Consider how much confidence you have in your followers and their abilities. The more you trust them, the further you can move back.

- ✔ **Experience:** When you're satisfied your followers are confident, skilled and experienced, you can lead from the back. The less confident, skilled and experienced your followers are, the further forward you need to move.

- ✔ **Numbers of people:** Be conscious of how many followers you're leading. The more followers you're leading, the more you need to move towards leading from the front.

- ✔ **Previous history:** Take note of the type of leadership your followers are used to receiving. Too sudden a change in the way you lead can come as an unwelcome surprise, at least initially. If you need to change, adjust your position gradually.

- ✔ **Responsibility:** Evaluate how willing your followers are to become involved or take responsibility. If they want to become involved and are very skilled, lead from the back. If they're less skilled, move towards leading from the centre or front of centre.

Understand the prevailing leadership style in your organisation. You're not going to get far marching against the prevailing wind. Here's the bottom line: You can lead from anywhere but you need to lead from the right place at the right time with the right followers.

Producing a leadership style to suit every occasion requires suppleness, flexibility and strong leadership muscles (see Chapter 3 for more on this subject). To develop a full suite of the four leadership styles, you can work on improving any that you consider weaker than the others. You can also find some good role models for particular styles and watch them closely. Look, listen and learn from the other leaders. When you feel comfortable with a particular style, give it a try and ask for feedback from your colleagues.

If the Hat Fits ...

Will Shakespeare wrote in his play *As You Like It*: 'All the world's a stage ... and one man in his time plays many parts.' People today play many parts at the same time, too. Here I describe the different parts (or roles) people play as similar to wearing different 'hats'.

You know how everyone wears different hats in different life situations. One afternoon you may be formal and focused in a job interview, and that night you may be letting your hair down on the dance floor. Like everyone, leaders wear different hats in their different leadership situations. This doesn't mean that people behave falsely; when it comes to leadership, playing many parts means leaders need to be flexible and able to rise to the demands of a situation by doing what other people expect of them and what they expect of themselves.

Okay, now try these questions. As a leader, how do you behave

- ✔ When delivering a speech on behalf of your organisation?
- ✔ When training your followers for a specific task?
- ✔ When you need to admonish a follower for behaving in an unsafe manner?

Right, so each of these situations requires you to wear a different hat. See? It's easy.

The more you think about it, the more you can see how many hats you wear in your professional, as well as your private, life. And, you can probably see how leaders often need to wear two or three hats at the same time!

This section explains the various leadership hats that you, as a leader, can wear. Don't be concerned; it's fascinating. (Or is that fascinator?) I put them on three different hat racks: one for your people hats, another for your information hats and a third for your decision-maker hats. Then I offer you a hat rack for your roles as an employee, colleague and follower, and another for the hats you wear in your personal life. (I do like to keep things tidy!)

Just as in fashion, some of these leadership hats may not suit you; and you don't have to wear each of them with perfect panache. But you do need to wear each of them with some degree of comfort. You also need to understand what each hat represents and know when you need to wear a particular hat.

If you can't wear a hat convincingly, appoint someone to wear it for you until you can wear it with ease. And be alert to the dangers of wearing some hats too often and others not often enough. All becomes clear as you read on.

People hats

Perhaps more than any other skill, leaders need to be able to work effectively with people. Leaders need to motivate, encourage, persuade, assist and learn from people. Leaders need to be able to explain 'bigger pictures', such as an organisation's vision and goals, or the need for change in an organisation (see Chapter 5 for more on vision and Chapter 14 for more on change). Leaders who don't wear their people hats well are, at best, mediocre leaders.

The formal top hat

Leaders wear a *formal* hat when they're acting in an official capacity, such as representing their organisation or followers at events, presenting awards, making speeches and signing documents, such as contracts or employees' timesheets.

To wear a formal hat successfully, you need a sense of grandeur and drama and a dash of charisma. You need to look and act like a leader. (Chapters 3, 4 and 7 have more information on how to work on these leadership character traits and skills.)

The guide hat

The *guide* hat is the one that 21st-century leaders wear most often. They wear the guide hat to

- Discuss goals
- Discuss the best way to get the work done
- Lead their teams every day
- Make sure team members are progressing on schedule

Wearing the guide hat, leaders make sure their followers understand what they're supposed to be doing and that the followers are rewarded — psychologically and materially — for doing their work. Leaders also wear a guide hat when they correct or coach followers who don't do what they're supposed to do. (Chapters 18 and 19 explain how to wear the guide hat to help followers improve their performance.)

To wear the guide hat comfortably, you need to excel at

- ✔ Coaching, solving problems and making decisions
- ✔ Organising resources such as time, equipment and funding
- ✔ Organising yourself and your followers (check out Chapter 6 on this subject)
- ✔ Planning ongoing work as well as special projects
- ✔ Watching each follower's progress and the progress of the team as a whole

The connector hat

Leaders wear the *connector* hat when they're communicating with people, both inside and outside their organisation. Leaders need to be completely comfortable wearing this hat because communication is a large and important part of everything a leader does.

To wear the connector hat, you need to be able to

- ✔ Bring people on side
- ✔ Communicate clearly one-on-one and with groups
- ✔ Keep your followers up to date with the organisation's plans and changes of plans
- ✔ Lead and participate in meetings effectively (see Chapter 13 for more on meetings)
- ✔ Quickly develop comfortable relationships with people

Information hats

Leaders need a lot of information, which they pull together from many sources. Some of it they gather with their eyes and ears, observing events that are happening around them, inside their teams, between people all over the organisation, and by listening carefully to what people say (and don't say). Leaders collect and collate information from spreadsheets and produce new spreadsheets, particularly using figures that show how their operations are tracking against their success measures. And leaders gather information through reading — professional journals, memos, reports and so on.

Leaders are also important sources of information to their teams, to their own leader and to other leaders in their organisation, as well as to people outside — sometimes individually and sometimes to groups through presentations and meetings, both formal and informal. Leaders present their ideas and opinions, lobby for resources, write reports and memos and promote their team's results and successes.

Because you're going to be wearing *information hats* a lot, you need to

- ✔ Be able to both give and gather information, using spoken words as well as written words
- ✔ Be attentive and perceptive
- ✔ Be comfortable speaking to people individually and in groups
- ✔ Know how to be an effective meeting participant and meeting leader

You can find more information about communicating in Chapter 7, and check out meetings in Chapter 13.

The observer hat

Leaders need to be ever watchful and alert to how their team and operations are tracking. Off the hat rack comes the *observer* hat. Leaders also wear the observer hat when gathering evidence from databases and reports, as well as through clues and signals, both subtle and obvious.

To successfully wear the observer hat, you need to

- ✔ Be sensitive to signs that indicate trouble is brewing
- ✔ Understand facts and figures that tell you how you and your followers are performing so that you can pinpoint individuals and problem areas that need your attention and help

The explainer hat

The *explainer* hat is for sharing information or explaining situations or data to followers, senior management, colleagues, work teams, customers, suppliers, other organisations, government bodies and the general public.

To wear the explainer hat successfully, you need to work confidently with your customers and followers in these ways:

- ✔ **Customers and suppliers:** You may need to work with customers to find ways to meet their needs or to explain your organisation's requirements to suppliers. The explainer hat enables you to show you're willing to work with your customers and suppliers to find the best way to obtain what you and your team need.
- ✔ **Followers:** You need to be able to confidently explain complex ideas, strategies, plans and results to your team and others in a clear, yet succinct, way.

The spokesperson hat

The *spokesperson* hat is also one to don when you're sharing information. However, this hat is a more formal hat than the explainer hat (refer to the previous section).

Reach for your spokesperson hat when representing

- Your followers to management — and management to your followers. For example, you may need to be spokesperson for both sides in discussions over workplace agreements or when announcing the results of a project.
- Your organisation to external people and groups.

Vision and loyalty figure highly when you wear your spokesperson hat. Pop this hat on when you need

- An understanding of the 'big picture' (this is covered further in Chapter 5)
- Sensitivity and empathy (see more on these subjects in Chapter 7)
- The ability to convincingly explain a point of view that may differ from your point of view — for example, when senior management decides on a course of action that adversely affects your team, but is for the greater good of the organisation
- The ability to see situations from another person's point of view (even when you don't agree with that point of view)

If you sometimes see a decision as unreasonable or inappropriate, you may be seeing only part of the picture and you may not have the information that your manager or the decision-maker has. In this situation, do your best to understand the background to the decision so that you can explain the decision to your followers.

Decision-maker hats

Leaders wear their various *decision-maker* hats whenever they're called on to make decisions involving people, methods, resources or plans. The decisions can be large or small, routine or complex; may affect a large number of people or only a few; may affect a large part of an organisation or only the leader's own team or area of responsibility.

To make decisions well, you need to

- ✔ Be level-headed enough never to act in haste
- ✔ Consider your followers as well as the wider organisation and, when necessary, the wider community
- ✔ Draw on your creativity as well as your ability to think logically
- ✔ Stay alert and clear-headed to consider all the possible decisions and their potential consequences

The initiator hat

Leaders wear the *initiator* hat when they're

- ✔ Looking for ways to improve procedures, systems or workflows; or ways to do them faster, easier, better or more economically
- ✔ Putting ideas together in new ways and coming up with new ideas
- ✔ Seeing similarities in seemingly different situations; and differences in seemingly similar situations

Followers look to leaders to make a situation better, to fix problems and irritations and to facilitate their progress, so get used to popping on the initiator hat whenever you need to find ways to improve a situation or fix problems. Followers want leaders to make pesky recurring problems go away too. (Chapter 11 helps you sort problems.)

Leaders who wear the initiator hat with skill and confidence are highly valuable and valued and are becoming more so every day. Learn to use your initiative to help you adapt to new situations and changing conditions, to identify opportunities not obvious to others, to think creatively and innovatively and to translate your ideas into action.

The disturbance-handler hat

Sadly, leaders occasionally need to put on their *disturbance-handler* hat to deal with matters of discipline such as unacceptable behaviour and breaches of safety protocols. And, even in the most orderly groups, unforeseen problems, conflicts and grievances occasionally arise. These situations call for leading from the front (refer to the section 'Leading from the front — a nose-to-the-grindstone leader' earlier in this chapter) to bring things quickly into line and restore harmony and performance.

When reaching for the disturbance-handler hat, you need to

- ✔ Be able to think clearly and analytically
- ✔ Find ways to turn arguments into agreements so that you return the situation to its correct footing quickly, before too much damage is done
- ✔ Listen carefully
- ✔ Speak assertively and persuasively

For some tips on how to wear the disturbance-handler hat well, have a look in Chapter 7, which deals with communication.

The resource-distributor hat

Leaders have many resources at their disposal, most of them in limited supply. Leaders use the *resource-distributor* hat when they need to work out the fairest or the optimal allocation of limited resources, while bearing in mind the needs of the rest of the organisation as well as their own followers. Time, money, space and facilities, people, materials and equipment all hang from the rim of this hat, like corks to keep the bush flies away.

To look the part in the resource-distributor hat, leaders need broad shoulders and solid planning skills peppered with experience. Be informed by the inevitable occasional mistake you're bound to make so you can wear this rather tricky hat effectively.

The negotiator hat

Most leaders work with individuals in their team and their team as a whole, with others in the organisation and with people outside the organisation to reach a variety of formal and informal agreements. They may negotiate for the best use of limited resources, negotiate wages and working conditions, negotiate for timetables and schedules or for specifications or prices. Wearing the *negotiator hat* elegantly earns you the respect of your followers and colleagues and retains your followers' trust and loyalty, based on the good agreements you reach on their behalf.

Negotiating successfully takes thought and effort, as well as self-mastery and the ability to remain in control of your own behaviour (more on this in Chapter 3). Negotiating also takes practice and, fortunately, you can hone your negotiating skills in your private life, as well as leading others in the workplace.

Colleague, employee and follower hats

Leaders wear hats in their roles as colleagues, employees and followers, too — and the best leaders turn these into very influential hats.

Here is when you wear these hats:

- *Colleague* **hat:** You're working with your peers. This hat is important to you. When leaders don't have the support of their colleagues and the other leaders in their organisation, they find maintaining their positions difficult.
- *Employee* **hat:** You perch this hat on your head, along with the other hats you need at the time, when you're leading in the workplace. This hat makes sure you live up to your organisation's values, adhere to its policies and conform to its various practices and protocols. This hat also ensures that you behave ethically, safely and responsibly.
- *Follower* **hat:** You're working with your own leader and the leaders of the organisation who are senior to you.

Personal-life hats

Sometimes as a leader, you may feel you need to be all things to all people. And you're right, because we're not finished yet. Your *personal-life* hats are important because they give your life richness and supply time to relax and generate creative ideas, mull over possibilities and think strategically — all key activities of leaders.

All work and nothing else is far from a well-balanced life for anyone, and especially for leaders. Leaders who neglect the variety of hats they need to wear in their personal lives can pay a hefty price in health, relationships and personal happiness. Their leadership itself can also suffer if the personal-life hats aren't given an outing — research shows that spending too much time on the work treadmill can also be bad for work performance.

Here are some of the more common personal hats that leaders wear:

- Friend
- Parent

- ✔ Partner
- ✔ Sibling
- ✔ Sportsperson
- ✔ Volunteer

Fortunately, you can draw on your experiences and the skills you build up from wearing your leadership hats to help you wear your personal hats more effectively, and vice versa.

In fact, your personal-life experiences almost certainly help you to be a better leader. Chapter 21 offers some tips on how to build a balanced life that can reward you both personally and professionally; and Chapter 22 gives you some tips on dealing with the stress that leadership can bring.

Chapter 3

Building Your Leadership Muscles

*R*eal leadership begins inside you. Ask almost any leader to think back over their leadership career and what they have learned most and benefited most from learning and they tell you the same thing — self-knowledge. Leadership muscles are built by understanding yourself and what makes you tick.

Ask followers to describe the best leaders they know and what the qualities they talk about can be summed up as 'strength'. Not physical strength. Leaders come in all physical shapes and sizes. Inner strength is what followers see in successful leaders and inner strength comes from your values as a leader and your mindsets as a leader. Inner strength comes from feeling positive and confident about yourself as a leader and as a person, from knowing where you're headed and knowing what matters most, from behaving ethically and from understanding how you work best. This concept isn't about 'self-love' so much as 'self-acknowledgement', which comes from a realistic assessment of your strengths and weaknesses.

With strong leadership muscles, you can build robust relationships with the people you lead and the people who lead you. You can cultivate your power and influence and earn the respect you need to lead effectively (see Chapter 8 for more information on power and influence). You can motivate and inspire people and reach the goals for which you're aiming.

And even though leaders come in all shapes and sizes, they need to look and act like leaders. Funnily enough, that begins inside, too.

You begin this chapter by thinking about your values. Then you discover the five mindsets that help you lead effectively. I also explain how to recognise your own working styles and how to look, sound and act like a leader. Finally, you work out your own personal path to leadership success following three simple steps.

Leadership Begins Inside

The human genome project has found that you and I share 99.8 per cent of our DNA with each other and with every other person in the world. (We also share it with chimpanzees, but let's put that to one side!) This means that 99.8 per cent of you is exactly the same as me, as your followers, as everyone else in your organisation and as every other leader in the world.

The difference, the tiny but all-important difference, that makes you unique is what's in your head and what's in your heart. Not the organs themselves, but the abstract qualities you can't see or touch — your values and your mindsets.

Your *values* are what you believe is important and hold close to your heart. Your *mindsets* are your beliefs, views and opinions about yourself, other people and the world around you. Your values and mindsets are the lenses through which you view your world, colouring what you see and hear, how you think about it and what you conclude. Your values and mindsets make you who you are and define you as a person.

Your powerbase — as a leader and as a follower, as a parent and a partner, as a human being — comes from your values and mindsets. They guide your thoughts, your actions and your decisions and, to a large extent, they determine how happy you are, how productive you are, and how good a leader you are. In fact, values and mindsets are what set apart the 'best' from the 'good enough'.

Knowing your values

What do you stand for? What do you hold dear? What is most important to you? Perhaps being honest, dependable and efficient, working hard and building a loving family. Perhaps having fun, learning from new skills, being physically fit or making a meaningful contribution. Maybe having status symbols, being liked or accepted by others, being in control or following tradition. Or maybe having compassion, humility, tolerance or adventurousness, or orderliness, initiative and perfection.

Maybe none — or all — of these suits you. No right and wrong answers exist for values and mindsets because, unlike ethics (ethics are the same for everyone — an absolute right and wrong), everyone's values are different. Knowing what you value is important because, as the saying goes, 'If you don't know what you stand for, you'll fall for anything.' Knowing what you stand for helps build your leadership muscles and allows you to act with the strength of integrity.

Most organisations have a values statement that sets out the important principles employees are to uphold in their day-to-day activities (refer to Chapter 5 for more on how to use your organisation's values to lead your followers). If you don't hold similar values to your organisation's values, you won't fit in, feel comfortable or do well — as a leader or as an employee.

Strengthening your mindsets

Do you know that every time you think a thought, a specific electro-chemical pathway in your brain switches on? (The technical phrase is *neural pathway* — a *neuron* is a brain cell, so a neural pathway is a series of electrical and chemical links between brain cells.) Just as a through-the-bush pathway becomes more worn with time, and more likely to be used the more it's used, the pathways in your brain become stronger each time they're used. This means that every time you think a thought, about yourself, others or the world around you, the more likely you are to think that thought again. And again. And again.

Eventually, a set of similar thoughts, or pathways, become a mindset that guides your actions. Knowing how you view yourself, your followers and other people you're close to, and how you view the world around you helps you make sure your mindsets are taking you towards a destination you actually want to reach.

Once established, your mindsets become self-fulfilling prophecies. Scientists are now coming up with rock-solid evidence showing that whatever you believe about yourself, others and the world around you has a way of coming true. Scientists believe that these beliefs are partially determined by your genetic programming and the rest are built up through your life experiences, particularly during childhood.

Even so, you can always examine, adjust and finetune your mindsets to ensure they're up to date and accurate so they can guide you more effectively. You can choose what you believe.

How self-fulfilling prophecies work

A *self-fulfilling prophecy* is a belief that continually reinforces and strengthens itself as you act on it, producing evidence that confirms the prophecy. Basically, you 'see' what you expect to see. Most people go through their lives seeing what confirms their beliefs and ignoring what contradicts them. If they can't ignore the contradictions, they re-interpret them so these apparent contradictions fit in a bit more comfortably.

Finding evidence that confirms what you already 'know' — and ignoring contrary evidence — is easy. In fact, your brain is wired to ignore information that doesn't fit into your view of the world because to absorb conflicting information creates what psychologists call *cognitive dissonance* — the conflicting information makes our brains hurt! (If you want to find out more about how your brain protects you from the pain of cognitive dissonance, see Chapter 11.)

Think for a minute about how you view your world, about what you believe about yourself as a leader and what you believe about the people you lead. Then think about whether these views serve you or sabotage you as a leader.

Based on an explosion of recent research, neurophysiologists and brain scientists are showing how people build and strengthen their neural pathways by using them, and how some people allow them to deteriorate by not using them. These scientists are also showing that, by the power of pure thought, you (and I and everyone else) can re-shape your brain internally and change the way you think and behave, as a leader and as a person. Neuroscientists call this phenomenon *brain plasticity*.

Getting Your Mind Around Mindsets

The way you lead pivots on your mindsets because your mindsets determine how you react to and interact with your world. Mindsets can expand not only your own productivity but also the productivity of your followers. Alternatively, mindsets can keep the goals you want to achieve out of your reach.

The following sections examine the essential mindsets — backed by social and emotional skills — that I believe are essential for you, as a leader, to succeed.

Mastering yourself

What do you think of yourself? Are you capable and competent? Kind? Smart? Dynamic? That's how good leaders think of themselves. Do you respect and care about yourself and others?

What do you think of your followers? Are they lazy losers? Careless? Untrustworthy? (The term for this is *Theory X.*) Strong leaders don't think of their followers that way. Successful leaders see their followers as capable people who do their best. (The term for this is *Theory Y.*)

What you as a leader think about yourself and the people you lead is critical for two reasons:

✔ **Anything you believe — it's true!** You see what you expect to see and get the results you expect to get. In other words, your self-fulfilling prophecies come true.

✔ **Even when you never say what you *really* think out loud, what you think affects everything you say and do as a leader.** Your followers can sense whether you think they're lazy and irresponsible. If that's what you believe, they won't want to follow you. Even worse — your followers may come to believe this description of themselves and begin behaving that way! By the same token, if you believe your followers are capable and dependable and you feel privileged to lead them, they can sense your thoughts and they're likely to move heaven and earth to live up to your high expectations.

Understanding self-esteem and self-mastery

Your *self-esteem* is how you feel about yourself — the sum of your feelings of self-respect and self-worth, the value you place on yourself as a person and as a leader. Your self-esteem can be high or low; it can empower you or make you feel small. Self-esteem combines with the value you place on others and your ability to control your responses and emotions to become the essential 'mental muscle' that is called *self-mastery*.

Without self-mastery, it's hard to achieve goals and impossible to be an effective leader. Leaders who master themselves feel comfortable and confident. They look for answers to problems, accept responsibility, stand straight and look people in the eye, and act with integrity. These leaders have the confidence to tackle tough tasks, learn new skills, make mistakes and learn from them and work with a variety of people who are different from themselves.

Listening to self-talk

Have you ever been tempted to say any of the following?

- ✔ 'I'll never get anywhere!'
- ✔ 'I'm so stupid!'
- ✔ 'I'm such a loser!'

If you ever say anything like that to yourself, stop putting yourself down right now! I hope these are more like the messages you give yourself:

- ✔ 'Great! Another job well done!'
- ✔ 'I haven't done that before but I'm sure I can figure it out.'
- ✔ 'Let me think this through for a minute.'

Watch your language when you talk to yourself — the loudest voice you ever hear is your own silent voice. When you talk to yourself about yourself or your followers, you eventually believe and act on those messages, which reinforces them. Nasty or nice, true or false, your *self-talk* — the silent messages you give yourself — become the 'truth' (see Chapter 4 for more on managing your self-talk).

And whether you know it or not, you talk to yourself constantly. You may even speak out loud. (That's a different topic that needs a different treatment!) You're probably not aware of your self-talk — most of the time self-talk is just a fleeting feeling. Sometimes, self-talk is a full-blown conversation. Here's my self-talk from this morning:

> 'I really should get up and put on my gym gear and go to the gym. But I'd rather get up and put on my jeans and finish Chapter 3. But if I don't go to the gym I'll feel guilty and lack energy all day. But the computer is calling me — I can hear it!'

Your self-talk gives you a handle on your self-esteem and on how well you master yourself. If it isn't making you feel good about yourself, guiding you with integrity or serving your leadership, stop the self-talk and change the message so that it does support you. Be your own best friend, not your biggest critic.

Your self-mastery guides your actions and generates your thoughts and your self-talk, and your self-talk confirms your self-mastery. The two feed on each and spiral around, upward, making you feel competent and able, extending and expanding your ability to lead; or they spiral downward, making you feel inept and bungling, limiting and shrinking your ability to lead.

Nine ways to master yourself

If your self-mastery needs a boost (and everyone's does from time to time), here are some ideas to follow:

✔ Acknowledge and celebrate your successes and achievements.

✔ Don't let someone else's bad mood affect your good mood.

✔ Don't make excuses for your mistakes — acknowledge them, fix them and look for the lessons they offer you.

✔ Don't put yourself or anyone else down and look for the best in yourself and others.

✔ Focus on your positive attributes and make the most of them, instead of dwelling on your faults.

✔ Hang around successful leaders, peak performers and people who make you feel good about yourself.

✔ Keep learning.

✔ Take care of yourself — you deserve it! Eat well, exercise, and participate fully in life.

✔ Take responsibility for what you say and do, for achieving your goals, for succeeding as a leader.

Here are two important questions for all leaders to ask themselves:

✔ What, if any, mental limits might you set for yourself?

✔ What, if any, mental limits might the people you lead set for themselves?

Helping followers master themselves

I once knew a sales trainer I'll call Dennis. His 'training uniform' was baggy, wrinkled brown trousers, rolled-up shirt sleeves and a loose tie that had seen better days. The message? I don't respect myself much and I don't respect you enough to bother dressing as though I do.

Here's how Dennis began his training programs: 'Listen, folks, I'm only going to say this once. This material I'm going to teach you is hard. It's technical. Many of you won't understand it. A few of you may get it — but only if you pay attention and try hard.' No wonder Dennis complained about how poorly motivated his trainees were!

By way of contrast, I once worked for a wonderful man named Hal McGhie. I was pretty much straight out of university, so perhaps you can imagine my lack of a tidy hairdo and my extremely short skirts. But Hal never said to me 'Kris, you look terrible. Fix yourself up if you want to work for me!' Just as well because I'd have crossed my arms, dug my heels in and protested, 'It doesn't matter how you're dressed — what matters is how you do your job!'

Instead, whenever Hal took me to conferences and meetings, he introduced me like this: 'I'd like you to meet Kris Cole. She's very professional.' After a while, I started thinking about that word — 'professional' — and slowly, my hair started getting a bit of a 'do', my hemlines dropped to more business-like levels and I started, well, 'smartening up'. Hal gave me something to grow into.

Leaders don't go around tearing people down. Instead successful leaders create opportunities for their followers to 'star'. Leaders help followers to master themselves through offering honest compliments and constructive feedback that helps followers to improve and build their self-confidence. Followers respect and trust leaders who make them feel good about themselves and their abilities, who expect the best from them and who offer help when they can see help is needed.

Setting high standards

When you were in school, you probably noticed that the coolest kids hung out together. Ditto for the smartest kids and the most athletic kids. You probably notice the same tendency in adults too — top performers hang out together just as complainers hang out together. That's not surprising.

If you have mastered yourself, you naturally have high standards and expect the best from yourself and for yourself — why wouldn't you? You have the self-discipline to keep trying until you get it right and you have the confidence that you can handle yourself, stay level-headed and remain articulate, even in difficult situations. You step up to challenges and bounce back from setbacks (the word for this is *resilience*). Settling for second best or falling for 'close enough is good enough' is not an option.

Expecting the best also means you expect the best from those around you. Who was the best leader you ever had? Chances are, that leader was someone who brought out the best in you and insisted on great performance and great results, someone who set high standards and expected you to perform. And chances are, you delivered.

Expecting the best doesn't mean having unrealistically high expectations, but it does mean setting challenging goals and working to achieve them. You can breed top performance all around you by setting high standards and expecting — in fact, insisting on — the best.

Here is a saying I believe is worth hanging wherever leaders and followers congregate:

> Mediocrity is a choice.
> So is excellence.

Setting goals

You may know the adage that three kinds of people make up the world: Those who make things happen, those who watch things happen and those who wonder what happened. Leaders make things happen.

Leaders don't dream or wish or rely on other people, or random events, to achieve their goals. Leaders set challenging goals that stretch and test themselves and their followers and draw on and expand everyone's skills.

Then leaders plan how to achieve their goals. They're action-oriented (this is known as being *proactive*). Leaders know that action, not hope, is what turns goals into reality. Solid achievements work; daydreams don't work.

Here's how to set great goals:

- ✔ Make your goals ambitious, but achievable.
- ✔ Make your goals specific so you know precisely what you want to achieve.
- ✔ Set a few goals and state them simply so they're memorable.
- ✔ Set goals in positive terms — aim for what you *do* want, not what you *don't* want.
- ✔ Set target dates for your goals.

Use great goals to fashion your own future and the future of the people you're leading by deciding what you want to achieve, planning how to achieve it and acting on your plans. (If you want to find more on goals, see Chapter 12.)

Staying alert

Leaders pay attention to what they're doing and what's happening around them. In other words, leaders are *mindful*. Staying on your toes keeps you out of 'ruts' and stops you from feeling that your job or your life is the same old, same old, day after day. Staying alert stops you from just drifting through life and helps you spot ways to make your life better and improve your performance and the performance of your followers.

Paying attention helps you to see the novel in the familiar, to operate flexibly and creatively and to turn stumbling blocks into stepping stones (or at least find ways to get around them) so you keep moving closer to your goals.

When problems arise, don't complain, make excuses; don't blame the economy or a budget that's too high, or other people. Don't wait for someone else to assess the situation and fix the problem; don't ignore the problem and hope it goes away. Don't say: 'That's not my responsibility.' All these responses just drain your power and energy. Instead, take responsibility for figuring out what needs to be done to produce the results you're after, work out how to make your solution happen and think through the consequences of your decisions and actions.

Focusing on what matters most

One maxim I like says that people get what they focus on — and it's true. A couple of years ago, I was in Sydney to run a training day for a group of leaders and I walked into a huge room they'd set up for the training session. To my horror, I saw the electric cable, practically at knee height, stretched to the computer for my PowerPoints. On one side of this high wire was the flip chart and on the other side was the big whiteboard I needed to use. I knew I'd be going back and forth between them constantly and I'd need to step over this high wire every time. The screen was fixed and because of the room layout, I couldn't re-arrange anything. I couldn't believe my situation! I raced around looking for an extension cable but, of course, I couldn't find one. Good old Murphy's Law in action again.

I figured I'd have to live with this distracting and dangerous situation, at least for a few hours until someone could find or buy an extension cord. Naturally, my first mental image was of me tripping over the wire, the computer flying through the air and me landing on my nose with the computer crashing on top of me. Since I truly believe people get what they focus on, you can imagine how quickly I changed that mental image to one of me stepping gracefully back and forth over the wire every time. Fervently, I kept repeating, 'I will remember to step over the wire.'

And guess what — I didn't trip once!

Concentrating on what could go wrong, what may make achieving goals difficult, or what you don't like about someone is begging for problems. Focusing on what you want to happen is a powerful invitation. Keep your focus on what you want, beginning with your overall aim as a leader and your key result areas and goals. (If you need to figure out what these are, see Chapter 4.)

Don't waste your time worrying about factors and events that are beyond your control. Focus your efforts on things you can affect, where they can count the most — and show your followers how to do the same.

Staying focused can even save your life

One of the first things racing car drivers learn is what to do when they lose control of a car and go into a spin. Most people's natural reaction is to focus on the trees they're about to hit; but if that's where you focus, that's where you end up.

Instead, racing car drivers learn to focus on the spaces *between* the trees, on where they *want* to end up — their desired destination in that situation.

Working Out How People Work Best

When you understand your working style and what you're good at, you're in a good position to

- Make the most of the opportunities that come your way.
- Select areas where you're potentially strong, for improvement.
- Try to avoid situations that highlight your weaknesses (yes, everyone has weaknesses).

Understanding your own working style also helps you spot the styles of those you lead and those who lead you. You can deal more effectively with followers because you know how to request information, give information and assign duties. (If you want to find out more about personality styles — which also affect working styles — see Chapter 9.)

Considering the many ways to work

How do you prefer to receive information? Perhaps in writing; that's certainly convenient and you can refer to it later, but you may well be up the creek if your own leader or some of those you lead prefer to listen or have a discussion. Sticking rigidly to the way *you* prefer to work works well with like-minded people but not with anyone who prefers to work in a different way.

Different people work in different ways and work best in different environments. For example, some people

- Enjoy detailed work while others cringe at the very thought of it
- Feel more comfortable in hierarchies, others in informal, relaxed structures

✔ Like a lot of variety in their work while others seek routine

✔ Like the chance to move about a lot while others are happier staying in one place

✔ Like to work with people in a team situation while others want to lead those teams

✔ Perform best in a highly structured and predictable environment, others in a hectic and unpredictable one

✔ Think through issues out loud by discussing them with someone else; others think through issues by quietly mulling them over; still others need to be active and prefer to roll up their sleeves and run a trial experiment

✔ Work best independently but with people nearby while some perform best working on their own

✔ Work best in small organisations or groups while others work better in large organisations or groups

✔ Work best with tangible items while others work better with ideas

Discovering ways to deal with information

Once you come to grips with the possible ways people deal with information and know how you deal best with information, your leadership abilities can take a giant step forward. Here's why:

✔ You can ask your followers to provide you with information in a form that you can absorb and work with most easily.

✔ You can explain to your leader and other leaders how you grasp and use information best so they can oblige you — after all, communicating with you efficiently is in their best interests.

✔ You can figure out how your followers, your leader and others you work with want to receive their information from you and accommodate their preferences. That way, they can easily understand the information you give them.

✔ You can even ensure that you assign work to the right person.

The result is wins all around for you, your followers and your colleagues.

People deal with information in different ways. Most people favour one way over the others and can work successfully with a second method of receiving and using information; and most people find that at least one way of receiving information just plain doesn't suit them.

Feelers

Feelers see situations and make decisions based on their own personal values. Feelers like to work with people, help other people and make them feel comfortable. If that description sounds like you, take the trouble to find out the background of plans and ideas that people suggest to you. Finding out this information helps you assess the merit of the ideas and feel more comfortable with your assessment.

Let the feelers you work with know you understand what motivates them and how they're, well, feeling. Always acknowledge how much you appreciate their help.

Intuitors

Intuitors have strong and often successful hunches. Intuitors are imaginative and enjoy playing around with abstract concepts and theories; this means they often enjoy creative work and tasks that involve long-term planning. While intuitors easily see the 'big pictures', they often miss the details. If that's you, ask your followers to explain where they're headed and decide how well their ambitions fit with your ultimate goals and vision.

Understand that the intuitors you work with may appear to talk in 'circles', and that creative and sometimes on-the-spot ideas can be hard to follow; and then intuitors can be impatient when questioned. The solution is to allow time for intuitors to talk through their ideas and then ask questions at the end. The wait can be very worthwhile. Be careful to phrase your questions to show that you're not being critical of their ideas — you're simply looking for a few more details to see their ideas as they see them.

Sensors

Sensors are down-to-earth, energetic and hard working and would rather be doing a task than thinking about it. Practical people with lots of common sense, sensors are the first to roll up their shirt sleeves and get on with the job (often before thinking it through). Sensors are great at getting projects and plans off the ground, setting up projects, negotiating details, troubleshooting problems and converting ideas into action. If that's more like you, tell your followers not to give you too much detail or 'fancy theory', but to be clear and to the point. Guard against (unintentionally) making non-sensors feel they're taking up too much of your time and you'd rather be getting on with something else — not everyone marches to your rapid drumbeat!

Understand too that the sensors you work with probably have short attention spans — possibly because they're so keen to be getting on with the job. Help sensors relax by letting them know you have a plan for getting the job done — and let them know fast. Get to the point and communicate in easily digestible sound bites.

Thinkers

Thinkers need time to think through an idea or issue to feel comfortable before they proceed. Thinkers are best at tasks involving facts and figures, research and analysis and problem solving. Thinkers are organised, realistic and strong on the follow through. If you're a thinker, ask your followers to give you an overall concept of a situation first and to present their information clearly and logically.

Thinkers also can easily spot mistakes and like to point out mistakes; when a thinker points out a mistake you make, reassure them that you can fix the problem. Always assure the thinkers you work with that you don't get carried away with idealism but stay grounded in reality, and that you're very careful when gathering your research.

Putting the task or the followers first

Perhaps when you meet with your followers, you're the type who gets straight down to business. Perhaps your leader chats about the weekend or asks about your family before moving on to the task at hand. Some people focus first on the task, others focus first on people. That doesn't mean that task-focused people don't like people and people-people don't want to work. It just means that some people naturally attend to the job at hand as their first priority and others put people first.

Neither scenario is right nor wrong. However, when you're a task-focused person who gets straight down to business, you probably become annoyed by people who want to begin a discussion or meeting with a chat about family, friends and weekend outings — of course this is annoying; they're *people*-people and you're a task person. People-people chat first because they care about you and your family; now that I've explained that, maybe you won't find this caring so annoying in the future.

If you're a people-person, hopefully you now understand why colleagues and followers who tend to get straight down to business can appear a bit impatient and abrupt. But of course they're not really impatient and abrupt — they just prefer to get straight down to business.

Okay, now you're thinking about the difference between people people and task people, and you're also becoming aware of the importance of not being too irritating to others. If you're a people-person and your leader focuses more on the task, don't begin your conversations and meetings with 'irritating small talk' that annoys your boss. And if some of your followers are task-focused, get straight to the point with them, too, and leave the small talk for an encounter in the tea room.

Looking and Sounding Like a Leader

You know and I know that leadership is more than how you dress, how you speak and how you carry yourself. That's not to say how you look, sound and stand aren't important, though. The way you present yourself is important and no-one can really think of you as a leader until you look, sound and act the part.

Leaders need to look cool, calm and collected because people take more notice of another person's body language and voice intonation than the words that person speaks. Make sure your body and voice tone match and enhance your words and your leadership image.

Habits build over time. Some habits are helpful, some are less so. You may not even be aware of the way you dress, walk and talk, or how the way you dress, walk and talk affects how other leaders and your followers assess you. So, allow me to get right down to a few basics in the following sections.

Seeing yourself as others see you

Marketing people know the importance of packaging, and the way you package yourself says a lot about how you see yourself and want others to see you. Your packaging — your overall presentation — includes

- ✔ The style of clothing you select
- ✔ The jewellery you wear
- ✔ The accessories you carry
- ✔ The way you put it all together
- ✔ The way you sit, stand and carry yourself

Packaging (or presentation) can give you extra confidence, help you achieve your objectives and enhance your image as a leader. Or it can trip you up. Read on to find out how:

- ✔ **Dress appropriately:** Wear whatever the other leaders and the people who lead you wear. (And make sure it's clean and pressed to show you respect yourself and the people you're leading.)

- **Drop the fiddling:** People who fiddle, fidget, twist and turn, shuffle, shift, sprawl, pace or constantly move their weight from one foot to the other look nervous and uncertain. The more you clear your throat, tap your foot or pump your leg, the more you signal: 'I'm uneasy'. Self-repair and self-grooming gestures (for example, adjusting your hair or clothing) also signal discomfort. Sucking on a pen or fiddling with a serviette, necktie or scarf make you look nervous and uncertain. Similarly, scratching or rubbing your head doesn't look cool, calm and collected, either. The antidote is to take a deep breath and stand or sit still, empty your mouth and your hands and keep them still too.

- **Look at people:** Always look directly at the people with whom you're speaking, not at your paperwork, your computer screen or your watch. Show you're listening and interested in what a speaker has to say by making eye contact; nodding and murmuring a soft 'Mmm' of agreement or understanding; and asking a follow-up question when the speaker takes a pause. Every once in a while, recap what the person you're talking to has said to show you understand and to encourage the speaker to continue. (See Chapter 7 for more tips on listening and on reading body language.)

- **Make a strong first impression:** Keep your hand movements open and relaxed, not extreme, jerky, sudden or quick. Stand up straight and hold your head up. An upright posture shows you're calm, composed, confident and competent. Pulling back your shoulders and holding in your stomach makes you look poised and self-possessed.

- **Watch your attitude:** Most people read 'Arrogant!' when they see hands on hips, in pockets or behind the head; and 'Timid!' when they see slouching, a caved-in chest and a hanging head.

Hearing yourself as others hear you

How you speak can undermine or strengthen your message. If you don't yet sound like a leader, you can do with a bit of practice. You developed your particular way of speaking, your characteristic voice tones, pitches, volumes and speeds during your life and you can continue to develop them to enhance their leadership qualities any time you want.

The volume and tone of your voice, for example, reveals whether or not you're nervous or in a hurry. Your voice can even signal how much you like the person you're speaking with. Your inflections proclaim not just what part of the country you're from and what your social background is; your voice can also show how confident you feel about what you're saying.

Avoid these sure signs of uncertainty:

- ✔ Constantly clearing your throat
- ✔ Mumbling
- ✔ Rabbiting on about nothing
- ✔ Speaking softly and hesitantly

Leaders speak steadily, calmly and strongly. Their words flow without awkward hesitations at an even pace. Successful leaders emphasise important words and phrases to make their meaning clear.

Keep breathing — deeply, not shallowly — when you're speaking. Breathing deeply produces a richer voice that's clear and steady. Breathing relaxes your vocal cords enough to pitch your voice at the right volume, so people don't have to strain to hear you. Deep breaths also deliver oxygen to your brain so that you can think clearly about the words you want to use and say those words clearly and confidently.

Moderating the speed and tone of your voice to make your voice sound similar to that of the person you're talking with is one way to ensure that person clearly hears what you're saying. It's the old saying: 'We like the people who are most like us.'

I have a friend in New Zealand who speaks as slowly as cold syrup. When we speak on the phone, I automatically slow down my usual zillion-words-a-minute pace. Everyone does this *matching* automatically with people they like and you probably already do this, too. The next step is to do it with everyone — even people you may not instantly 'warm' to. Matching the way the other person speaks makes the other person feel more comfortable with you and therefore is better able to absorb what you're saying.

Acting Like a Leader

The most professional package in the world soon crumbles when it isn't backed by results. Leaders have to look like leaders — and act like leaders.

Strong leadership muscles enable leaders to lead 'from the inside out'. When you're aware of your values, understand how you work best and have supportive leadership mindsets, acting like a leader is easy (acting like a leader is really difficult if you don't have these prerequisites). With a bit of thought and effort, you can show you're a real leader by the reputation you develop for 'delivering the goods' for your organisation and 'doing the right thing' by your organisation and your followers.

What you see isn't always what you hear

Voices are complicated tools that come in many variations — high, low, clear, husky and so on. Whatever type of voice you have, you can vary its use to provoke all sorts of different responses from the people who are listening to you speak.

The following features combine to produce the overall impact of your voice. Most importantly, the way you use these features to direct your voice can add (or detract) from how much you sound like a leader:

- **Articulation:** Impressive leaders speak clearly so they're understood. To find out how articulate your speech is, record yourself presenting a speech. Now play back the recording and listen to whether you avoid running words together, whether you sound the consonants on the ends of words, whether you pronounce every word correctly and so on.

- **Emphasis:** Leaders make their meanings clear by emphasising particular words and avoiding monotonous monotones.

- **Energy:** Leaders engage people by speaking with enthusiasm. Remember, energy can be contagious.

- **Inflection:** Leaders sound certain, confident and convincing by speaking with a 70 to 80 per cent downward inflection at the end of their sentences. Try to avoid the Australian tendency to put an upward inflection — à la *Kath & Kim* — in your voice at the end of a sentence. Upward inflections make you sound nervous and uncertain.

- **Pitch:** Leaders sound authoritative and credible by speaking with a lower pitch — similar to a television newsreader's pitch — rather than a high, flat or sharp pitch.

- **Rhythm:** Impressive leaders are easy to listen to because they speak at a well-modulated pace, not like a rifle spitting out bullets.

- **Speed:** An efficient speed is three words to the second. Time yourself and see how closely your normal speaking pace resembles that speed. Smart leaders speak even more slowly when they want to highlight a point or sound more thoughtful and serious.

- **Tone:** Leaders breed confidence by speaking in a can-do and matter-of-fact way that's positive and cheerful, thoughtful and quiet, straightforward and clear — not harsh, sharp, whining, nasal, raspy, belligerent, accusing, placating, patronising, bored, bossy, helpless, dry or dull. A clear, brisk voice that says: 'I'm in charge'.

- **Volume:** Leaders speak to be heard — neither shouting nor whispering.

Behaving ethically

Values aren't the same for everyone, but ethics are, at least for everyone in the same culture. Ethics are an absolute choice of right and wrong. Occasionally, leaders are faced with ethical dilemmas and situations that may be legal but are nevertheless not ethical.

Here's a little ethics test. A situation is ethical when

- It's legal.
- You accept someone doing the same to you.
- You're comfortable for your actions to become public, for example, reported in the media.
- Your mother would approve.

If you can't agree with each of these points, don't do whatever it is you're considering!

When you're pulled in many directions by people, often with their own differing interests (your followers, your own leader, people outside your organisation and so on), deciding which path is the best to follow can be difficult.

When you're faced with a dilemma and not sure what way to move, apply your values to the options available to you. Then check your decision against the four-point ethics test. Consider, too, how your decision may affect those around you.

Easy? No. That's what leadership is all about.

Building trust and confidence

Trust is an essential bond between leaders and followers. Without it, a team can't achieve much.

Trust has three interesting qualities:

- **Trust is an absolute:** You either trust someone or you don't.
- **Trust is fragile:** Trust takes time to build, but seconds to destroy.
- **Trust works two ways:** Leaders need to be able to trust their followers to do their jobs and behave appropriately. Followers need to be able to trust their leaders to support followers' rights and best interests and treat the followers fairly.

Mirror, mirror, on the wall ...

One of the most highly respected diplomats in the early 1900s was the German Ambassador in London. He was such an impressive leader that he was expected eventually to become Germany's foreign minister or chancellor.

But the ambassador resigned abruptly in 1906 rather than preside over a dinner to be given by Germany for the United Kingdom's King Edward VII. It seems that Edward, who succeeded his mother, Queen Victoria, to the throne, was a notorious womaniser and he'd had his courtiers make it clear what kind of a 'dinner' he expected.

On hearing of King Edward's fancies, the ambassador declared: 'I refuse to see a pimp in the mirror in the morning when I shave.' And he resigned his post.

I don't know whether that's a 100-per-cent true story, but it makes a vital point: People need to live according to their (and their society's) ethics and to live in line with their own values.

The mirror test helps you decide what to do when you're faced with a hard choice. When faced with a dilemma, ask yourself: What type of person do I want to see in the mirror tomorrow morning? You can make your choice accordingly.

Even in virtual teams where people seldom or never meet face-to-face, leaders need to build a team culture based on trust and confidence so that everyone performs and achieves results. (See Chapters 15 and 16 if you want to find out more about building a team culture and leading virtual teams.)

Developing a reliable and competent reputation

Leaders are people who do what they say they're going to do when they say they will. When a meeting starts at two o'clock, leaders are seated and ready to begin, at two o'clock. When leaders promise to phone followers or others before noon, they phone before noon, not at ten past. Leaders deliver on their promises, large and small — successful leaders know that if they don't deliver, they're not only letting others down, they're letting themselves down, too.

By completing projects successfully, by communicating effectively, by being dependable and consistent, by honouring your promises and coming up with helpful ideas and suggestions, you become someone on whom other people can rely.

Five ingredients of trust

Lots of factors go into the pot of trust, some adding a nice but expendable 'zing' while others are essential. Leadership researchers describe five indispensable ingredients of trust that leaders need to display in order to earn the trust of their teams and their own leaders:

- **Competence:** Technical and people skills

- **Consistency:** Reliability, predictability and good judgement in difficult situations

- **Integrity:** Honesty and truthfulness

- **Loyalty:** Willingness to look after people and save face for them

- **Openness:** Willingness to share ideas and information

Here are some ways to build trust with your followers:

- Build enthusiasm and inspire confidence in your followers.

- Face up to tough issues honestly without being confrontational or judgemental.

- Give credit when plans and projects go well and accept responsibility when they don't.

- Show your followers that you're honest and competent.

- Show your followers that you trust them by asking their opinions and including them in decisions — this way your followers know where they stand.

You can build your reputation as an effective leader in many other ways. Here are a few more for you to consider:

- Avoid chopping and changing priorities.

- Avoid setting vague goals.

- Be sincere and considerate.

- Do more than is asked of you.

- Take on extra tasks and responsibilities, especially those your own leader doesn't want.

Giving and earning respect

Effective leaders respect followers and other leaders by valuing them as people, whatever their skills, talents or quirks. Respecting others is easy when

- You know that everyone has their own way in which to contribute.

- You look for people's strengths and find ways to build on them.

✔ You put yourself in their positions.

✔ You're able to see situations from other people's points of view.

Successful leaders never flaunt their status or play one-upmanship games or promote themselves by putting others down. These leaders make followers feel appreciated and supported and treat everyone politely. Common courtesy is the mark of a true leader.

Displaying good judgement

Sound judgement means making calls based on strong evidence, informed knowledge and clear understanding of the subject and the situation. The opposite is when people refer to making a decision 'by the seat of your pants'. Seat-of-the-pants decisions include decisions made to advance your own interests; decisions based on prejudice; decisions based on emotions; or personal likes and dislikes; and decisions reached simply because they're quick and easy.

Now look who's boasting . . .

I don't know about your mother, but mine taught me never to boast. Nothing's worse than a braggart, full of hot air but no real substance, don't you think? While you avoid boasting of your achievements, even unintentionally, you can still project a positive image. Here are some ideas to get you started:

✔ Aim, every three months, to come up with one good, solid, workable and innovative improvement idea to present to your followers, your fellow leaders or your own leader.

✔ Build your reputation outside your organisation. Network with like-minded leaders and colleagues, speak at external conferences and write for academic, industry or trade journals.

✔ Tell others what you do, what projects you're working on, what your achievements are and how your organisation benefits from the work you supervise. Keep your reports objective.

✔ Meet regularly with your leader for an update on what you and your followers have achieved, what you're still accomplishing, what other problems you're resolving and generally report how you're reaching your goals. Be objective and factual.

My boomerang does come back

Have you ever noticed that if you smile at someone, even a stranger, they generally smile back?

Or if you're friendly to someone, that person is friendly in return?

Human brains are wired with *mirror neurons*, which are programmed to return like with like.

That's the *boomerang principle*. (Technically speaking, you call this *psychological reciprocity.*)

What does this mean in everyday life? Simple: When *you* treat people with respect, *their* respect boomerangs back to you.

Instinct and intuition can be important in good judgement but don't rely on instinct and intuition alone. Leaders are after the right answer, not just the quickest answer. Success generally has more to do with direction than speed, and taking the time to explore a situation and think through a decision generally helps you move in the right direction. Even when you feel pressured to come up with an answer, take the necessary time to consider and find the right answer. (To find out more about how to make sound leadership decisions, see Chapter 11.)

How do you disregard pressure to make an instant decision or give an instant answer? The best way is to practise being comfortable saying something like, 'I don't know yet' or 'Let me think about it' to avoid the need to give a seat-of-the-pants answer and buy yourself time to find the right answer. To use that time well, you may

- ✔ Ask the opinion of experts or people with experience in a similar situation.

- ✔ Look at the situation from every angle you can.

- ✔ Mull your ideas over and consider the options open to you, their effects on other people and other parts of the organisation, including 'downstream' effects, which may occur later.

- ✔ Put the situation on your brain's back-burner to percolate for a while. That way your subconscious can gather your earlier thoughts and work on the answer, which usually results in better solutions anyway.

- ✔ Reach your conclusions in line with your values and ethics.

Similarly, if someone comes to you with a problem or just wants to chat through an idea, don't feel you have to jump in with an answer before you have all the information. Ask a few questions and listen a bit longer. The other person feels better about the progress of the conversation when you listen and show genuine interest. As a bonus, when the two of you explore the situation together in some depth, you're rewarded with more insights into the topic. Gaining more knowledge helps you offer a sound opinion.

Be confident in your conclusions — don't change your mind just because others may disagree with your decision. Leaders are true to themselves and the effort they bring to a decision. Strong leadership muscles give successful leaders the courage to do what they believe in.

Identifying Your Personal Path to Success

Your future begins first in your mind, then in the goals you set and, finally, in the actions you take to move towards your goals. Think about the future you want to create for yourself, plan how to achieve that future and keep working towards your goals.

The three simple steps to success are (in this order):

- **Set your goals:** Your goals are your desired future achievements, and they guide your present actions and decisions. Without goals, you're in serious danger of just muddling along.

  Write down a few challenging *result goals* (your overall aim). Then break them down into smaller, more quickly achievable *activity goals* (activities you need to complete to achieve each result goal). Make all your goals positive and as specific as you can make them and set time frames for each goal.

- **Develop action plans:** Turn your activity goals into an action plan by putting them in a To Do order. Keep your To Do plan handy and in sight so you can refer to your list frequently to check your progress and keep yourself motivated. (You may not achieve every goal 100 per cent, but you can achieve much more when you write the goals down and plan what you can do to achieve them. I guarantee it.)

- **Keep at it:** Every bit of effort you make towards achieving your goals helps. As the Italian proverb says:

  > Persistence makes the impossible possible, the possible likely and the likely definite.

A goal without an action plan is just a wish. Ask any highly successful person in any walk of life what is the secret to their success and they all say goals, an action plan to achieve their goals, and following their plan — through the tough times, frustrating times and failures.

The power of persistence

If you think having a dream, turning your dream into a set of goals and planning how to achieve those goals is enough, think again — achieving success isn't always easy. The path to success is often more like three steps forward and one step back. Remaining true to your dream and sticking to your plan is an important part of success. Here are some examples to illustrate what I'm getting at:

✔ **Ford facts:** Why was the Model T called the Model T? Because Henry Ford went through A to S before succeeding in making a car he could sell.

✔ **Pasteur's perseverance:** French scientist Louis Pasteur's tenacity — as much as his brains — led to his linking germs to disease, rescuing the French silk industry from ruin, developing inoculations against anthrax and chicken cholera, developing a treatment for rabies in humans and dogs and founding the discipline of bacteriology.

✔ **Edison's light at the end of the tunnel:** Thomas Edison considered the invention of the electric light bulb to be a 2000-step process. Had he not, he'd have given up long before his 2000th attempt failed!

✔ **Chuck's first flight:** This is my favourite. Chuck Yeager, a combat pilot and the first man to break the sound barrier, threw up on his first flight as a passenger. He vowed never to fly again. But he stuck with it instead!

Part II
Leadership Is Personal

Glenn Lumsden

'That book on leadership he read has really worked wonders.'

In this part . . .

Strong personal skills are the bones that support your
leadership. Before you can begin to lead effectively,
you need a swag full of personal skills. In this part, I give
you the tools you need to harness your personal power
and pick up the weighty responsibilities of leadership in
a way that inspires your followers to follow you willingly.
I explain how to concentrate on what matters most and
how to master the time available to you. You find out how
to communicate as a leader — with words and without
words — one-to-one and to groups, in person and from
a distance. I describe how to forge strong alliances and
networks to fortify you in times of need and to help you
celebrate in times of success.

Chapter 4

Take the Lead? Me?

*T*his statistic may surprise you, but it's true: Up to 70 per cent of leaders sometimes fear they don't really belong in a leadership role and that they're about to be rumbled. Deep down, many leaders feel they're 'winging it' and someone is going to find out and expose them as a fraud. Feeling like a fake is so common, the syndrome actually has a name: *Impostor syndrome*. So don't worry if you feel a bit uncomfortable taking the leader's role, especially in the early days.

Most followers aren't shocked to know that every leader's confidence flags once in a while. What followers don't want, however, are leaders who fail to stay true to their beliefs and values. Followers want leaders with strong leadership 'muscles', leaders who act with integrity and who respect themselves and their followers. Followers want leaders who bring out the best in them by stretching them to do more than they ever thought they could. Followers want focused leaders who keep their goals in sight and who make projects happen.

In this chapter, I explain how to build your confidence — and how to cope if your confidence crashes. I show you how to work out your own leadership vision and introduce you to the most important areas that need attention from you in your leadership role. Finally, I pass on some important advice you may find helpful, particularly if you're a new leader finding your feet.

Boosting Your Confidence

Right! Now that you're a leader, you never have to worry about nerves or crises of confidence again. Right? If only.

If your knees shake or your hands sweat just when you want to make a terrific impression, if you think you're making a right decision but you're not quite sure, if you have a tough problem to solve or a difficult conversation to hold and you're afraid you may blow it — take heart. I'm going to share with you three proven ways to boost your confidence.

Managing your self-talk

No doubt you feel confident about some areas of leadership, whereas others can bring on the horrors for you. These feelings are natural — everyone is confident in some circumstances but not in others.

Your level of confidence has a lot to do with your self-talk, the silent messages you give yourself — the 'I can do it' or 'I can't do it' type of inward instructions you invariably give yourself. (Refer to Chapter 3 to find out more about how important self-talk is.)

If you provide a haven to a harsh inner critic, know this: Chances are that your inner critic is seldom, if ever, accurate. Even so, the discouraging silent instructions that your inner critic hands out to you can hold you back and stop you from trying or from giving a job your best shot.

Switch off any voice within you that crushes your confidence. Whenever your inner critic pops up with a negative line, replace that slur with a supportive thought that buoys you up. That's how you can talk yourself into becoming the best leader you can possibly be.

Calming the nerves

If you're like most people, you breathe quickly and you hold your breath high in your chest, or even your throat, when you feel nervous or uncertain. Shallow breathing actually works against you by preventing you from thinking clearly and speaking confidently, making you even more nervous.

Confidence versus arrogance

Leaders need to be confident, but where do you find the fine line between confidence and arrogance?

Arrogant people think only of themselves. They not only believe they're perfect — they believe they're more perfect (I know you can't be more perfect than perfect!) than anyone else. Arrogance leads to all sorts of unpleasant results.

People with high self-esteem and self-confidence have a high regard for others as well as for themselves.

You can easily balance self-respect with respect for others and you can be sure then that people won't find you arrogant.

In a difficult situation, you can relax by taking three deep breaths. Just three breaths are enough to calm you down and deliver oxygen to the thinking part of your brain. Taking deep breaths makes your voice sound better, too. With three deep breaths, you can think properly and speak like a leader.

Now smile. A sincere smile achieves these great outcomes:

- ✔ *Endorphins*, those 'feel-good' hormones that help you look confident and calm, are released when you smile.
- ✔ Nerves usually take a back seat when you smile.
- ✔ Smiles are catching.
- ✔ Smiles make you look more interesting and approachable.

When you're lost for words, ask a question. Really listen to the answer. The more absorbed you are in hearing someone's thoughts or opinions, the more you forget about your nerves.

Working to your strengths

There's a saying that encapsulates the spirit of this section:

> If you're a runner, run.
> If you're a bell, ring.

Recognising your natural talents, and *using* them, is hugely satisfying.

You perform best when you're working in the areas your natural skills and inclinations take you. Once you work out what you do best — which activities and situations are your strengths — you can concentrate on working in those areas to further enhance your skills. When you don't identify your strengths and build on them, you may find yourself running on the same spot. At worst, you may be left behind by others who move on and out-perform you.

Funnily enough, lots of people know what they're *not* good at, but not what they *are* good at. If that applies to you, go and find out what your special skills and talents are. One way is to ask people who know you well — they may give you some answers that can astonish you! Much of what you're best at is probably so 'second nature' to you that you don't even realise the particular qualities that help you lead well.

You can also monitor your own performance by noticing what you most enjoy doing, what tasks and activities seem to come most naturally and easily to you and what projects you seem to be good at completing. Notice which tasks you dread and which tasks you anticipate. Think about the types of relationships that you most enjoy and the standards of results and time frames that you achieve most easily.

Don't do some tasks just because you're good at and enjoy those tasks at the expense of other tasks. For example, if you're great at explaining information, don't be tempted to over-explain — know when to stop.

Now I don't want to rock your confidence, but identifying any areas where you lack aptitude is important too. These areas are to be avoided. Continually exposing your weaknesses erodes your self-confidence and self-esteem. To avoid being a bell trying to run or a runner trying to ring, delegate what leaves you numb and what you find crushingly difficult.

Trying to develop and improve skills in areas you have absolutely no talent in is a waste of time and effort. Chances are your hard work may result in your becoming little more than mediocre. After all, rugby players don't try to play in every position on the field. Should speedy wingers spend time improving their scrumming skills? No! They're far better developing their natural talents by preparing to run with the ball when it's released from the pack.

Having said that, I'd hate for you to think that just because you may not be skilled at a particular task now, you can't *become* a success in that field. You're probably potentially talented in lots of areas. The point is that you need to recognise the big difference between an as-yet undeveloped talent and a field where you don't have — and are never going to have — any ability.

Taking on an 'acting' role

Acting is a great way to get results when you're not brimming over with self-confidence. For instance, if you're about to chair your first meeting, you can expect a few butterflies. To get those pretty wings flying in formation, you can act as though you're calm and confident, even though you may not feel that way. Similarly, if you're leading someone you haven't warmed to yet, act as though you really do like that person and you can speed up the process of forming a harmonious working relationship.

Acting also helps when you don't know what to do or say in a particular situation. The solution: Think of someone who knows exactly how to handle the situation: Think about how they behave, and then mentally step into their shoes and act as though you're that person. For instance, if you need to mediate between two quarrelling followers and you're a bit uncertain about how to proceed, think of someone who mediates well. Ask yourself what that person would do and say in situations like this one.

Acting starts you moving in the right direction and may even produce the result you're after. And the next time you're in a similar situation, you know what to do because you now have experience. The more you use your new ability, the more that skill becomes part of your repertoire.

Acting becomes reality with repetition

Leonard Nimoy, who played Mr Spock, that super-cool, super-logical fellow with the pointy ears in the original series of the famous TV show *Star Trek* said that playing Spock had a huge effect on his life and his thought processes.

Even though Nimoy didn't consider himself a particularly rational or logical person, spending so much time acting as though he were rational and logical reshaped his life and the way he now thinks. By acting as though he were logical and rational in his role as Mr Spock, he became logical and rational.

Behaving as though you already have the qualities you want gives you energy and inspiration and builds the behaviour and memory patterns that can last your entire life.

Faking it until you make it

Do you remember that childhood tale about Robert the Bruce? He was hiding in a cave with nothing to do but watch a spider trying to climb high up the mouldy, slippery wall to build a web, only to slip back time and time again. That little spider never gave up. The moral to this story is: If at first you don't succeed, try, try again. That's excellent advice, provided you try a different approach. If you keep doing what you always do — climbing the same path time and time again — you won't achieve your objective.

This scenario begs the question: What different approach are you going to try? This is where faking it comes in. If you don't know what to do, fake it. In other words, keep trying different approaches until you find a way that works for you.

Knowing Why the Boss Picked You

The two points I'm about to list are essential not only for building your confidence but also for succeeding as a leader:

- ✔ Have a clear leadership vision.
- ✔ Know exactly in which areas you're responsible for achieving results.

If you don't have this knowledge, your energy and efforts are aimless, you won't achieve what you want to achieve and your leadership is destined to flounder.

Once you establish your purpose as a leader, and your most important areas of responsibility, you have your own personal guidelines upon which to base your leadership. Your leadership vision and key responsibility areas help you decide where to concentrate your energies, efforts and attention and help you to decide how to deal with difficult and challenging issues.

Determining your key result areas

Leaders need to be right on top of their jobs. That means that leaders (and followers, for that matter) need to be able to state, without hesitation or doubt, their most important areas of responsibility and accountability. These areas are generally known as *key result areas* (KRAs) and are where your priorities lie.

Each of your leadership functions and all the many tasks you carry out slot neatly into a KRA, giving you an overall framework for managing your time and effort. (Some tasks, such as coaching a follower or streamlining a workflow, become a bonus because they help you get results in two or even three key result areas.)

For example, a leader on an assembly line may have the following key result areas:

- Administration
- Continuous improvement
- Health and safety
- Leadership
- Machine utilisation
- Output — quality, quantity, cost and timeliness
- Staffing

A team leader in an office may have these key result areas:

- Continuous improvement
- Data entry management
- Document preparation, storage and retrieval
- Equipment maintenance and upgrades
- Leadership
- Liaising with internal customers

Keep your key result areas short — just one or two words, and don't use verbs — these are areas of responsibility, not tasks that you do. Each KRA contains many individual tasks, which together help you achieve results. You can't list your KRAs in any order of importance because each area is equally important. If you drop the ball in one area, your leadership as a whole suffers.

Once you establish your own KRAs as a leader, set yourself one or two challenging goals in each area to work towards over the next, say, six months. Make these goals specific, measurable, ambitious and easily trackable so you know how you're doing. (If you want to know more about how to set goals, you can find information in Chapters 5 and 12.)

Don't use your key result areas as an excuse for not accepting responsibility for other important duties that may come your way.

Discovering your purpose as a leader

I have a very important question: Can you state your overall aim as a leader? Think about it. In the meantime, here's my overall aim: To help people, teams and organisations to reach their full potential so that they and Australia prosper.

My overall aim can also be expressed as my *leadership purpose*. To me, my leadership purpose says: This is what I do and why I do it. All leaders need a short statement like this to guide their actions and help them decide what matters most. (By the way, I didn't write that aim in two seconds; it took quite a bit of thought, writing, re-writing and polishing, so don't worry when you discover that writing your leadership-purpose statement takes a bit of thought, too.)

To write your leadership purpose, think about

- ✔ How you want to lead your followers
- ✔ How you want your followers to work together
- ✔ What you want to help them achieve that benefits you, them and your organisation

When you run into a problem or dilemma, your leadership purpose and key result areas can guide you. When you're too busy to scratch yourself, your leadership purpose and key result areas can help you decide what to do next. When you have a decision to make, your leadership purpose and key result areas can help you make up your mind. In fact, your leadership purpose and key result areas can guide everything you do and say as a leader.

Tips for New Leaders

Becoming an effective leader is a journey of continuous learning and self-development which, even for the most gifted, is an arduous (but rewarding) process. If you're becoming a leader for the first time, know this: Decades later, you may recall your first months in leadership as a transformational experience. Expect to feel disoriented, overwhelmed or confused — and at times expect to feel all three at once. You may well find that being a leader isn't anything like you expected and that being a leader is too big a job for just one mere mortal. (Uh-oh — there's that impostor syndrome again!)

However wracked your nerves may be, your followers expect you to know everything there is to know about leadership! They look to you for leadership from Day 1.

Chilling out

The skills you use to succeed as a follower are very different from those you use to succeed as a leader. No doubt you're technically competent, and that's easy to prove to your followers, but that isn't really the know-how your followers are interested in. In fact, acting like the smartest kid in the room, jumping in to solve every problem for your followers and constantly telling everyone what to do undermines your credibility as a leader.

The expertise your followers are interested in is your ability to lead and they expect you to prove your leadership skills to them. You need to look, sound and act like a leader (refer to Chapter 3). Even if you're an old hand at leading, be prepared to demonstrate your leadership skills to a new group of followers. Followers never accept your track record as proof you're an inspiring leader.

Don't worry when a gap exists between your current capabilities and demands of your new role as a leader. Everyone has something still to discover and everyone keeps discovering new skills throughout life (at least, I hope so). You can increase your skills by doing your job, reflecting on what worked and what didn't, figuring out why, and figuring out how to improve. You can discover new skills through looking at and listening to other leaders and from your followers.

You can also increase your skills by making mistakes. Mistakes are inevitable. When you make a mistake, remember Henry Ford — he didn't put a reverse gear in his first car, yet he and his business survived (and so did most of his Ford car drivers). You can live with your mistakes (believe me, you can). Think of your mistakes as a guide to better performance in the future. Work out what went wrong so you won't make the same mistake twice. (If you keep making the same mistakes, you're not learning from your mistakes and you won't be a leader for much longer.)

Moving from 'me' to 'we'

Probably what won you your leadership appointment was your sterling individual performance, but individual performance isn't what leadership is about. Your goal is no longer only about getting the best out of yourself but getting the best out of your followers, too. Your goal is about helping your followers do their jobs to the best of their ability (see Chapter 10 for more on how to bring out the best in your followers). Your goal is about developing the skills and potential of each of your followers, together and as a group. (To find out more about moulding individual followers into a team that works well together, see Chapters 15 and 16.) Your goal is about stepping back and sharing the limelight.

The transition from being an individual contributor to leading other individual contributors may be challenging, but changing the 'me' mentality into a 'we' mentality is a necessary shift in attitude.

Leading one follower versus leading all followers

Leading each follower individually is not the same as leading all followers together. For example, you may think you're making a decision that relates to only one follower, but think again. Every decision you make about an individual follower is noticed by, and affects, all your other followers.

Even if you're trying to build or strengthen your relationship with one follower, when you make an exception for that person, you're likely to regret the unexpected effect on the team. When followers pop their heads around your door and ask seemingly harmless questions, such as 'Hey, okay if I take Jane's parking spot now that she's left?', don't give a snap answer. Take a day to think about the consequences. For example, you may find other followers then demand parking spots, or the parking spot may be coveted by an employee in another department who's been waiting years for a company car spot.

Every decision you make has consequences. Working on a series of one-on-one relationships with your followers can be fruitful in some ways, but it can also neglect a fundamental aspect of leadership — harnessing the power of the group as a whole. Think through the impact of all your decisions on your followers and on other parts of the organisation.

Earning your authority

If you're a new leader, you probably realise by now that followers won't give you authority free of charge — you have to earn your authority. Just telling people what to do won't earn you the trust, respect, cooperation and commitment you need.

Followers are extremely sensitive to any integrity gap between what their leader does and says. Your authority comes from your credibility as a leader and the strength of your personal leadership 'muscles'. Show your followers your character and what you stand for. Show your values and your intention to support your followers. Build yourself a positive image (a good reputation is an asset no leader can afford to be without). (If you want to know more about building your leadership muscles and earning authority, you can find the info in Chapters 3 and 8.)

Building your team's culture

Every group of followers has an unwritten code of behaviour and rules, known as *norms*. The norms form a culture unique to each team and each organisation. The norms say: This is how goals are achieved around here; this is how our team members work together; this is how 'fast' we work and how much emphasis we put on 'getting it right'.

Watch your team and the way it operates and think about what that tells you about its norms. If a team's norms don't support the team's overall aims, the team is likely to end up with poor results. (To find out more about understanding and building your team's norms and culture, see Chapters 8 and 15.)

Leaders need to be highly attuned to their groups' cultures in order to ensure that culture leads to the attitudes, behaviours and performance levels that produce results. At first, sit back and observe the culture in your group of followers. If you want to make any changes, try to introduce them gradually, one at a time. (If you're not sure how to introduce changes and make them stick, you can find out in Chapter 14.)

Work to shape a team culture that allows all of your followers to fulfil their potential — individually and together. Make sure the culture supports your organisation's vision and mission, too. (If you want to know more about how a team develops a culture and how to build a culture in a way that supports your leadership vision, you can find that information in Chapter 15.)

Going for an early win

Ah, those first 100 days of leadership bliss. That's how long your unofficial honeymoon — when you can impress your followers and your own leader — lasts. This period is your arbitrary deadline — 100 days has a nice roundness to it.

In your first 100 days as a leader in a particular job, show your followers that you have some authority and influence so they can rely on you as a leader. Go for an early win for your team members or do something to make them feel special. This way your team members can see you as an ally in reaching their individual and team goals. Show them that you have influence in the organisation and that you can use your influence to the benefit of your followers. For example, get your followers access to scarce resources, such as training, or get them equipment that can make their jobs easier.

Now go for another early win that your own leader can appreciate — aim to succeed in a project that fits with your leader's goals or aspirations.

In your first 100 days, if you can make quick and easy wins look as nightmarish and difficult as possible, you can earn extra kudos. Take care not to step on toes, though. Think about what you want your early wins to be, think about the possible ramifications and think about how to best achieve your goals before you jump in and make too much of a splash in your new job. I strongly recommend you avoid making too many changes too quickly.

Try to spot the *unofficial leader* in your team — the person everyone turns to for help or advice, the person who seems to be the unofficial spokesperson for the team. Once you get this person on side you have the rest of your followers on side, too. (See Chapter 15 for more information on the influence of the unofficial leader.)

Fitting in and standing out

When you're new to an organisation, you can put in place a number of checks to help you decide how to behave as a leader. On the one hand, you want to fit in. On the other, you want to stand out and show you're dependable, can add value to the team, can deliver more than is expected and have plenty of ideas to offer. Here are some ways to suss out the existing culture so that your leadership won't flounder because of a 'poor fit'.

- ✔ Figure out whether the culture is a team or an individualistic culture — for example, do the rewards go to those who achieve on their own, or to a whole team of people who achieve together?

- ✔ Find out whether your own leader expects you to introduce big changes or just steady improvements.

✔ Notice what happens at meetings. In some organisations, meetings are places to thrash out difficult issues. In other organisations, people meet merely to ratify decisions that are made before the meeting.

✔ Observe who gets rewarded and why.

✔ Spot how conflict is dealt with — openly, under wraps, or not at all.

✔ Take a look at the people around you and form some guidelines for yourself about your image. It's important to follow the unwritten (but real) uniform code of the other leaders in your organisation as well as that of your own leader — flashy or subdued, casual, smart casual or corporate, stylish or conservative.

Avoiding the most common mistakes of new leaders

Most new leaders find that leading isn't what they expected. Leading is filled with surprises, unexpected lurches forward, dismaying steps backward and struggles to live up to what everyone expects from you. The more quickly you become comfortable in your leadership role, the more quickly you reap the huge satisfactions that effective leadership brings.

To help you navigate your tricky but all-important first few weeks, I have a list of the most common problems I've heard leaders describe. (I sure wish someone had given me this list when I started out in the business.)

✔ **Becoming overwhelmed by a web of relationships and conflicting demands:** Other leaders, your own leader, your followers, even people outside the organisation, such as your customers or suppliers, all want to influence you and your decisions. So don't think you get to call all the shots. Think of Solomon and his wisdom and do your best to reconcile conflicting expectations, needs and demands. Avoid the soft option, the quick-and-easy option and the seat-of-the-pants option.

✔ **Focusing on the rights and privileges of leadership:** If you think rights and privileges are what leadership is about, you're in for a rude awakening. (Have a look at Chapter 2 for more rude awakenings.)

✔ **Making too many changes too quickly:** You may have heard the saying: The new broom sweeps clean. That may well be true for new brooms. Oddly, some new leaders think of themselves as new brooms. This concept is not just a poor analogy, it's also a mistake.

- ✔ **Thinking that asking for help or advice is a sure sign that appointing you to a leadership role was a huge mistake:** You're not expected to have all the answers, but you are expected to know how to find them. Ask for help when you need help. Your own leader, a mentor, a trusted friend, another leader you trust — inside your organisation or outside — can probably offer support. Take the time and trouble to build strong networks to increase the number of brains you can pick. (If you haven't built good networks yet, find out how in Chapter 8.) Coaches, mentors and strong role models can help you see how your peers and followers see you. These people can also point out your skills and your weaknesses and offer constructive help, advice and support.

- ✔ **Thinking that becoming a leader is becoming a boss:** Chances are you really won't be the boss of very much at all in a leadership role. A leader's daily routine is pressured and busy. Leaders hop from one task to another and often feel that their time is not their own to use as they want. Leaders have to keep a myriad of balls in the air, so get used to pressure, a fast pace and interruptions. Learn to be flexible and adaptable and not to 'sweat the small stuff'.

- ✔ **Thinking your job is to keep your department running smoothly:** Your real job is to add value and instigate changes to enhance the way your department operates. (You can find out more about this subject in Chapters 5 and 20.)

At least in the beginning of a new job, respect your followers' culture, or the bits of it that support your aims as a leader. Sit back, observe, listen and file away any information that can help you. Chat with each employee: Tell me about your role. What do you like best around here? What would you change if you could? Ask questions like these. Get a feel for what's going on.

Yes, you have your ideas and you want to mould your team to help you achieve them, but you also want to avoid foot-in-mouth disease, so keep your mouth shut until you know what's going on. The more you know about your followers, the more you can explain your vision and aims to them in a way that draws a positive response. Once you're integrated into the organisation, and into your team, you can introduce any changes you need to make — gradually.

Chapter 5

Leading in the Right Direction

*H*ere's a question for you: What's the difference between a leader and a show-off? To me, a show-off wants to dominate a stage, to be the centre of everyone's attention. Leaders don't seek centre stage. *Leaders* aim to achieve goals. However, leaders can't achieve goals unless followers are willing to follow and assist their leaders.

One definition that I like to use is this: Leaders enable followers to achieve shared goals. These words emphasise the important fact that leadership depends on other people; in other words, leadership depends on *followers*.

Leaders need to provide a stirring ambition to energise their followers and point each one of them toward the same ultimate goal. Only then can leaders inspire, encourage and guide their followers to a specific result.

In this chapter, I show you how to inspire your followers and keep your followers geared to what you're trying to achieve. I show you how to put together plans to achieve your goals, how to protect those plans and how to execute them. And after you absorb all that information, I have another challenge for you. Just when you think your plans are in place and working well, you discover that leaders need to finetune procedures and work flows.

Taking Your Team to Success

Values, vision and *mission* set the scene for the goals you want to achieve and how you want to achieve them. A leader can't lead effectively without values, which guide every follower, and a vision and mission, which act as beacons, beckoning people towards the goal they want to achieve.

Every leader's first duty is to establish values to guide their own and their follower's actions, and to uphold those values. Demonstrating them every day clearly signals to followers how they are expected to act, too, and leaders need to acknowledge when followers live up to the organisation's values (and pull them up when they let those values down).

Every leader's second duty is to create a vision and mission and to become their guardian by ensuring that followers understand, are enthused by and are committed to their visions and missions.

Having all the followers properly prepared in this way is sometimes called 'getting your ducks in a row'. If you fail to get your ducks in a row, you relegate yourself and your followers to humdrum mediocrity and, ultimately, your goals remain out of reach.

The fourth member of the leadership quartet is the *strategy* — the road you guide your followers down to achieve your vision, mission and shorter-term goals.

If followers pull in different directions, the values become a hallucination, the vision, mission and strategy fade into the distance and the goals become mere wishes. When everyone in a team works together (is *aligned*) toward the same overall objectives, they can achieve amazing results.

So what exactly are these values, visions, missions and strategies that are so essential to success? I explain them this way:

- ✔ *Values* state what the organisation believes is important and worthwhile and describe how the organisation as a whole and the people in it behave toward each other and toward the people outside it. (For information on a leader's personal values, refer to Chapter 3.)
- ✔ *Vision* describes what leaders want to achieve and what inspires them. The vision is the 'big idea', the inspiring destination the organisation is aiming for that followers can rally around and adopt for themselves. The vision enables people inside an organisation to know that what they're doing makes a difference, and the vision shows people outside an organisation that the organisation intends to make a difference.

✔ *Mission* points the way to the place of your vision.

✔ *Strategy* is the more specific map you follow to reach your goals.

Leaders need the entire quartet. Values guide people's actions and decisions and the vision, mission and strategy flow down through an organisation, becoming more and more detailed as they gather specific information regarding different teams' and people's roles and the contributions those teams and people make to the final goal.

These days, visions, missions and strategies aren't set in stone but are fairly flexible, so that organisations can nimbly adapt to changing circumstances as needs arise. However, flexibility doesn't undermine importance. Visions, missions and strategies are essential to running an organisation because, as the saying goes, if you don't know where you're going, you're probably never going to get there.

Finding the beacon that marks your destination

Think of an organisation's vision as a beacon — a bright and burning light atop a difficult challenge that the organisation's leaders and followers are daring to reach. The light atop their destination provides a vividly clear marker of where everyone wants to be long term. Here are two current examples of beacons that mark significant ambitions:

✔ **Amnesty International:** This organisation aims to help build a 'world in which every person enjoys all of the human rights enshrined in the Universal Declaration of Human Rights and other international human rights standards'.

✔ **Microsoft:** This organisation aims to 'enable people and businesses throughout the world to realise their full potential'.

(Microsoft's previous vision was 'to have a computer on every desk'. When Microsoft was close to achieving that vision, the company moved on to its current vision.)

Notice how concise, precise and unforgettable the Amnesty International and Microsoft visions are. The result of this simplicity is that followers within the organisations can easily understand, remember and act upon these visions.

I know of a large accounting firm that has this vision:

To make a lot of money for the partners.

The partners can't understand why their employees are not too enthused by that vision. The moral of that story is to make sure your followers find advantages for themselves too, because when an organisation or its leaders are the only beneficiaries of your team members' work, the vision won't engage or enthuse your followers.

Reaching for the beacon

A mission explains how the organisation intends to move towards its vision. For example, Microsoft says it plans to help people and businesses realise their full potential 'by developing innovative software that transforms the way people work, learn, and communicate ... and by using our resources and expertise to help expand social and economic opportunities in communities around the world'.

Amnesty International's plan to help everyone enjoy human rights is to 'undertake research and action focused on preventing and ending grave abuses of the rights to physical and mental integrity, freedom of conscience and expression, and freedom from discrimination, within the context of its work to promote all human rights'.

Lofty visions and missions like those of Amnesty International and Microsoft stretch, challenge and inspire people. These goals may not be easy to achieve but they're goals worth working for (at least to the people inside these organisations). But if you, as a leader, fail to make these goals an inspiring touchstone for your followers, then the goals become just a set of meaningless words. If you fail to make your goals believable, they may only raise a smirk.

Moving towards the beacon

The strategy gets a bit more specific about how the organisation moves towards and achieves its vision and mission. Strategies don't have to be long or complex — in fact, the simpler, the better.

Woolworth's strategy, for example, is said to be to be a 'high volume, low margin, discount retailer'. These six words guide the company's entire business. More than that, these six words are measurable and they reveal the company's targeted outcomes. As well, the six words are designed to steer the company towards greater competitiveness and a stronger position in the marketplace. These six words describe a powerful way to do business that everyone in Woolworths can understand and follow. Now *that's* a strategy!

The leadership quartet of values, vision, mission and strategy are an organisation's four guiding principles and focus everyone on what's most important. They need to be top of everyone's mind and guide everyone's actions, acting as reference points for everyone's decisions.

Creating a Team Purpose

Your next step is to design the future for your own group of followers. You do this by crafting a *team purpose* statement that describes the team's unique contribution to achieving the organisation's vision and mission. Your team purpose statement also expresses how the team benefits from fulfilling its purpose. A clear and concise team purpose serves as your team's special vision, binding the team members together and guiding their behaviour and decisions.

You need to live and breathe the team purpose every day to signal its importance. Now you have the beginnings of a very powerful, focused and successful team. (See Chapter 15 to find out how to build on this strong foundation.)

Crafting your team purpose together

The process of designing a team purpose is as important as the end result. Gather your followers together and review your organisation's values, vision, mission and strategy. Then talk about how your followers can contribute to achieving the vision and mission — individually and together.

Next, ask these questions of the team members:

- How do you want to work together?
- What do you want to achieve together?
- What type of team do you want to create?
- What do the team members want to be seeing, hearing, feeling, saying, doing and thinking when the team starts achieving its goals?

Write everyone's ideas on a big whiteboard and then discuss each idea. Guide the discussions towards finding agreement on a statement of your team's purpose. You want a statement that inspires everyone, generates enthusiasm and can guide your followers' activities and decisions. You're looking for concepts, ways of working and ultimate results that your followers agree are important and exciting, as well as concepts that they're proud to share and put into practice. (See Chapter 13 for more on how to lead a good discussion.)

Next, whittle down your team purpose into one sentence with which everyone can identify and will want to support. I find this formula of words helps:

To ... so that ...

The first part of the sentence explains *what* your followers do and the second part explains *why* they do it. Here is an example you can use as a guide:

A team in a sporting goods store agreed on this team purpose:

To advise and assist our customers in a friendly, stimulating and enjoyable environment so that they keep purchasing from us and we meet or exceed our measures of success.

Once you have your team purpose stated in one simple, short sentence like this, you can agree one or two broad aims for the team to work toward over the coming months. Think generally. You probably have many goals you would like to reach, but what do you and your followers most want to accomplish? What worthwhile achievements could you set your sights on? Dream big. Set a few targets that can really make a difference and contribute toward fulfilling your team purpose.

Making your team purpose sing

Once you and your followers have agreed on a concrete team purpose and on goals that unite and focus the team members, don't just frame and hang them on a wall. Live your team purpose; breathe your goals and keep them alive and at the forefront of everyone's mind. If you don't stay focused on and committed to your agreed team purpose and goals, your followers won't either.

Your next essential duty is to clear away any obstacles that are preventing or making it difficult or awkward for your followers to achieve their team purpose and goals. Have you ever wanted to do something but kept bumping into silly and inconvenient obstacles that got in your way? If you have, you understand that nothing is more frustrating and disheartening. Hitting your head against a brick wall is simpler. Eventually you tire of trying and give up. (If you need to find out more about how to identify and remove the obstacles that get in your followers' way, check out Chapters 10 and 11.)

Fire them up!

You can generate enthusiasm for your team purpose and overall aims in many ways. Here are some ideas to get you started:

✔ Put them on your stationery or on an automatic sign-off for inter-team emails.

✔ Put them on posters, coffee mugs, mouse pads or computer wallpaper.

✔ Begin every meeting by going around the table and hearing from everyone about one contribution they're making to the team purpose.

Now you're getting the team moving. Making an effort to display and reinforce your team purpose encourages your followers to become familiar with them.

Planning, Doing and Checking

Can you imagine a bus company where the drivers are told: 'Go and collect a bus, cruise around the streets, take a break when you feel like it — the timetable always works out all right in the end'? Or perhaps a football team whose leader says: 'Okay, team, get on the field and do your best! Get the ball when you can, try to score and try to stop the other side from scoring. Got it?' Or maybe a political party trying to win an election and the leader says: 'Right! We've got eight weeks! Get out and win the electorate's hearts and minds!'

I call these non-plans 'recipes for disaster'. What followers in their right minds would even *want* to follow leaders like these?

When leaders don't provide a plan that each follower understands and is willing to follow, the right hand won't know what the left hand is doing. Chaos reigns, tempers flair and crises flourish. Ironically, everyone ends up working harder than necessary and for worse results.

Putting together a plan

People need plans because plans

✔ Assure followers (and leaders) the job is under control

✔ Enable people to know what to do and when to do it

✔ Give people a way to track their progress towards a goal

✔ Inform people about whether they've been successful

✔ Keep followers (and leaders) on track toward their vision and purpose

✔ Keep the job running smoothly

✔ Show people what others are doing and how they can help the others

Developing a successful plan takes a bit of thought, but the time and mental effort is well spent. In fact, you can say that leaders who fail to plan are planning to fail.

Whenever you need to develop a plan, enlist your followers for these reasons:

✔ The involvement of your followers ensures they understand what the plan is trying to achieve, what the plan entails and why.

✔ The involvement of your followers ensures your followers are committed to the plan.

✔ The plan benefits from the variety of followers' ideas and insights.

Begin with your overall aim

What do you want to achieve? The answer gives your followers an end result to hold in their minds, which gives meaning and purpose to everything they do.

State your overall aim in one sentence, using positive language (what you *do* want, not what you *don't* want). The Verb–What–Why formula is a great way to state your overall aim.

Verb	What	Why
Develop and implement	a plan	to improve ...
Develop and implement	a plan	to resolve ...

You can mix and match this Verb–What–Why cocktail, meaning you don't have to keep them in that order. How's this for an inspiring overall aim:

> Dream up the best fete ever (Why) and come up with a plan (What) to make it happen (Verb).

A clear aim stating what you intend to achieve combined with a plan puts you in the driver's seat. If you don't have a clear destination in mind, why bother getting into the car?

Now get a firm fix on what your aim, once achieved, is going to look like. Ask these questions:

- ✔ How can you and your followers know how well your plan is working?
- ✔ How do you, your followers and the organisation benefit from achieving your plan?

Finally, write down your overall aim and ultimate measures of success and put them where you and your followers can see them. This helps keep your aim front-of-mind and helps keep you and your followers focused on the plan. You can put your aim and measures of success on a banner screensaver or laminate your aim and measures of success and hang the poster on a wall where everyone congregates and can see it every day. That way, you can post progress updates beside it so the team can see their progress and feel proud of their accomplishments.

An overall aim that is extremely ambitious or long term can overwhelm your followers and make them feel despondent. When that happens, your followers tend to give up trying. Be sure to break down large or long-term plans into milestones of manageable size and develop a separate plan for each milestone.

Deciding what to do

As someone once said: 'Even if you're on the right road, you can get run over if you just stand there.' Knowing your overall aim isn't enough. You also need to know what needs to happen in order to achieve your aim.

Concentrate on what you want

A few years ago, roundabouts sprang up around where I live in the Adelaide Hills. I have no idea why, but here's what I imagine happened:

Some bright spark on the local council decided it would be a good idea to reduce the number of car accidents in the area and appointed an investigator to find out which council areas have the fewest accidents and why.

'I've got it!' the investigator shouted triumphantly. 'The council areas with the fewest accidents have lots of roundabouts!'

'Great,' said the bright spark. 'Engineering Department, go and build roundabouts! Put in as many as you can! That'll do the trick!'

Here's my message: Concentrate on results (achieving fewer accidents) not activity (building roundabouts).

The easiest way to figure this out is to *brainstorm* — just write down ideas as they occur to you, asking yourself what needs to be done. Write all your thoughts down as steps or activities. Don't worry about whether you're listing the steps in the right order and don't worry if you repeat an idea in a slightly different way from the first time. You benefit by including your followers in this process, too. (See Chapter 11 for more tips on brainstorming.)

Now edit. Combine any repeats, cross out any activities that aren't necessary or put those activities to one side under a 'Nice to do when time allows' heading. Try to begin each step with a verb.

Then put the steps in order. What needs to happen first? Next? And next?

When working out how to achieve a goal, you can work backwards if you become stuck. Start with your overall aim. Ask: What needs to happen before I can finally reach this goal? When you work out that final step, ask yourself how you get to that step. And when you get that second step, ask yourself what you need to do to get there, and so on. Eventually you reach the situation where you are now at the start of the project and your steps to your goal are laid out in front of you.

Now you have the order planned, add in the details. Assign target dates and responsibilities to each activity. Write down clear, measurable and achievable action steps for you and your followers to take:

- ✔ How should this step be taken?
- ✔ When should this step be taken?
- ✔ Where should this step lead?
- ✔ Who should take this step?

An aim without an action plan is just a wish. Develop your plan with execution in mind. A plan that shows what needs to be done — as well as who is responsible for doing what task; the way to do each task; and when and where to make the task happen — makes tracking your progress easy. Thorough plans also make it easy to spot problems that may arise so that you can fix them.

Establishing clear measures of success

Leaders don't just swing into action and hope for the best. Leaders know exactly whether, and to what extent, they're reaching their aims as their plans progress.

You've already determined an overall measure of success for your ultimate aim. Now the time's come to establish success measures that quantify the most crucial elements of your plan's success; these are often called *key performance indicators* (KPIs).

You and your followers can find out in two ways whether your plan is rolling out as expected:

- ✔ You can measure your progress as the plan unfolds with *lead indicators* (measures that tell you what's happening now).
- ✔ You can wait until D-day (deadline day) and find out whether you succeeded by using *lag indicators* (measures that tell you what has already happened).

While both measurements are useful, using only lag indicators is like driving down the road just looking in your rear-view mirror — all you know is where you've been but you won't have much idea of where you're heading. And if you feel a bump, you won't know what you hit until it's too late! Lead indicators help you see the bumps coming so you can avoid them. Try to use lead indicators as much as you can to track your progress.

Cricketers don't win matches by keeping their eyes on the scoreboard. Cricketers win by keeping their eyes on the ball. Think of lead indicators as the ball and lag indicators as the scoreboard.

Get your goals clear and know which are the most critical and sensitive activities and which activities give you the maximum impact for your efforts. The big pay-off activities are where you focus your efforts and the most critical and sensitive goals are where you pay special attention to measuring your progress. Here's how to decide what to keep your eye on:

- ✔ Choose which activities or steps are particularly important to the success of your plan — tasks that, when they're not done well or not done on time, can create a major obstacle to achieving your goal. These are the activities, be they output, costs, quality, quantity, safety, timeliness, sales, customer satisfaction or whatever else, which can put a serious dent in your plan's progress if not completed correctly.
- ✔ Decide exactly how you can tell whether these critical activities are going according to plan. Make them measurable, using lead indicators wherever possible. Select specific events or measures that give you and your followers useful information quickly, easily and accurately.

Enlist your followers to develop ways to monitor your plan's progress. That way, your team members know you're not just checking up on them. They understand why the success indicators are needed.

Using measures of success adds another layer of protection to your plan because you have built in ways that you and your followers can see how your plan is progressing. You can spot problems, and you can identify when congratulations are in order.

Securing your resources

Another planning task is to make sure all people involved in executing a plan have what they need. Think about what resources you need to organise for each step and how you can obtain them.

- ✔ **Equipment and material:** You may need to beg, borrow, buy or upgrade some equipment or materials (for instance, raw materials or procedure manuals).
- ✔ **Funds:** Ensure enough money is in the kitty to purchase any resources that you need.
- ✔ **Time:** Your followers need enough time to carry out your plan; if they don't have enough time for what needs to be done, free up some time from their other duties.
- ✔ **Training:** You may need to provide some or all followers with special training to carry out your plan.

Protecting your plans

You probably know of Murphy's Law; maybe you've even experienced it:

Anything that can go wrong will go wrong.

Maybe you know O'Leary's Law, too:

Murphy was an optimist.

Three steps to success

This three-part sequence to success is an oldie but a goodie, so it's worth repeating. When you have the answers to these three questions, you have the basis of a workable plan:

- ✔ Where are you now?
- ✔ Where do you want to be?
- ✔ What is the best way for you to get there?

Now make a list of the people on your team who can help you and list what you need them to do and when. Then decide how you and they can know they're doing the job well and consider whether you need any special resources. And you're on the way to achieving your goal.

The sad fact is, plans are seldom perfect, so you need to think about what can go wrong. You may be able to prevent a mistake happening. When you can't, at least you can plan how to deal with the problem if it does happen.

Put on your 'doom and gloom' specs and look for weak spots in your plan. As well, look for events that can cause a problem. Be sure that you're equipped to deal with all *contingencies* — those potential problems that have a habit of blowing in from left field when you least expect them.

Here are some tips to ensure your plan is working. Check the following:

- ✔ **Estimated time:** Find how long an activity is likely to take to complete to make sure you haven't underestimated time.

- ✔ **People or events:** Think about whether any people — perhaps people outside your team — or any events can stop your plan from working as well as you want it to work. Develop a plan that can prevent any damage before the harm happens or, better still, figure out a way to turn those people or events around into a positive. Just in case, develop a plan to deal with the problems you identify when damage does occur.

- ✔ **Projected costs:** Make sure you haven't underestimated the costs.

- ✔ **Resources:** Be sure you have everything you need and that you haven't underestimated the resources required for the job.

Think about what signals would alert you to problems as they arise and make sure your followers know the signs, too. Work out with your followers a series of standby arrangements you can put into effect when problems do occur — you want to be ready ahead of time, because once a problem has struck, it's too late to start re-planning.

Any time you make a plan, forces are about that can act against your plan. At the same time, forces are about that can help your plan. 'Forces' come in the form of people, events or situations. Always be aware of the hindering forces, so that you can minimise the most likely 'derailers', and the potential helping forces, so you can make the most of them.

Run your plan by an expert or someone who has experience in something similar. An expert's familiarity with similar situations, as well as that person's distance from your plan, can help the expert spot flaws that you and your followers may miss.

Questions that protect

When you and your team members are thoroughly familiar with your plan, get together for a brainstorming session to spot potential problems. Try these questions:

✔ What can go wrong?

✔ How can the team recognise something's about to go wrong?

✔ What can the team do beforehand to prevent a problem happening?

✔ What can the team do if the problem occurs?

✔ What can the team anticipate that may help the plan succeed?

✔ What can the team do to make the most of these potential assisters?

Once you know what can go wrong, you can prepare for it. Prevent the problem if you can. If you can't, minimise the negative effects.

Bringing people on board

Generally, bringing in your followers at the early stages of developing a plan is preferable. If that's not possible or desirable, communicate your plan after the development stage so that your followers understand and commit to the plan. Everyone involved in carrying out the plan needs to understand why the plan is needed, the plan's ultimate aim, how the each team member contributes to the plan and precisely how each team is to contribute to the plan's success. This way, everyone can commit to the plan's success.

Think about who else you may need to tell about your plan — for example, your own leader, other leaders you work with and other people in your organisation who may be able to contribute to your plan's success.

Implementing your plan

Now the time has come for the rubber to hit the road.

If you file your plan away, it won't be much use to you. Write reminder notes about tasks to be done, tick off what's been done already and comment on how well each task worked. If necessary, adjust your plan and finetune the details as the plan unfolds.

To keep your plan flowing along smoothly:

✔ Create checklists to jog your memory about what to do and to provide critical guidance in an 'emergency' situation.

> ✔ Make cross references on your checklists to make sure important steps are carried out.
>
> ✔ Put charts in obvious places and tick off activities as they're done, so everyone can see the progress.

Track your progress

If your plan is veering slightly off course, you need to find out quickly so that you can bring it back on track before too much harm is done. Keep on top of how your plan is unfolding by using your key measures of success to compare what's happening with what you expected to happen. Walk around and keep your eyes open — this may not replace more formal monitoring, but watching what's happening around you is a great supplement to tracking your formal measures of success.

When you meet with your followers individually, discuss how the plan is rolling out from their points of view. When you meet with them as a group, review how the plan is progressing, check that everything is up to date and find out whether anyone has encountered any problems. Keeping your followers' attention on the overall aim of your plan and on the progress towards achieving your goal is vital. Otherwise, your followers can quickly lose interest and stop trying.

Spending a lot of time monitoring your progress isn't necessary — spend just enough time so that you are able to take action quickly when the plan is failing for some reason. When the plan is rolling out as expected, thank the people whose efforts have contributed. When the plan is lurching to one side a bit, point people in the right direction.

Half-time in the dressing room

Many sport teams meet at half-time to review how the play is progressing and what the players need to do to lift their performances a notch or two.

Build a half-time review of play into your game to discuss the progress of your plan.

When you review the plan's progress with your team members, evaluate how the plan is rolling out and how your followers can lift their performance a notch or two. Most importantly, avoid laying blame when the play isn't going as you hoped. Instead, concentrate on finding ways to make the game plan work better.

Make sure your followers can watch their progress and recognise their successes so they can take corrective action or alert you to problems if you need to become involved. This also enables team members to generate their own positive feedback.

Don't over-monitor your team members as they work. You can become so wrapped up in checking and double-checking that you spend all day squinting at progress reports. A good move is to only keep an eye on activities that may experience problems. Be sure to point out the successes as well as the problems when you're checking on progress.

Review your successes and setbacks

Well, you did it. You led your team of followers through a plan to a successful outcome. The first move is to celebrate your success. Take some time out to acknowledge how hard you all worked and revel in your achievements. Make a speech, hand out silly thank-you presents, buy everyone a coffee and a muffin. Your team members deserve a reward and so do you.

But that's not the end of leading your plan to fruition. Once the initial glow has worn off, don't sit back with a 'Phew! That's done!' Invite your followers to a review meeting. You want to identify what went surprisingly well and what didn't go as well as you expected. More importantly, you want to find out why. The purpose is not to embarrass or blame anyone — that's the last thing good leaders do. The purpose is to find out what factors led to the successes and the, ahem, disappointments.

Ask these questions in this order:

- How did the job go?
- What went well?
- How can the team ensure something similar goes as well next time?
- What didn't go as well as expected?
- How can the team ensure a similar situation is more successful next time?
- What can the team do more of in future?
- What can the team do less of?

Don't ever celebrate mediocrity. Don't let your followers gloss over or ignore mistakes and activities that can be improved next time. No fudging, ignoring, pretending, denying, excusing or spinning. Look for the hard truth. Get problems out in the open; ignoring problems doesn't make them go away. Ideally, people say: 'You know, I can really do better. Next time I'll ...'

The easiest way to get to the bottom of what went well and what went not-so-well is to try the *Ask Why Five Times* technique. For example, imagine that a particular task in the plan wasn't completed on time:

- ✔ **Why wasn't the task completed on time?** Because the supplies needed weren't available.

- ✔ **Why weren't the supplies available?** Because the supplies weren't delivered.

- ✔ **Why weren't the supplies delivered?** Because the supplier forgot about the order.

- ✔ **Why did the supplier forget the order?** Because nobody reminded him.

- ✔ **Why didn't someone remind him?** Because confirming the delivery wasn't on the plan's checklist.

Ah — next time, you can make sure you include details like that on a checklist.

Look for the setbacks and successes that occur as your plan unfolds and pick out recurring root causes. Isolate clear actions for the future, write them down and file them to use the next time you and your followers develop and implement a plan. That way, you and your team keep getting better and better.

End the review meeting on a high note with a positive summary and outlook so your followers can move onto the next project with positive energy.

Improving — Always Improving

If you're thinking 'Ah, *now* I can sit back and relax', I have some news for you. Leaders never sit back and relax. They, and their followers, always look for ways to make their work better. Leading is a never-ending cycle. You get one job working, tweak it, refine it, perfect it and polish it. The Japanese have a word that sums up this process — *kaizen*.

That one very positive word is far, far more valuable than these six very negative words:

We've always done it this way.

In fact, those six words can cost you and your team dearly. If you keep doing the same task, you keep getting the same result. Hanging on to old ways of doing a job is a recipe for never changing, never growing, never trying new ways, never improving. Those six words are a recipe for stagnation and, ultimately, failure.

Leaders know how important it is to innovate and streamline, and to keep improving, to keep finding ways to do a job differently and better. If you don't keep adding more and more value, you and your followers may soon be overtaken and left behind.

Here are six sets of six words that replace 'We've always done it this way':

- ✔ How can I do this better?
- ✔ How can I do this cheaper?
- ✔ How can I do this differently?
- ✔ How can I do this easier?
- ✔ How can I do this faster?
- ✔ How can I do this efficiently?

These six words trigger a different mindset — one of innovation, continual improvements, flexibility and progress. The theme is about doing the job just that little bit better. This is smart thinking because doing each of 100 tasks 1 per cent better is much easier, yet still more effective than doing a whole job 100 per cent better. These six sets of six words, and their one-word shorthand version, *kaizen*, safeguard your future as a leader and your organisation's and followers' futures.

And in the same way that many hands make light work, so do many brains produce better ideas. Closely involve your followers in the quest for innovation and continuous improvement. After all, the people at the coalface are the ones who feel the hiccups and headaches, know where the bottlenecks are and see where the duplicated and wasted effort, energy and materials are. Your followers are in a perfect position to come up with sensible solutions and all sorts of ideas that you may never imagine.

No leader, no group of followers, and no organisation can afford not to be in a permanent *kaizen* state of mind. Here are ten ways to keep getting better in the *kaizen* way:

- ✔ Be alert for bottlenecks, wasted and unnecessary steps in a procedure, wasted materials and wasted energy and effort. Remove them.
- ✔ Conduct small experiments with different ways of organising and carrying out work, refine these methods and keep improving them.
- ✔ Don't assume the way you always do a job is the best way.

✔ Encourage creative ways of planning a new project or completing a new task.

✔ Identify the silly little practices that annoy people and obliterate those practices — just like that!

✔ Keep looking for ways to tweak, polish, refine and perfect what you and your followers do, even when you already do your jobs well.

✔ Look at where errors are made and look for ways to make those errors never happen again.

✔ Review your team's performance regularly. When a task is completed, gather your followers to review how the work was done and to see what knowledge was gained. Discuss with the team members how everyone can use this information to do an even better job next time.

✔ Sit down regularly, one-on-one, with your followers and talk through what they do, step by step, looking for ways to streamline their jobs and do them faster, more easily or more cheaply. After a while, your followers begin to review their jobs automatically and won't need you to guide them.

✔ Watch how others do similar tasks and see what you can adapt from their methods.

Chapter 6

Getting the Job Done

*L*eaders' days are hectic — filled with interruptions and unplanned but nonetheless important ad hoc meetings and conversations. In fact, most leaders confess they can't get everything done in a day that they'd like to get done — simply because they don't have enough time.

Yet, despite the fact that they're so busy, leaders achieve results because they know how to pinpoint their energies and efforts on what matters most; and they know how to prevent countless potential time wasters from draining their time. Leaders are efficient. They're able to work smoothly through the jobs they need to complete, find information and items when they need them and avoid back-tracking, getting stuck in bottlenecks and re-working mistakes.

In this chapter, I explain how to set priorities so you can concentrate on what matters most, and how to make sure you don't ignore the lower-priority matters. Here you find out how leaders start their days, organise themselves and take charge of time so that they achieve results. Finally, I share with you five proven ways to send your productivity and effectiveness soaring into the stratosphere.

Knowing What Matters Most

A laser uses just the same amount of energy to punch a hole through solid metal as a bulb needs to light the inside of a refrigerator. That same amount of energy can also send to the moon a beam of light so strong that it can be reflected back to earth. With enough attention on the right subject, you too can achieve such strength of leadership.

Leaders are busy people and can't afford to waste their time on activities that don't add value to their own areas of accountability, to their teams or to their organisations. They can't afford to waste time doing something a second time because they didn't do it properly the first time. Leaders attend to what matters most.

You may care passionately about all sorts of subjects — global warming, drought, war, pestilence. But if you spend a lot of time complaining or worrying about these matters, you can enter the danger zone of using these problems as excuses not to get on with activities that bring results. The outcome is that you end up underachieving.

 Similarly, responding to every task and every issue that crops up is not a successful way to operate — trying to do too much is a recipe for working hard but achieving little. You end up feeling rushed and never quite 'caught up', which is stressful and unhealthy. Because leaders lead hectic lives, feeling in control is particularly important.

In fact, the busier you are, the more you need to take time to step back and isolate the vital activities that lead to the greatest results. Stepping back and checking your priorities helps you

- Avoid 'wheel spinning' and achieve more
- Avoid emergencies and crises because you have dealt with matters in a timely manner
- Feel less harassed and stressed and more confident in your ability to lead
- Stay in control of how you use your time

Some activities have a bigger pay-off than others. These activities add value to the work you perform and bring you closer toward your leadership vision and your ability to get results in your key areas of responsibility. These activities are important and require your attention. That makes sense — when activities don't contribute to the results, then why bother with those activities. (If you don't have a leadership vision and know your key result areas yet, refer to Chapter 4.)

Once you're clear about your purpose as a leader and your key result areas (KRAs), you have to deal only with moments of choice. You can give your attention to your KRAs or you can fritter away your time and energy. Everything you do either moves you toward your aims or away from them. You're either paying attention to the right activities or you're not.

Many of a leader's most important duties have little or no urgency about them, making it tempting to put them off. But that's a trap. If you put off your value-adding contributions as a leader — activities such as planning, training your followers and building relationships — you ultimately find yourself so far behind that it's difficult to catch up. Make the work that matters most — your 'weight-bearing work' — your first priority.

Dealing with lower-priority work

Leaders can deal with less important 'lightweight' work — activities and tasks that don't directly contribute to their leadership vision — in three ways:

- ✔ Deal with the work later when you have time or when you want a short break from your more important tasks.
- ✔ Delegate the work to a follower who wants to learn those tasks.
- ✔ Dump the work in 'the round file' (that's what I call my waste bin when I don't want to admit I'm tossing something out).

This brings me to the Four Ds — a method to use whenever someone or something tries to snatch your attention. You may be distracted by an incoming email, a document dropped onto your desk, a telephone call or a team member or fellow leader popping in to ask a question or give you some information. Use the Four Ds, in this order, to decide how to deal with the situation:

- ✔ Do it now (if it adds value).
- ✔ Do it later.
- ✔ Delegate it.
- ✔ Dump it.

Make a firm decision and refuse to let less important tasks get in the way of doing more important tasks. (You can find out more about how to delegate successfully to your followers in Chapter 12.)

Effort and energy don't always produce results

For many years, I used a conference centre in Western Australia that was part of a large hotel/resort complex. It was a pleasure to go there because the place ran like clockwork. The same friendly people greeted me when I arrived, including the manager, John — who, by the way, never seemed to do much but was always around, keeping an eye on his staff, chatting to guests and making sure everyone was happy.

One time when I went back, John had left and been replaced by two people. But nothing seemed to work properly. Coffee didn't arrive on time for coffee breaks, meals ran overtime due to slow service — I won't go on. Yet those two replacements, even though they were the leaders of the complex, ended up rushing around, shirt tails hanging out, delivering the morning coffee themselves, never having the time to stop or speak to their followers or their guests. Suffice to say, without John leading it, the place had become a disaster and, sadly, closed down a few months later.

Effort and energy don't necessarily produce results — but effort and energy on the right activities always produce results. When you set priorities and concentrate on what matters most, you can get amazing amounts done. If you don't set priorities and stick to them, you end up rushing around and working frantically — like John's two replacements — but achieving little.

Deal with unimportant and non-urgent tasks when you have a few minutes of slack time or want a quick mental break, especially the too-little-to-be-bothered-with-now jobs and the jobs you dislike. This is also a good time to go through your To Read email folder if you're at your desk.

Asking the question that makes time work for you

Everyone has periods when the workload is heavy. When you're constantly under pressure and feel overwhelmed, you can make some changes before your health, wellbeing and personal life are adversely affected. The reason is simple: The way you spend your days is how you spend your life.

And I can confidently say that as each of your days progresses, matters that scream for your attention pile up. I can also assure you that if you attend to whatever 'calls' the loudest, you are likely to squander your day dealing with tasks that add little or no value. To combat the 'squeaky wheel' syndrome — attending to whatever makes the most noise, whether it's truly important or not — keep asking this question:

What is the best use of my time and attention — right now?

That one question keeps the priorities in the spotlight. That question also prevents you from being sucked in by so-called emergencies. Attending to one of these emergencies won't move you any closer to your goals or add any value to your leadership. Always evaluate 'emergencies' and all other incoming work against what matters most. Then you can decide how to deal with the work using the Four Ds described in the previous section.

Getting Your Days Off to a Great Start with a To Do List

The astronomer Carl Sagan once pointed out that not all birds can fly. What separates the flyers from the walkers is their ability to take off. Pretty much the same holds true for leaders who are 'flyers' — getting their days off to a great start gives them enough momentum to keep making progress and not get mired down as the day unfolds.

The surest way to get your days off to a great start is to make a To Do list at the end of every day. To Do lists help you track your commitments and keep egg off your face, making you look professional, organised, competent, capable and on top of your leadership role.

Write down what matters most — the jobs you need to do, people you need to meet, activities to check, important documents to prepare — whatever adds value and helps you achieve goals that are worthwhile in the areas that are most important to you as a leader.

Don't program every minute of your day — leave some slack time to spend with your followers and other leaders and to deal with matters that unexpectedly crop up. If your To Do list includes lots of tasks, prioritise those tasks. (You find out how in the following section.)

First thing the next morning, start on your high-priority tasks. Remove items from your list as you complete them and keep referring to your To Do list to guide the rest of your day. (If you use a paper To Do list, rewrite it when it gets too messy.)

Choosing e-lists or paper reminders

If you gave a To Do list a try and didn't stick with it, maybe you weren't using the right type of list. You can choose paper lists or electronic lists.

The most common paper To Do lists are kept in spiral-bound notebooks or diaries. You're best to opt for paper if you

✔ Can easily recall where on a page you wrote or read a particular detail

✔ Enjoy a hands-on approach

✔ Find the visual overview of a paper plan or diary helpful

✔ Remember best by writing down details

Paper To Do lists are cheaper and faster to write up than their electronic counterparts — and they don't run out of batteries. On the downside, you don't have a security password to keep out nosy people. And if you lose your paper list, you don't have a backup.

On the other hand, if you try a paper To Do list and decide paper isn't for you, chances are you're going to love an electronic list. E-lists suit when you

✔ Don't need the visual overview to keep your head clear

✔ Have a good memory for dates and numbers

✔ Move around a lot

✔ Prefer using a word search to trying to remember where you wrote your details

✔ Think clearly using a keyboard

Electronic To Do lists are light and compact. You can cut and paste without rewriting and you can find information easily with a keyword search. You can back up lists on your computer and, if you don't complete a job, you can expect the list to save automatically. Many types of e-lists have other handy features, too, such as access to email and the ability to store a long list of contact names and numbers.

The drawbacks of e-lists are that note taking is tedious and time consuming. You can't use computers as easily as a notebook in meetings and the risk of crashes and data loss makes your toes curl.

Whether you go for a paper or electronic version, divide your To Do list into sections representing your main types of activities. Here are some examples:

✔ Coaching

✔ Items to follow up

✔ Meetings

✔ Projects

✔ Telephone calls to make

Choose four of five of your most common and important task areas. Grouping activities together helps you work on them together, which increases your efficiency.

Setting priorities with ABCs

Once you have your To Do list written out, give an 'A' to the most important items, those you definitely want to do tomorrow. Give a 'C' to those activities that can wait if they need to, and the rest are 'B's.

Begin every day working on your 'A' priorities. As the day progresses and matters you need to deal with crop up, deal with them or put them on your To Do list to deal with later or to delegate. Then return to your 'A' priorities because they really add value to your leadership. When you complete your 'A' priorities, move onto your 'B' priorities.

Do your 'C' priorities when you want a bit of 'light work', a rest from the 'heavier work' and when you find that a 'C' priority has hung around on your To Do list for some time and you're sick of seeing it there. Or perhaps you transferred a 'C' priority to a new list several times. Think about your 'Dump it' option. If you don't want to dump your 'C' task, do it now and get it out of the way.

If you don't need the ABC system because your To Do list isn't 'busy' enough, try highlighting the 'musts' that you must get done the next day.

Organising for Efficiency

Attending to what matters most makes you *effective* — 'doing the right things'. You also need to be *efficient* — 'doing things right'. That means not doing a job in a roundabout, long-winded way that takes extra time and effort. Instead you can tackle a job in a smooth way that avoids backtracking, bottlenecks and wasting time.

Efficient people get jobs done properly. They complete tasks more quickly, probably better and certainly with less frustration than inefficient people do. When you're both effective and efficient, you're on top of your role as a leader, respected and looked to as a role model. Expanding your efficiency can be easy if you take the advice in the following sections.

Why is your To Do list not working?

Leaders are so busy that they really can't afford not to have a To Do list. If you tried one but didn't find it helpful, figure out why so you can overcome the problem. Are you

- ✔ Attending to 'squeaky wheel' unimportant tasks while leaving undone the tasks that add value?

- ✔ Avoiding doing some of the items on it for some reason?

- ✔ Becoming busy doing your followers' work instead of your own?

- ✔ Failing to commit to achieving the tasks on your list?

- ✔ Finding your environment so hectic or so filled with emergencies and crises that planning is difficult?

- ✔ Ignoring your priorities?

- ✔ Jumping into tasks in the middle, without first figuring out how best to tackle them?

- ✔ Lacking the self-confidence to tackle the more difficult jobs?

- ✔ Leaving tasks because you find them difficult or boring, or because you have too many interruptions?

- ✔ Neglecting to update your To Do list or refer to it as the day progresses?

- ✔ Opting to do what is easiest, quickest, or whatever catches your attention because your self-discipline is failing you?

- ✔ Testing the water instead of plunging into a task?

- ✔ Tending to put tasks off until the deadline looms?

- ✔ Thinking: 'I probably won't have time to finish it anyway!' so you don't even start?

- ✔ Trying to do too much?

Loving lists

I can't function without lists. If you try to rely on your memory, some important task is bound to slip through the cracks, and sometimes those tasks can be very important jobs. Lists help reduce stress by taking some of the load off your brain — you don't have to remember everything. All the jobs you haven't done yet won't prey on your mind, cluttering up your thinking processes and distracting you from the job at hand.

Lists are the bridge between thinking and action. Writing down tasks also increases the likelihood of your completing the task.

I talk about To Do lists in the previous section. Now the time has come to look at other types of lists. You can make lists for projects, points you want to make at a meeting or during a phone conversation, or a list of information you need in order to make a decision. You can make lists on a pad of paper or create a simple electronic task list, and you can make them as detailed as you need to by showing various categories, such as due dates, milestones and progress notes.

Most leaders simply brainstorm their lists; and when a list is long or complex, efficient leaders may tidy up the list by dividing it into topic areas or putting the contents in timeline order. Some leaders also keep a pad of paper and a pencil by their beds so when they wake in the middle of the night with their minds racing, they can dump their thoughts on paper and go back to sleep, confident that their thoughts are captured and not forgotten.

Tidying up

Searching for items or information you need increases your stress and eats up precious minutes that all add up to wasted time. Moreover, clutter is unsightly and emotionally draining. It distracts you and prevents you from paying attention to the job at hand. ('Clutter' is any item that isn't being used and isn't where it belongs — away in its 'special place'.)

If you don't want to make your life or the lives of your followers any harder than necessary, cast out clutter and streamline your storage. Make sure everything has a place and, if an item isn't being used *right now*, put that item back in its place — otherwise, it's clutter. The place for everything that is frequently used is closest to where you use it, at a convenient arm's reach or less. The place for less frequently used items may be further away but where the items can be clearly labelled and easily accessed.

Make this your motto:

Don't just put it down — put it away.

You won't notice the seconds it takes to put items away; and, if you put off putting it away until later, you probably won't get around to it. That's how chaos builds up and gradually overwhelms you, and you're faced with the tedious and time-consuming job of a major tidy-up.

Tidiness sends a strong message that you and your followers have 'got it together' and are in control and reliable. Get into the habit — and ask your followers to do the same — of spending a few minutes at the end of each day tidying your work areas and making sure the folders, files, books and bits and pieces you work with — staplers, pens, pencils, paper clips — are stored away where they belong.

At the end of the week, spend ten minutes evaluating any paperwork and electronic files that have accumulated to see what you can discard or delete, and file the rest. Be ruthless about culling. Label your paper and electronic files and folders clearly and meaningfully so you don't waste time searching for information, and show your followers how to do the same.

Profiting from a great follow-up system

Failing to consistently honour your commitments blows an otherwise good reputation. If you say you'll contact someone by 3.00 pm, do so — 3.30 pm isn't good enough. You have a right to expect others to honour their commitments to you, too. When a person agrees to give you some information by Friday, expect it by Friday. Put it on the follow-up section of your To Do list and if you haven't received it by, say, noon on Friday, give them a quick, polite reminder.

Set up a reliable follow-up system. Whenever you agree to do a task or need to follow up a promise, or whenever a colleague has agreed to provide you with some information or documentation, note the details on a special section of your To Do list, or set up an electronic reminder to alert you. When you follow through and the task is completed, remove or delete that entry from your list.

When you note matters to follow up or follow through, make your life easier by jotting brief reminder notes of the circumstances, the person or people involved and their contact details. You're training your followers to honour their obligations and leading by example — two other important jobs of leaders.

If you lead from a desk

No doubt you have enough interruptions and distractions to handle without adding to them unnecessarily. That's why keeping your desk clear is important. Apart from whatever you are working on right now, have only four or five items on your desk. They are

✔ Computer screen

✔ Keyboard and mouse

✔ Telephone

✔ To Do list if it's a paper one

Even your in-tray should be on a console or filing cabinet out of arm's reach so you won't be tempted to check every time a document or file is dropped into it — that would only disrupt your train of thought. The same goes for the visual and auditory computer alerts that announce an email has arrived — turn the noises off unless a key part of your role is responding quickly to emails. If you use SMS on your mobile phone, turn off the sound. If you use instant messaging, use the Busy button when you don't want to be interrupted.

Tackling the Time-Eating Monsters

Everyone has time wasters that devour the time and steal the attention from more important matters. If you're like most people, 44 per cent of your time wasters are of your own making and others aren't. Perhaps you can recognise some of these time wasters:

- ✔ Busy work (doing a little job for the sake of doing it, even though the job doesn't really need doing)
- ✔ Emails
- ✔ Incessant interruptions
- ✔ Procrastination
- ✔ Surfing the Internet
- ✔ Telephone

You need to know how to stop wasting your own time and how to deal with the time wasters your environment throws at you. That way you can prevent those monsters from continually munching away, leaving you with no time or energy left to lead properly. You also need to be able to show your followers how to deal with their own time-eating monsters.

Stamping out procrastination

Everyone puts off tasks once in a while, but if you put off too much too often, you feel stressed and you undermine your self-respect and your leadership.

If putting off tasks is your downfall, here's a three-pronged attack for the procrastination monster:

- ✔ **Commit to a deadline:** Set a start deadline, a finish deadline, or both. If you're a chronic procrastinator, try setting a false deadline — when a job is due to be complete in four weeks, set a deadline for three weeks.
- ✔ **Recognise the consequences:** Know how completing the task you're postponing helps you to achieve your leadership vision. On the flip side, recognise the consequences of not completing the task or not completing the task well enough.
- ✔ **Slice the task into small To Do steps:** Commit to doing as many of those small steps as you need to every day until the task is complete. Feel free to spread the steps over several days if you need to do so. But most people find that once they have gained momentum by completing the first small step or two, it's easy to keep going.

You probably find more satisfaction in getting a job done and out of the way so the job isn't hanging over your head like the Sword of Damocles. 'I won't be able to finish this, so I'll do it later' is a guarantee that you're never going to get the job done. Simply make a start — revising is easier than creating.

Don't wait to get to work on the important tasks until you're in the mood. Set up a system, or a set of 'rules' for yourself that gets your nose to the grindstone every day. Set a target for what you want to achieve and keep working toward your target until you reach it.

You probably aren't a chronic procrastinator — leaders can't afford to be. But you probably have chores you don't enjoy and some you even dislike that you keep putting off. You still need to do those chores, though. You don't have any choice.

But you do have a choice about how you do a job. You can do a job with an 'I have to' attitude or you can do a job with an 'I want to' attitude. The 'I have to' choice means you do the job half-heartedly, resenting every moment and getting the job over with as soon as possible. That approach won't help you do a good job or give you any pleasure from doing the job or from seeing it finished. That attitude makes you miserable.

Your other choice is to change the 'have to' into 'want to'. That one-word change makes those dreary duties more agreeable and helps you do them better and take some pride in the results, too. In fact, that one little word can make you twice as productive.

What's stopping you?

Many situations can conspire to stop you getting a job done. Here are some culprits:

✔ Do you have a block that says, 'I don't feel like it'? Sorry — not good enough. You're a leader, snap to it!

✔ Is fear of failure preventing you from starting? Think: Here's a chance to learn. Or think: Here's a chance to boost my confidence.

✔ Is it fear of success and fulfilling others' expectations of you? Think: Here's a chance to show my value and expand my repertoire.

✔ Is it fear of finishing and finding yourself in a vacuum? Think: The time has come to get on with the job.

✔ Do you need more information or resources? Figure out what you need and how to get what you need so you can get on with the job.

✔ Are you not really committed to doing a job because it's someone else's priority (not yours)? Find a way to become more committed and to want to do it.

✔ Do you just plain hate the job? You have two choices — gut it out or farm it out. Do either, as long as the job is done.

If you're thinking 'I really don't want to do this', find a reason to want to — even if you're only doing the job to get it done and out of the way, so you won't feel guilty about not doing the job, or so you can feel proud or relieved once the job is finished.

When you replace 'I have to' with 'I want to', you can attack irksome chores with a positive outlook and take some pleasure in doing those jobs well. From now on, say 'I want to' whenever you have a tedious task to do.

Banishing 'busy work'

We live in an action-oriented culture with an ethic to always look busy, but leaders know not to squander their time being busy on marginal tasks that add little or no value to their leadership or other important responsibilities. Nor do they do 'busy work' just to avoid other, more difficult (but important) work!

'Busy-ness' doesn't count, and doing something just because you enjoy it isn't a good enough reason to do it. Doing busy work at the expense of more important work generally leads to firefighting when the monster of undone important work rears its ugly head.

Working hard isn't the same as being productive, and working hard doesn't make you a leader. If you want to be a successful leader, don't kid yourself that merely looking busy is in your best interests or is satisfying. Only do work that adds real value to your leadership responsibilities.

Taming the telephone

The phone rings; you answer it. You may be in a crucial meeting, but you answer it, rudely leaving the other person twiddling thumbs and wasting time. Or you may be in the middle of an important project, but you stop and answer the phone, breaking your concentration and allowing your train of thought to evaporate.

Don't let the telephone become a monster that controls you. Use telephones strictly as tools of convenience. When you're in a meeting or busy and can't afford to be interrupted, put the ringer and message machine on silent or forward your calls to someone else.

When you make outgoing calls, try to make several in one block of time. Organise your calls so that you know what points you want to cover and have any information you need ready to hand.

Conquering email excess

Use emails as a tool of convenience, too. Here are some quick and easy tips to keep from being crushed by emails:

- ✔ Ask people who are sending you information you don't need to send the information to an appropriate team member instead of to you.
- ✔ Check your emails twice a day (once in the morning and once in the afternoon) or when you have a low-energy period or want a quick break (unless your job demands more instant responses).
- ✔ Don't start your day on emails, especially if this is a productive time of the day for you.
- ✔ Transfer emails to an appropriate folder unless you can deal with them in less than two minutes. Delete all emails that don't warrant a short response.

When you're composing emails, help the recipients out with a clear subject line. State your main points in the first two lines, and keep the email to less than one screen in length. And don't forget the rules of common courtesy — include a salutation (Hi John, Dear Sally) and a sign-off (Cheers, Best wishes) and remember your 'pleases' and 'thankyous'.

Enduring endless interruptions

Here's a scary statistic for you: People in busy offices are interrupted every three minutes and five seconds on average. How can anyone ever get anything done! Most leaders have between three and nine minutes between interruptions. Many interruptions are important; but equally, many interruptions are intrusive and irritating.

Interruptions destroy productivity. Ninety minutes of uninterrupted time is equivalent to four hours of interrupted time, so you need to know how to tame the time-eating monster of interruptions by avoiding some interruptions, limiting others, and dealing gracefully with the rest.

Avoid interruptions

People aren't your only interruptions; noise is distracting, too. Noise interferes with your concentration and creates confusion and tension. Eliminate as much needless noise as you can. Yes, I'll say this again and again — turn down the noisy ring tone on your phone and silence your computer alerts, computer command tones and voice mail and SMS alerts.

Angle your desk and chair so that passers-by can't easily catch your eye and interrupt you. If you can't change the furniture position, place a plant on your desk to prevent easy eye contact. Make your space work-like and less inviting to drop in to — for example, don't have a spare chair near you, a dish of lollies on your desk and so on.

If you really need to concentrate, close your door or head off to a quiet place where you can work without interruption. (Remember to let your team members know where to find you before you go.)

Limit interruptions

The sad truth is, some interruptions you just can't avoid. But that doesn't mean you have to deal with them — at least not all of them — and you don't need to deal with every interruption immediately.

First, decide whether the interruption really is necessary and when it isn't necessary, end the interruption quickly by referring the person to someone else or by arranging a more convenient time to get together. Ask people who interrupt you how much time they need, to encourage them to think through their problem and help you plan your day.

If people want information from you, decide whether you're the best person to supply it — if not, steer them in the right direction. Ask whether they need the information straight away — they probably don't and you can add that job to your To Do list to deal with when it's more convenient.

If someone is offering you information, decide whether you need that information and whether you prefer to have it in writing or schedule a more convenient time to meet and discuss the information.

Speed conversations up by standing up when someone comes in; and if they're a notorious 'visitor', say you were just off for a cuppa — would they like to join you? This action makes it easier to take your leave gracefully. Try keeping a pen in hand, poised for action, mentioning a priority you're working on, glancing at your watch frequently — anything to shorten the interruption. (If the visit is important, stop what you're doing and give the person your full attention. For more on this subject, see the following section.)

Have a mental (or written) note of 'important' phone calls you need to make so when you want to close the meeting, you can excuse yourself and explain why. If the interrupter doesn't take the hint, say you'd love to talk more and you can catch up later because you have a lot to do. That shows your time is valuable, too.

Cope with interruptions

If you need to deal with an interruption right there and then, try to break what you were working on at a natural stopping point and jot a note to yourself where you were up to and what you intend to do next; that gets you up to speed quickly when you return to the task. Then put away the task so it won't distract you, and give the interrupter your full attention.

Pareto's Law, or the *80:20 Rule,* tells you that 20 per cent of people are probably responsible for 80 per cent of your interruptions. Identify who your serial interrupters are and work out some more satisfactory arrangements with them; for example, agree to meet at specific times, weekly or daily or whatever is appropriate and ask them to keep a list of talking points and questions for those meetings. Agree on the length of the meetings and think about combining the meetings with something else, such as a cup of coffee or lunch.

Working Smarter Not Harder

Do you remember the story of Hercules battling the Hydra? Every time Hercules cut off one of Hydra's heads, three more heads appeared. The harder and faster Hercules fought, the more easily the monster overpowered him.

The head-slicing trick doesn't work with time-sucking monsters, either. Working smarter does.

Working harder and faster reduces your productivity and increases your stress. To avoid ending up frazzled and burnt out, concentrate on one meaningful task at a time and get it done properly — first time. Go for quality, not quantity.

Respect other people's time

Set a good example by respecting other people's time, too. For example:

✔ Don't use your voicemail to screen calls for hours on end.

✔ Return calls to avoid seeming rude, disorganised or unreliable.

✔ Start calls you make by briefly outlining what you want to discuss and ask if the person is free to talk for a few minutes.

Slow down and do more

Rushing causes mistakes. Too much rushing even damages your immune system. Leaders know that just because they have a lot of work to do, they won't get the work done any faster or better if they rush — quite the opposite.

When you're rushing, your brain releases hormones that cause your muscles to tense, your heart to beat more rapidly and your body temperature to rise. When that happens, you need to put in a lot of effort before you see any results. So rushing is basically a recipe for stress, confusion and mistakes.

Smothering recurring problems

One way to make your life easier is to tackle recurring and predictable problems and find a way to prevent them from occurring in the first place. For example, when your team members continually interrupt you with the same questions, put a system in place to answer those questions automatically; or show people where they can find the answer themselves. In other words, don't keep chopping off a head — smother it!

For the monsters you can't prevent, figure out what you can do to lessen their impact and have a backup plan that you can swing into action when the problem rears its ugly head.

Putting your down time to work

If you're like most leaders, you're too busy to waste your time while you're waiting to see someone, standing in a queue, or waiting for or sitting on a train or plane. You can't recycle wasted time, so put that *down time* to good use.

Always have one or two small portable tasks with you, such as articles you want to read and a notepad so that you can jot down ideas, even when down time catches you unawares. Use the time to think up ideas, or simply relax if you decide that's the best use of your time. Carry a list of people you need to telephone; have their numbers on the list and keep dot points of what you want to discuss. (When you make those calls in a public space, respect others by keeping your voice down or stepping outside.)

Working in your prime time

You may have noticed that you have your own *prime time* when you can most effectively tackle your most difficult tasks. This is when your energy level is at its peak and when you're thinking most clearly.

If you're a morning person who wilts in the afternoon, attend to more routine matters in the afternoon and schedule the morning, when you're at your best, for important activities — important presentations, critical meetings, projects and decisions that need careful thought. If you can't, have a high-protein lunch, eat a piece of fruit and get some fresh air beforehand.

If you hit your stride later in the day, do your most important work and your serious thinking and then attend to more routine matters in the mornings. If you need to have an early start to the day, hit the deck running by organising items and information you need the day before; eat a high-protein breakfast or fresh fruit, and get some fresh air.

Whether you're a morning or an afternoon person, you also experience six to eight peaks of energy, lasting one and a half to two hours each, separated by 10- to 20-minute troughs of fatigue during which performing at your best is impossible. Work smarter not harder by scheduling some quality time-out for these troughs — get some fresh air; take a walk to the shops to pick up something you or your team needs; phone home; eat a piece of fruit or stand up and drink a glass of water.

Don't let lack of sleep steal your time. Sleepiness cuts your concentration, produces poor thinking and shrinks your productivity. You are more alert and work more easily and faster when you're well rested.

Evicting multi-tasking madness

So much to do; so little time. The temptation to knock off several tasks at once is big. But this work practice is usually a mistake.

You end up doing nothing very well unless the tasks are all so routine that you could do them in your sleep. But as soon as something needs a bit of thought, care and attention, multi-tasking doesn't work. Multi-tasking becomes inefficient, makes easy work hard and piles on the stress. In the long run, multi-tasking takes more time, not less, because you end up doing jobs a second or even a third time to get them right.

In short, splitting your attention between several tasks at once actually shrinks your productivity. Too much multi-tasking can even reduce your memory and your ability to concentrate for lengthy periods. Value, not velocity, gets better results in less time.

Instead of multi-tasking, group your work into like activities. Write emails, read reports, then make a few phone calls. Doing similar tasks in one block of time means you don't need to keep switching mental gears, which saves you time and helps you get into a smoother work groove. Organise tasks into like groups on your To Do list to make this easy.

Multi-tasking only pops information into your short-term memory. If you can't resist multi-tasking, work on active tasks where mistakes won't matter, never on tasks you need to remember.

Taking time to think

Leaders often feel pressured to come up with answers but generally they're better to take time to think through a question first because the *right* answer is better than the *quickest* answer. You need to be comfortable with saying something like 'I don't know yet' or 'Let me think about it' to buy you some time to find the right answer. Then you can mull over your ideas, think about your options and let those options percolate on your brain's back-burner for a while. That also means your subconscious can get to work, which usually improves the result.

The myth of multi-tasking

When you multi-task, you're really just switching quickly from one task to another and back again. Every time you do this, the brain has to do a quick 'Now where was I?' catch up. Even if you're not conscious of it, your brain has to make the decision to switch tasks, then switch tasks, and then warm up to the new task. That might take only half a second, but the switching all adds up to wasted time.

Meanwhile, your brain struggles to keep tabs on all the jobs you're doing. You just can't think clearly and concentrate properly on any one task when you're trying to do several jobs at once. That's why you're generally much better doing one job and sticking with it for as long as you can.

Similarly, if someone comes to you with a problem or just wants to chat something through, don't feel you have to jump in with an answer. Ask a few questions and listen a bit longer. The other person feels better about you and the conversation because you're listening and you're showing some genuine interest. As a bonus, when the two of you explore the issue in depth, you're rewarded with more insights and can generate a better solution or plan of attack.

Employing intelligent laziness

'If a thing's worth doing, it's worth doing well.' I heard that adage a thousand times when I was a child. And generally speaking, that advice has stood me in good stead. If a job is important, it is worthwhile to give that job the time it deserves and doing that job 'right first time'.

Sometimes, though, less is more. Sometimes, high standards can lead to overdoing a job that doesn't warrant much time, fuss and focus.

Sometimes close enough *is* good enough! Know which tasks not to spend too much time and effort on for too few results. Do a 'good enough' job on lightweight tasks.

The busier you are, the more you need to discriminate between the jobs that deserve all the effort you can muster to do them well, and those that don't merit your full concentration and care. Otherwise, you can end up spreading yourself too thinly. Following this principle of discerning laziness allows you to do less and achieve more.

Chapter 7

Communicating as a Leader

Most leaders spend 75 per cent of their time communicating, and 93 per cent of their conversations are spontaneous. Communication is central to almost every aspect of leadership. In fact, saying that when you don't communicate well, you won't succeed as a leader, is not an exaggeration.

This chapter looks at how to listen to other people and how to help others listen to you; how to persuade people to your point of view; and how to prevent misunderstandings and disagreements from escalating into arguments. I explain that your body language is essential to communicating effectively and describe how to support your messages with positive, confident body language. I also describe the fail-safe five-step method that leaders use to prepare and deliver a speech.

Speaking Begins with Listening

Leaders understand the difference between listening and hearing. When leaders listen, they don't say much, but they're still involved. They think about what they're hearing and what it means from various perspectives, including the speaker's and their own. They also listen 'between the lines', for the meanings that may be behind someone's words, for what isn't being said, and for people's intentions, hopes and fears.

Listening with your heart, mind and eyes as well as your ears makes listening a very active process. You can't respond meaningfully and appropriately to another person's comments until you fully understand that person's point of view. In order to deliver a message others can understand and accept, you need to get on your listener's wavelength, and that can't happen unless you have listened well enough to know what that wavelength is. Then you can structure your comments in a way that people can grasp what you're saying. At this stage, you and your listeners can be said to be speaking the same language. That's why speaking begins with listening.

The easiest way to get someone to listen to you is to listen to them first. Then they feel obliged to listen to you, too.

Listening like a leader

Ironically, the words *listen* and *silent* contain the same letters. But the differences between listening and being silent are many.

Here are some tips to help you listen effectively while you're being silent:

- ✔ **Listen to the whole story:** If you just go for key words, you're likely to misunderstand the message.
- ✔ **Pay attention mentally:** Clear your mind; squash any negative, judgemental, sarcastic or otherwise critical thoughts.
- ✔ **Pay attention physically:** Lean slightly towards and watch the speaker, nodding occasionally or saying 'Mmm' as they make a point.

Most people can think faster than people talk, which gives you a lot of free mental time when you're listening. To use that time wisely, quieten any inner chatter going on in your mind and set aside your opinions and thoughts. Mentally summarise the speaker's main points and ideas as you listen. Listen for the meanings behind the words — what is the speaker *really* saying? To listen between the lines, get to what's below the obvious and apparent surface.

Using your E. A. R. S.

You have two ears and one mouth for two important reasons:

- ✔ **To listen:** Listening is twice as difficult as speaking. (If you don't believe me, listen to this fact: Your blood pressure and temperature rise and your pulse quickens when you're concentrating on listening to someone speak.)

> ✔ **To remember:** Remember to use your ears and mouth in that same two-to-one ratio.

I made up an acronym to help you really understand what a person is saying to you. This acronym is E.A.R.S. — explore, affirm, recap, silence.

Explore

You can explore what a speaker is saying by asking questions that bring out more information:

✔ How would that option work?

✔ What do you think led to this situation?

✔ What does that entail?

✔ What happened next?

✔ When did this begin?

Keep asking questions to probe and clarify the speaker's point until you're satisfied that you understand the point the speaker is making.

Affirm

Affirm you're listening to a speaker by nodding your head and softly murmuring 'Uh hmm' or 'Mmm' and leaning slightly forward, towards the speaker. Showing you're listening and paying attention encourages the speaker to continue — nothing is worse for speakers than feeling they're speaking to a brick wall.

Be careful never to 'Uh hmm' and 'Mmm' too loudly or too much in response to somebody else's presentation. Some people overdo this method of responding and their enthusiasm can make concentrating on the speech difficult for the people nearby and for the speaker.

Looking at the person speaking also shows you're paying attention and helps you listen better, too — when your eyes wander, so does your mind. Concentrate on what the speaker is saying — don't think about what you're going to say next.

Recap

When the speaker seems finished or moves on to another point, the time has come to recap. A *recap* is a short summary of what you understand from the speech so far, covering the speaker's feelings or meanings or both. Recapping shows you have, indeed, been listening and taking in the information.

If what the speaker is saying is quite complex, you can interject with a quick question that summarises the information to make sure you're not misunderstanding anything. Alternatively, you can ask a question to clarify what the speaker is saying to help you better understand the point. The speaker won't mind because, while interrupting is rude, checking you're still following the speaker isn't — in fact, checking your understanding is a compliment to the speaker because you're showing how determined you are to understand the speaker's point.

When recapping, keep your voice neutral and your words objective. As soon as you're satisfied with the answers, close your mouth and keep listening; because your silence, after recapping, draws out even more information.

The art of asking questions

The 18th-century French philosopher and author Françoise Marie Voltaire said, 'Judge a man by his questions, not by his answers.'

How skilfully do you ask questions?

If people often answer your questions with 'Yes' or 'No' or just a few matter-of-fact words, perhaps you're asking too many closed questions and not enough open questions.

Closed questions can be answered with a 'Yes' or 'No' or just a few words, so they work well when you want to confirm information. Open questions can't have a 'Yes' or 'No' answer, so they encourage a full response, helping you gather information and find out more about what the other person is thinking.

Ask one question at a time, then pause and wait for the response. Give your conversational partner time to think. Don't ramble on, don't answer the question you just asked and don't fill their thinking time with nervous chatter. And remember to listen to the answer!

Carefully aimed questions guide a conversation and move a discussion along. Good questions draw out the full story, clear up confusion and ferret out information, details and facts.

If you're ever stuck for something to say in a conversation, ask a question. Most people appreciate the opportunity to talk about themselves and their thoughts and opinions and are happy to answer you, as long as your question is halfway decent. To keep the conversational ball rolling, offer your own experience and thoughts, too.

Silence

The adage that silence is golden didn't happen by chance. I think of silence as a vacuum that begs to be filled. The trick is to let the other person be the person who fills the vacuum.

When you recap and you're confident you understand the speaker's message, sit back and switch back to listening mode. Pause and look at the speaker expectantly and wait to hear what the speaker has to say next. Don't worry when a short silence occurs — the speaker is probably thinking quite deeply about what to say. Don't feel you have to help, because your waiting allows the speaker to 'dig deep' to find the right thoughts. The silence may seem long, but silence never lasts more than a few seconds.

Use your E. A. R. S. especially when

- ✔ You can see conflict, disagreement or misunderstanding arising
- ✔ You can sense the situation becoming tense or emotional
- ✔ You want to listen carefully to what someone is saying

Taking a walk in someone else's shoes

Leaders need to understand the points of view of their team members, other leaders and their own leader — especially when disagreement arises. Being able to understand other people's points of view helps leaders pick up information they might otherwise miss; learn more about the people with whom they must negotiate; and work out how to communicate better with those people.

Taking a walk in someone else's shoes means you have *empathy* — you take the trouble to see that person's world from that person's point of view. You don't need to agree with other people, just understand what speakers are saying to you and from where they're coming. To walk in someone else's shoes, you first have to take off your own — that temporarily frees you of your own opinions, prejudices and assumptions while you're taking that walk, making room to let the other person's ideas in.

Everyone tends to assume that their own point of view is more accurate and correct than other points of view. The fact is, every person's point of view is different and each is probably correct, at least to a point. The more points of view you're able to see empathetically, the more clearly you can understand the situation and the more effectively you can lead.

Different points of view

You probably remember the fable of the elephant and the six blind men, each of whom believed the elephant to be completely different because each had touched a different part of the elephant's body. The man who felt the animal's large side saw the elephant as a wall; the man who felt the tusk saw a spear; the man who felt the trunk thought of a snake; the man who felt a leg imagined a tree; the man who felt an ear thought of a fan; and the man who felt the tail imagined a rope. Each man was correct from his own perspective, but none of the men saw the whole elephant.

Checking it out

You know the saying about assumptions — to *assume* something is to make an 'ass' of 'u' and 'me'. I don't know about that saying, but what I do know is that most assumptions are reached in the blink of an eye, as the brain tries to make sense of confusing and contradictory information. That means uncovering your quickly-formed assumptions can be difficult.

Nevertheless, try to stay vigilant and alert to any assumptions you and your followers may be making so that you don't become caught up in your assumptions. Treating assumptions as if they were facts is dangerous. Make a point of verifying your assumptions in order to avoid the embarrassing and expensive decisions and unnecessary conflicts that can result from assumptions that may prove wrong.

Giving Your Words Power

The people of West Africa have a saying: 'When the mouth stumbles, it is worse than the foot.' For leaders, casual conversations don't exist. Think carefully about the words you use because your words matter and they have power, whenever you say them and in whatever situation.

The more important your message, the more carefully your followers listen to what you say. Your followers discuss with each other what you say and analyse your words. Listeners also embellish your words with their own meanings, experiences, hopes and fears to the point where, if you're not careful, your message ends up with an entirely different meaning than the one you intended.

Once the words are spoken, you can't take them back

You have your own characteristic way of talking, called an *idiolect*. This word describes your unique manner of speaking and includes the style of words and expressions you use and the way you put them together.

Over time, people's idiolects become automatic and words just tumble out of their mouths. To keep your feet out of your mouth, pause and think about what you want to say and how you want to say it before you speak. Take particular care to do this if you're an outgoing person, because extroverts tend to speak before they think.

Choosing your words with care

Sweet words win you cooperation and commitment rather than clashes and confrontations.

Sweet words alone aren't enough, of course. Depending on your purpose, you can choose words that are forceful or weak, impartial or emotive, clear or vague, courteous or challenging. But you can always keep your words polite.

Choose constructive words

Leaders use words that are memorable and set a constructive tone to a conversation. Table 7-1 shows you how constructive words sound less critical, 'pushy' and daunting than their negative counterparts, so they encourage cooperation and reduce resistance.

The way you talk colours the way you think and the way you think shapes the way you lead. To avoid sounding like a vague, negative or weak leader, choose clear, positive, powerful words. This helps you think and act clearly, positively and confidently, too.

Table 7-1	Using Constructive Language
Instead of saying	*Leaders say*
'You have to …'	'I need you to … so that …'
'You never …'	'How about …'
'You're not listening.'	'Let me run through that again.'
'What's the problem?'	'How can I help?'
'I can't do that until Monday.'	'I'll be able to do that on Monday.'
You and I have got a lot to do today.'	'You and I have a full day ahead of us.'
'That will be difficult.'	'Here's how we can make this happen.'
'This is a problem.'	'This is a nuisance. What can we do about it?'
'That's impossible.'	'We can make this work if …'

Choose objective, factual and specific words

Leaders avoid exaggerating and choose objective words and factual, descriptive words over words loaded with double meanings, criticism or emotions. As a result, their comments come across as considered and fair, which soothes people and makes them more open to listening. See Table 7-2 for examples.

Table 7-2	Using Objective Language
Instead of saying	*Leaders say*
'You're rude and curt when you're on the telephone.'	'You speak very quickly and succinctly when you're on the telephone.'
'You're not making any sense.'	'I'm not clear about what you mean.'

Leaders don't use jargon. Instead leaders select specific and strong words that say precisely what is to happen. That way, no team member needs to guess or make what may be a dangerous assumption. See Table 7-3 for examples.

Table 7-3	Using Specific Language
Instead of saying	*Leaders say*
'I'll send it.'	'I'll courier it' or 'I'll fax it'
'I'll contact you soon.'	'I'll phone you on Monday morning' or 'I'll email you tomorrow'

Choose strong words

Avoid these weak words and phrases that can water down your message:

- Appears to be
- Could
- If
- I'll do my best, but ...
- I'll see what I can do
- May
- Might
- Possibly
- Probably
- Seems to
- That should be okay

Weak words spoil your message and invite people to ignore what you're saying. Powerful words sink in. Don't say, 'I'll try to have it by Friday.' Instead, say, 'I'll have it for you by Friday,' if that's what you mean. Or if you can't yet guarantee delivery by Friday, say, 'I'll email you as soon as I can tell you which day I'll have it.'

Choose words that the other person uses

Listen to the way the people you're with speak, and listen to the type of words they use — for example, are their words formal or informal, to-the-point or flowery, correct or colloquial? Do they use technical terms or everyday terms, long words or short words? Make your words hit home by using similar types of words and expressions in your communication with them.

Conversations flow more smoothly and people feel more comfortable with people who speak the same way they speak. Communicating in the same style as the people you're talking to increases their willingness to cooperate.

Butting 'but' from your vocabulary

Who would think that a simple little word like *but* harms relationships and spoils conversations? 'But' is a danger zone. 'But' butts away the other person's point of view. 'But' is a verbal hammer that wipes out the conversation and screams 'I disagree!' or 'Look out! Here comes bad news.' Here are some examples:

- ✔ 'I take your point, but ...'
- ✔ 'I understand what you're saying, but you've forgotten about ...'
- ✔ 'That was a good report, but you should have ...'
- ✔ 'You did a good job, but you made a mistake with ...'

Avoiding 'but' prevents tension and disagreement. The same holds true for 'however', which is just a longer version of 'but'. Substitute both 'but' and 'however' with 'and' for a positive result. Try these examples:

- ✔ 'I agree and ...'
- ✔ 'I appreciate your views and I'd also like to take into account ...'
- ✔ 'I understand what you're saying, and here's what I think.'
- ✔ 'That was a good report, and next time, you could ...'
- ✔ 'You did a good job, and the only thing to fine-tune is ...'

'But' blocks conversation and progress; 'and' builds conversation and progress. 'And' shows you're listening and hearing what the other person is saying. 'And' oils the wheels of a discussion because this little word acknowledges what someone has said and expands on the discussion. When you use 'and' you're working *with* a person's comments; with 'but', you're working *against* a person's comments. 'And' helps prevent arguments by allowing two points of view to stand: 'Here is what you think *and* here is what I think.'

Using magic words and magic phrases

No child ever received anything in my house without using the magic words 'Please' and 'Thank you'. Successful leaders use these words a lot, too, because these words make a leader more approachable. These words also enlist cooperation and build strong team relationships.

'Because' is another magic word that leaders favour. Explaining why takes the heat out of criticism and sounds more sincere and less patronising when offering praise. Explaining why also encourages the other person to keep doing what you praised.

'Because' is less useful when you need to say 'No' tactfully. For example, instead of saying 'I can't because ...' say 'I can as soon as ...' or 'I can once ...'

Here are some magic phrases and questions that leaders use:

- ✔ **Do you have a minute?** Ask this question before launching into a conversation with someone who may be in the middle of something else. Use this question when you telephone someone, walk up to someone's desk or approach people while they're walking somewhere. The question shows you're considerate of other people's schedules and tells them that they're free to say, 'Later is better'.

- ✔ **I'm not following what you're saying.** When you use these words, you avoid accusing the other person of being confusing or of having woolly thinking.

- ✔ **Tell me if you're not following what I'm saying.** This offer invites people to ask for clarification when they need to understand information.

- ✔ **Would you mind if I make a suggestion?** This question stops you from ramming unwanted advice down people's throats and is far better than saying 'I know just what you should do.'

Table 7-4 shows you phrases that leaders avoid and those they use instead.

Questions that begin with 'Why', such as 'Why did you do that?' tend to make people defensive. Instead, ask: 'How did this come about?' or 'What led to your decision to do that?' or 'What makes you say that?'

Table 7-4	Using positive phrases
Instead of saying	*Leaders say*
'You'll need to ...'	'So that I can ... I need ... from you.'
'We can't go to lunch until one.'	'We can go to lunch at one.'
'No, because ...'	'Yes, as soon as ...'
'It can't be done because ...'	'Here's how we can do it ...'
'It's only my opinion ...'	'I think ...'

Helping People to Listen

People don't listen to you just because you're a leader. You still need to make listening to you worth their while by making the information interesting or important, and you need to present your information clearly and succinctly, so that you're reasonably easy to listen to and what you say is memorable.

Whether you're speaking to one person or several, you need to think through the best way to put your information across so that people can receive it.

If you're a person who generally speaks at the same time as you think, try gathering your thoughts first and then expressing them. Doing this can help communicate your message better.

Thinking through your message first

The next time you're tempted to jump into a conversation, remember — thinking about what you want to achieve and how best to proceed before beginning to speak helps you guide the conversation to the outcome you want. Think about

- How you can best begin the conversation and dovetail your words with what your listeners already know and what they want to hear.

- How you want the discussion to proceed. For example, you may want people to just listen and agree, to examine and help resolve a problem, to suggest ideas, to put forward opinions or to help develop a plan.

- What you want to achieve (your goal). Generally, one clear aim is better than several.

- What you want to get across with your main message.

When people disagree with what you're saying, they tune out about 75 per cent of the information you're giving them. Think carefully about how to word controversial and 'bad news' messages so that the messages fit in with what people already know or believe. This way your listeners are more receptive to what you're saying.

Setting the scene

Setting the scene with your first sentence or two helps oil the conversational wheels and alerts people to what they're about to hear. Begin by sketching out your plan for the conversation. You may decide to say something like one of these opening lines:

> Bruce, I need to speak with you about presenting next week's report. Do you have a few moments now?

or

> Sheila, would you mind running through how you plan to do this? I want to make sure that we're on the same wavelength.

Saying up front what you want to discuss, and even why, helps people listen and understand more easily and guides your discussion towards the desired end, saving time and confusion. But before opening your mouth, listen to your mental chatter and make sure your thoughts are positive and that they support your intentions. Otherwise, your thoughts may guide your foot right into your mouth!

Gaining your listener's attention

Use the WIFM — What's In It For Me? — rule. The 'Me' refers to the other person, the person who's listening to you. Ask yourself: Why does this person want to listen to what I am saying? What are the benefits to the other person?

Give people a reason to listen and include the WIFM rule as early as you can, even in your first couple of sentences, because when people know how they benefit, they usually listen more open-mindedly and enthusiastically. (Remember to be subtle with your WIFMs, though.)

Help people focus their attention by letting them know what's coming:

- ✔ 'There are three important points I'd like to make. First, ...'
- ✔ 'The question we need to answer is ...'
- ✔ 'In summary, I suggest we concentrate our efforts on ...'

You can also give people a reason to listen by tuning your messages to reflect what's important to them. Show your listeners that they can benefit from what you are about to say with lines like these:

- ✔ 'I have something important I'd like you to hear.'
- ✔ 'Here's something that may interest you.'
- ✔ 'I have that information you requested.'
- ✔ 'Here's some information that may help you.'

Keeping their attention

Stay up-beat because people tend to tune out grumps. Talking about solutions, not problems, keeps your listeners listening, as does using body language that is *congruent*, or agrees with your words. Look like you're worth listening to by following these simple rules:

- ✔ Don't cross your arms or hunch your shoulders.
- ✔ Look people in the eye.
- ✔ Speak up so you can be heard.
- ✔ Stand or sit straight.

(For more on how to look and sound like a leader, refer to Chapter 3.)

Repeat important messages often, using different mediums. You may need to repeat very important messages in several different ways to individuals and groups several times and reinforce your messages on Intranets, on posters, in memos and in emails.

Turning Arguments into Agreements

Differences of opinion, differences in priorities, differences in outlook — all differences make life interesting. Differences can also make people uncomfortable and lead to quarrels and hurt feelings. Successful leaders are more interested in cooperative, workable relationships than in being 'right'. Everyone gets more done, more pleasantly, when they behave as colleagues rather than as adversaries.

When you see a disagreement as a 'fight' or a competition, the inclination is to stick to your opinion like glue and not admit the other person has a point. You force your ideas and solutions on them and ignore what they may believe or need. And, since losers have a way of getting even, you're likely eventually to pay for that tough stance.

Successful leaders spend time and effort turning arguments into agreements by

- ✔ Changing the way they look at a situation and by moving towards a joint understanding of where the parties are and where they want to be
- ✔ Looking for ways to turn the situation around so as to retain the other person's goodwill

> ✔ Taking a step back to see the problem from a different angle
>
> ✔ Thinking, 'Here's a point of view that's different from mine — here's a chance to learn something new'
>
> ✔ Thinking: 'How can I best find agreement on this?'

Instead of dwelling on disagreements and concentrating on differences, leaders are quick to turn a quarrel into a goal that both parties want. 'You and I want the same result', is a common refrain of leaders when they seem to be headed for, or find themselves in the middle of, a disagreement.

When you move your attention off what you're disagreeing about onto something you both want to achieve, all you need to do is figure out how to achieve that goal — together. A joint aim turns any argument into an agreement because mutual goals place people on the same side. You can increase cooperation by sitting next to, not opposite, the other person, which literally puts you on the same side.

When a discussion gets to a point where you can't go forward positively or when you feel you or the other person is in danger of 'losing it', wind up quickly and come back to the topic later. This gives you a chance to restore your composure and your objectivity, both of which are critical to avoiding arguments.

Timing is important. Hold your tongue and wait to discuss sensitive matters until the time is right and the other person has time to talk, and until you both can go to a quiet and private place. Before you share your opinion, ask yourself: 'On what am I basing my opinion?' If you can't support your opinion with facts, experience or expertise, think again before speaking up. And remember you are a leader, and leaders learn to live with people's quirks, traits and mannerisms because they know they can't change someone's personality to suit themselves.

Catching a conflict early makes the dispute much easier to sort out. Once the misunderstanding is resolved, think about what led to the dispute and what warning signs were present that you may have missed. This increases your awareness of looming conflicts and helps you prevent the same or a similar problem from occurring again.

(For more information on how to deal with differences of opinion, see Chapters 15 and 18.)

Watching Your Body Language

Have people pulled the trick on you where they say 'Oh, there's something on your chin' while rubbing their cheek with their hand? Naturally, your hand goes to your cheek, too. What people *do* is far more powerful than what they say and that's particularly true for leaders.

Body language is a silent language that speaks louder than words. Followers watch a leader's every move like hawks. Followers interpret leaders' words and decide what their leaders really mean based on their unspoken messages. If you're not aware of your silent signals, you may be communicating oceans of information accidentally and involuntarily. Your walk and your talk may not match, causing your followers to lose faith in you.

By becoming more aware of your body language, you can convey less of what you don't want and more of what you do want. When your verbal and non-verbal messages are in harmony, your followers (and everyone else around you) are more apt to trust you, believe you and follow you.

What you do says even more about you than what you say. Every movement you make sends a message. The way you sit, stand and move tells people how interested you are in them and in what they're doing. Your body language conveys how delighted you are (or are not) to be where you are. Body language also tells your followers how you feel about yourself. How you orient your body towards (or away from) people, how much eye contact you make and how you tilt your head sends messages about what you're thinking and whether (or not) you like the company you're in. When you move or change your stance, seating position or facial expression, you reveal your attitudes and feelings. The way you dress, the jewellery you wear and the accessories you carry announce how you view yourself and how you want others to view you.

The way you say your words influences how believable your words are. The way you say your words affects how much support, cooperation and help others give you, how willingly they accept your assignments and ideas, and how willingly they implement them. (If you want to find out more about how to look and sound like a leader, check out Chapter 3.)

The Cantonese people have a proverb that warns us to watch out for the man whose stomach doesn't move when he laughs. If you want people to believe you, make sure your stomach moves when you laugh.

Double reinforcement

Your body language reflects what's going on inside your head and your heart and then loops back to steer your thoughts and feelings.

The next time you're feeling a bit uncertain, lift your head high and start moving with energy. Confident, positive body language makes you feel confident and positive, helping you achieve what you set out to do, and to achieve it much more easily.

Here are some quick and easy body language tips to help you communicate as a leader:

- Float your ribcage up by pulling in your waist.
- Hold your head up.
- Pull your shoulders back and down.
- Sit or stand up straight.
- Smile.

Delivering on Your Feet

Leaders are often called upon to speak to groups of people, and most leaders initially quake at the thought. (Some experienced leaders still shiver in their shoes.) Lack of knowledge, lack of preparation and lack of confidence cause nervousness and you can overcome all three by planning, organising and practising your presentations.

The next sections show you the key activities you need to apply to your presentations in order to deliver your messages competently and confidently, with commitment, conviction and credibility.

Planning your presentation

Every speech needs a great deal of preparation and thought — even impromptu speeches rely on earlier preparations. The more thought and effort you put into a presentation beforehand, the better you can stand up and deliver when the time comes.

The first step is to decide what you want to achieve. You may want to inform, to gain cooperation and commitment or to spur people into action. Take a blank sheet of paper and write down your aim in one clear, short sentence, right in the centre of the page. Then circle your aim.

Now put yourself in the shoes of the people who are going to be listening to your presentation and ask yourself:

- How can your presentation benefit your listeners?
- How much do your listeners already know about the topic?
- What opinions, attitudes or prejudices may your listeners have toward your message?
- Which presentation styles are likely to gain the interest and attention of your listeners?
  - A clear plan of action
  - A step-by-step strategy
  - 'Blue-sky' ideas (exploring possibilities for the future)
  - Creative ideas
  - Costs, facts and 'hard numbers'
  - Demonstrations
  - Details
  - Examples
  - Highly technical explanations
- Which presentation techniques may turn off your listeners?
- Why are your listeners going to care about what you have to say?

A sound audience analysis like this helps you develop compelling objectives for your talk and structure your presentation for maximum persuasiveness.

Developing the structure of your speech

Now the time has come to develop and organise your presentation. Coming up with an outline only takes about ten minutes; filling in the details takes a bit longer — how much longer depends on the length of your presentation.

Here are some handy steps to follow:

1. **On the piece of paper you used to circle your goal, quickly write down all the points you can make.** Just one or two words are fine — enough to jog your memory. Let your ideas flow. When you're brainstorming ideas, don't think through each idea at that time, just write down your ideas, in any order, as they occur to you.

2. **Now cull your ideas.** Bear in mind who the people in your audience are and what your objectives are. Cross out any points that don't contribute directly to your goal. Next, number the topics that are left in a logical order so that the sequence of topics makes sense to your audience. Put your most important points first and last because people tend to remember the first and last ideas they hear.

   Depending on how long you're speaking, try to end up with between one and five main ideas. More than five ideas may confuse your listeners.

3. **Create an overall theme.** Choose appropriately numbered and easy-to-remember names for your theme, such as Ten Commandments, Seven Deadly Sins, Three Stooges and so on.

4. **Now number the points you listed.** Numbering helps your listeners follow the sequence. Numbers keep the listeners' attention and make your talk seem professional and organised. Numbering your main points also helps people take notes, when appropriate, and helps your listeners remember what you're saying.

Your main message

Now develop the main part — or *body* — of your talk. Introduce each main point with a self-evident truth or a familiar or simple idea with which your audience can agree or identify. Then make your point smoothly and cleanly, targeted at your objectives and avoiding non-essential information. Illustrate and strengthen your main points with facts, figures or other evidence, explanations or examples. Be sure to weave in your listeners' WIFMs (the benefits to your audience that we discussed earlier in this chapter).

Three powerful techniques leaders use

Leaders know how to make their messages memorable. Some favourite ways to make messages memorable include painting pictures, drawing out feelings and telling stories — all powerful ways to hold interest and give people information so they remember it. Here's how to achieve these three methods:

✔ Leaders paint pictures by choosing words that form images in the minds of their listeners.

✔ Leaders seek to draw out the feelings of their listeners by describing situations and events so clearly that listeners feel as though they are at the scene the leader is describing.

✔ Leaders tell stories that win their listeners' understanding and cooperation.

Your supporting material

Think about how you can help your audience follow your talk, pay attention, stay interested and understand and accept your information more easily. And think about what can help you make or reinforce your points effectively. Handouts, overhead slides and demonstrations all have their place when these resources add to your presentation. (If they don't add value to your presentation, then get rid of them. They're a hindrance.)

If you decide to use PowerPoint, don't use it as a crutch — slides are not your speaking notes and they don't merely outline your talk. Slides are meant to enhance your presentation, not deliver your information for you. So avoid standing in front of your audience, reading one slide after another. Your listeners can read just as well as you can. Don't turn your back on your audience to read a slide, either — turning your back to people is rude and muffles your voice. Remember — you're the presenter, not your technology.

Try to avoid giving out copies of your slides until after your presentation. This way, your listeners aren't tempted to read ahead rather than listen to you. The same holds true for handouts. Unless you want the audience to refer to them during your talk, keep them until the presentation is over.

You may decide to organise some supporting material at this point, too. But having too many slides or using slides that are too 'busy', too crowded and too hard to read confuses people. And too many fancy computer effects lead to Death by PowerPoint — the death of your presentation, I mean. Less is more. Use a nice big font, lots of headings, dot points and lots of white space in your visual aids.

That's the body of your speech. Now top and tail your presentation with a strong conclusion and a short, engaging introduction.

Your introduction

Your introduction makes people either sit up and listen or decide to let their minds wander to more interesting matters. Here are some ways to grab your audience's attention:

- Ask a provocative question.
- Ask a rhetorical question.
- Briefly state the problem, the solution you offer, and the results your listeners can expect.
- Cite an example that illustrates your key point or call to action.
- Make a startling statement.

- ✔ Open with a relevant quotation.

- ✔ State an interesting or surprising fact or statistic.

- ✔ Tell a relevant example-type or once-upon-a-time-type story.

- ✔ Tell an anecdote.

Your conclusion

Make the conclusion to your presentation circle back to your opening comments. As the saying goes, 'Tell 'em what you've told 'em.' Hammer home your main points one last time and perhaps add a punchline to leave a final impression on the minds of your audience.

Follow the *KISSS* principle — Keep it Short, Simple and Sincere. If you want your listeners to take any action as a result of your presentation, be very clear about what you want your listeners to do. Tell your listeners how to take that action and when to take it.

Finally, thank your listeners for their attention and, if appropriate, invite questions.

Practising your way to perfection

Here is where the real work begins. You may know your topic thoroughly, but you still need to practise your presentation — as often as possible.

Don't leave practising until the last minute and don't practise all in one hit. Frequent short sessions are far more effective. You benefit just as much from practising in your mind's eye, sitting on the bus or in your garden, as you do from your 'out loud' sessions. Aim to have at least one full stand-up, out-loud rehearsal, though.

What annoys an audience?

Research shows that presenters who are guilty of any of the following win the foot-in-mouth award, rather than the silver-tongue award:

- ✔ Lack of preparation and organisation

- ✔ Poor structure

- ✔ Poor visuals

- ✔ Reading from notes

- ✔ Repetitive habits (nervous ticks, repetitive gestures, ums and so on)

- ✔ Speaking in a monotone

- ✔ Speaking too softly

The Golden Rules of Speaking

Here are six golden rules to help you present your best-ever speech (and yes, I did mean to repeat the most important point):

✔ Be yourself.

✔ Prepare thoroughly.

✔ Relax.

✔ Think only about communicating with your audience (not about yourself or your nerves).

✔ Listen to what you're saying.

✔ Be yourself.

Practise doesn't mean memorise. *Practise* means knowing your speech so well and being so comfortable with what you're going to say — and how you're going to say it — that you only need key points to prompt you. Place these key points either on index cards or on one sheet of paper so you can see them at a glance.

Don't bring your full 'script' to your presentation because you may be tempted to just stand in front of your audience and read all the words. Reading your speech is a known way to send your audience to sleep.

Gradually whittle your speech down into key points as you practise your presentation. And, as you practise, get used to glancing at your brief notes and looking back up to your imaginary audience. This style of practice helps make your delivery natural and fresh. You can watch your audience's reaction and concentrate on delivering your message.

Taking centre stage

Before you begin, take five minutes to collect your thoughts and think about your message. Then, take three deep breaths and relax before you step on stage.

Now you're in the limelight, here are some more healthy tricks to keep you in charge of your presentation:

✔ Feel free to refer to your notes when you need to and, if you lose your place, pause, find the right spot, return your eyes to your audience and make your next point; no-one minds you pausing.

- ✔ Keep breathing.

- ✔ Keep up the lights if you're using slides. Dimmed lights signal your listeners to take a little nap.

- ✔ Move around a bit but don't pace or rock.

- ✔ Never worry about impressing people, only about making your meaning clear. Keep nerves at bay by concentrating on your message and ensuring your audience is with you. Purposeful gestures and a lively voice transfer nervous energy into positive channels and make you look and feel more confident, enthusiastic and in control. (After all, if you aren't enthusiastic about what you're saying, your listeners won't be either.)

- ✔ Stand tall and look around your whole audience (not into just one or two corners, at one or two people or straight ahead). Make four to six seconds of eye contact with listeners (shorter eye contact can make you look shifty).

- ✔ Think of your presentations as expanded conversations. You may need to adjust your language and manner slightly, but aim for the enthusiasm, animation, gestures and naturalness of your everyday conversations.

After your presentation

The way to get better and better at presentations is to review your 'performance' afterwards.

Replay it in your mind. If the presentation has been videotaped, replay the tape, just as sportsmen do to review their performances after a game. Ask yourself:

- ✔ What did you do well that you want to remember to do next time?

- ✔ What sections of your presentation can you polish and improve next time?

Jot down a few reminder notes (and refer to Chapter 4 for more information on how to improve by using the improvement cycle).

Using a lectern?

When using a lectern, stand squarely behind the stand and keep still. Avoid rocking and fidgeting by standing with your feet shoulder width apart. Slightly bend your knees — if you lock them, blood flow decreases, and decreased blood flow increases nerves. Pointing your toes directly at the audience, one foot slightly ahead of the other, enables you to stand straight without appearing stiff.

Just before you begin speaking, calmly look at your audience and take a deep breath. Then exhale through your nose. The deep breath aligns and straightens your body and helps you to relax.

Chapter 8

Who You Know Matters

Swans look serene on the surface of a glassy lake, but underneath the water, the swans are paddling like mad. The same scenario exists in any organisation. On the surface, clear lines of leadership and communication appear to exist, as do agreed ways of reaching decisions and procedures for dealing with problems and disputes. But underneath, the scene is very different.

Below the apparently calm surface, organisations teem with political machinations and in-fighting, undercover coalitions, underground information networks and surreptitious finagling.

This chapter explains how to suss out the expected ways of conducting yourself as a leader and how you ignore them at your peril. I explain the importance of knowing who the significant people around you are and why getting to know them works to your advantage. And I explain how to build your power base and play politics properly.

Making Love Not War

Two events happen whenever people come together. The first is that a set of shared values, beliefs and attitudes quickly builds up (the *culture*) and a characteristic way of doing particular activities emerges (the *norms*). These unwritten codes of behaviour regulate such matters as how people talk to each other, how people conduct themselves in meetings and how quickly and carefully people do their work. An organisation's culture and norms even affect the way people dress and how energetically they walk.

The second event is that people jockey for position in the pecking order. This is known as *politicking*. Everyone wants to be able to exert influence and to be known for some quality they make their own — to be the 'expert', the 'thinker', the 'comedian' and so on. Some people want to be at the top of the pecking order; others are happy just to be part of the hierarchy. Some people want to control people and events around them; others are happy to quietly do their bit. The overriding goal, though, especially for leaders, is to acquire and keep power and influence.

Culture and norms, politicking and power and influence affect every leader. To be successful, you need to fit in with the established ways of behaving in your organisation in order to be accepted by the people working around you. You can't escape becoming embroiled — to some degree — in politics. The amount of power and influence you gather are ingredients of your effectiveness.

Conforming to the status quo

A group's culture and norms are the rules by which people operate when they are together (and also when they are apart). The culture and norms determine what people do and don't do and how they do their particular tasks. Culture and norms cover all sorts of matters, such as

- How much fun followers and their leaders have as they go about their jobs
- How people deal with conflicts and differences of opinion
- How people discover and solve problems
- How people keep their work areas (tidy, messy, cosy, businesslike)
- How people walk, talk, dress and behave
- What leadership style people expect
- What people consider to be important
- What people focus on (the job at hand, results, people and teams)
- What the organisation's atmosphere is like (relaxed, formal, tense, energetic)
- What types of behaviours and traits people value, reward, respect and frown on
- Whether or not people take risks

Leaders identify these unwritten rules and observe them because they know that anyone who breaks those rules is ostracised, punished and pressured to conform. Leaders manage their own images so they fit in with and contribute to their group's and their organisation's culture.

Each of the smaller groups in any organisation, including a leader's own group, has its own *subculture* that is a variation on the culture and norms of the wider organisation — a slightly different common language, dress code, rituals, preferred hangouts, performance expectations, work ethic and so on.

Get to know the subcultures of the team you lead and the other groups that you encounter. Once you're aware of what makes one group that little bit different from the others, you can overcome some of the barriers you may bump into by making an effort to blend in when you deal with these other groups. (If you want to find out more about culture and norms, refer to Chapter 4, and for how to build a subculture with your followers that supports your joint goals, see Chapters 15 and 16.)

Knowing who's who

To network and politick effectively, you need to know who's who in your organisation. This is known as the *informal organisation* or the *shadow organisation*. For example,

- ✔ Who has influence and who doesn't?
- ✔ Who has power and who doesn't?
- ✔ Who is in the inner circle?
- ✔ Who is excluded from the inner circle?
- ✔ Who do you need to go to for advice or support?
- ✔ Who do you need to get on side?
- ✔ Whose opinions do you need to seek?
- ✔ Who do you need to avoid?

This subtle web of relationships is what really makes organisations tick. Hidden networks of associations and norms, unspoken alliances and coalitions of influence make up the who's who of organisations and the groups within those organisations.

To find out who's who around you, read between the lines of what goes on between people. For example, watch who

- ✔ Attracts people looking for opinion, advice and assistance
- ✔ Decides what the various coalitions want and need

- ✔ Generates ideas
- ✔ Has the opinions that really count
- ✔ Is in the important networks and cliques
- ✔ Is what to whom
- ✔ Moulds people's opinions and sets the pace and the trends
- ✔ Persuades people to their way of thinking
- ✔ Sets the patterns of loyalty
- ✔ Socialises with whom

Once you know who's who, you can decide who to include in your networks and whose power and influence you want to embrace.

Building valuable networks

A *network* is an informal web of relationships inside and outside your organisation that you can call on for help, support, advice and information. In return you extend the same value to others in your networks. Networks increase the information available to you and expand your sphere of influence. Networks can even help you win a promotion — leaders who are promoted more often network more than twice as much as leaders who are promoted at 'average' rates.

Networking is not about promoting yourself or what you're selling, landing a job, digging for donations or ingratiating yourself to gain an advantage. Networking is not about seeing and being seen, petty politicking or immediate gain. Benefits come after relationships and trust have been established and sustained, and after you build a reputation as a leader who's dependable, who knows useful information and who can offer helpful opinions and advice. Only then can you seek assistance or feel comfortable offering assistance.

What is political competence?

Political competence is the ability to understand what you can and cannot control, when to act and when not to act, who might resist your ideas and proposals, who might support them, who to bring on side and how to build coalitions of support.

Knowledgeable leaders with strong leadership muscles who politick and network well can end up with a lot of power and influence, especially when they have influential mentors. Leaders without power and influence become outmanoeuvred, overlooked and overridden.

Networking is about connecting with others and building supportive relationships by adding value through sharing knowledge, perspectives, opinions, advice and contacts. Don't become so one-eyed on producing results and leading your team that you don't take time to lay the groundwork for the future — part of which is building good networks. If you think you're too busy to network, you need to master the art of delegation. (Find out more about delegation in Chapter 12.)

As the traditional hierarchical pyramid in organisations has *flattened out* due to downsizing and restructuring — some organisations have dropped entire layers of middle management — the official power that was held by the leadership hierarchy has moved to people with good networking and politicking skills. So build useful networks inside your organisation by getting to know influential people and being in the right place at the right time. Volunteer for committees and projects that involve prominent leaders from other parts of the organisation and make a solid contribution. A circle of people who are prepared to speak up on your behalf, keep you informed, guide you, and spread the word about your abilities greatly strengthens your political muscles.

Don't stop inside your organisation. Build deep and wide networks that include a range of people with different backgrounds, knowledge and skills, different perspectives on the world and different specialisations. Network with people from other industries and walks of life. This broadens your knowledge and helps you to understand more about what's happening outside your organisation and gives you a smorgasbord of resources to draw upon.

Casting wide your net

Leaders mix with a wide range of people both inside and outside their organisation. Inside your organisation, you can build *operational networks* that help you meet your obligations and obtain results. Operational networks are based largely on trust and include your followers, your own leader and other leaders, and other internal and external people who can support you. You can also plug into the *expert network*, the *career-advice network*, a *social network* and an *ideas-generating network*.

Leaders also build *strategic networks* that include leaders from other parts of their organisation and from outside their organisation. These networks can alert you to trends and opportunities, provide information and help build your influence.

Personal networks, made up mostly of external people from professional and industry associations, can help you develop as a leader and as a person through coaching and mentoring and can provide important referrals and information.

Successful networking takes practice. Networks thrive only when they're used, so take every opportunity to contribute to your networks and receive the benefits they offer. Never wait to network until you reach the point where you're desperate for help.

Finding a mentor

All leaders need people to help them navigate their tricky and complex leadership journey because no leader in history has been appointed with all the knowledge, wisdom and experience one person needs to succeed. Lucky leaders have someone to guide them, to help them through the stickier patches, to walk them through tough decisions, to encourage them when they falter, to help them learn from their mistakes and to introduce them to the politics of their organisations. These guides are called *mentors*. Mentors are very special people and an important part of every leader's network.

Mentors usually choose the people they guide, often choosing people who remind them of similar qualities in themselves. Or they choose people who show characteristics the mentors like and are therefore keen to show these people how to succeed. If you notice a leader from your organisation — not necessarily your own leader or even one from your area — spending time with you, offering advice and support, be sure to pay attention.

If you don't have a mentor yet, make your own luck and find one. Get to know one or more wise, experienced and influential people who can advise you. Look for keen listeners who don't tell you what to do but help you figure out the best solutions, who are well respected and who you can rely upon to keep your conversations confidential. Offer to buy these people coffee and ask if you can pick their brains for ten minutes about a specific issue, problem or question. Once these people get to know you and understand that you're serious about improving your leadership skills, they may continue to spend time with you and give you the benefit of their knowledge, support and experience.

The first mentor

In *The Odyssey*, Homer tells us about Odysseus. Before he left for the siege of Troy in 1194 BC, Odysseus asked a friend to care for and teach his son, Telemachus, to advise the boy and to be his friend. The name of the guide Odysseus chose was Mentor.

Tipping the Balance with Power

The more power and influence you have, the more you can achieve results. Power gives you some control over the behaviour of others and power can get you what you want. But being a leader doesn't automatically mean you have power or influence. These are rewards you must earn.

Leaders have limited — very limited — amounts of official power that comes from their leadership position. Most leaders rely on their unofficial power, or influence. Influence comes from many sources — for example, knowing the right people, knowing a lot about a subject others care about, being able to obtain scarce resources or even having a forceful personality or the gift of the gab and so on. (Plenty of non-leaders also have influence, based on these qualities.)

Knowing who's who and networking with influential people can increase your power and influence. But you need more than that to build a power base. Recognising the six types of power and knowing how to use them is a good starting point.

Understanding the six types of power

Six types of power can help you become a successful leader.

The first three types of power in the following list are based on formal power and the second three are based on informal, or unofficial, power, which comes from a leader's personal characteristics. *Note:* The six types of power start with the weakest and move on to the strongest.

Here are the three formal powers:

- ✔ **Position power:** You hold this power as a result of the mere fact that you are a leader. However, followers who follow your instructions only because you are the leader do so grudgingly and poorly. Position power is a very weak form of power, so use it only as a last resort.

- ✔ **Coercive power:** This power is based on your ability to punish and withhold rewards. Followers may do or not do as you ask so that you don't give them a hard time, refuse to give them overtime or assign them boring tasks. Fear-based power isn't particularly effective because, after a while, fear loses its grip on followers.

✔ **Reward power:** This power is the opposite to coercive power and is a stronger pull for most followers. Leaders often grant favours or provide small incentives to establish an emotional debt. You can assign interesting jobs, let followers have a bit of leeway when they take or come back from breaks, recommend them for training, and so on. You can praise your followers, too. Friendliness and praise are rewards you can use to encourage and thank followers for doing as you ask.

Now here are the three informal powers:

✔ **Proximity power:** This means you have access to powerful, interesting and/or influential people. Or you have interesting information that you can share, such as explaining the reasons behind a decision or passing on behind-the-scenes information about events in the organisation. People may or may not like or respect you, but they are willing to hang around you and do what you say because they want to hear the goss or bask in the glory of your achievements. Although, having friends and associates in high places can give you some power, at least for a little while, proximity power is empty power when other forms of power don't support it.

Be careful with gossip. Leaders can't afford to make negative or malicious comments about anyone — it breaks trust with the people they say them to, earns them a reputation for talking behind people's backs, and destroys their image of integrity.

✔ **Expert power:** This means you have skills or expertise in areas that are useful to others, or that you have the wisdom of experience that people respect. You can help people by drawing on your expert power. Followers are generally happy to follow if they believe that their leader knows best.

✔ **Personal power:** This means that people like and respect you as a person and that you have created a bank of goodwill by behaving fairly and consistently and by building good relationships. Your followers and other leaders follow you because they want to be supportive and cooperative — in their eyes, you earn their support and you deserve their support. When you have personal power, people seek out your company, your opinions, your advice and your assistance.

Power isn't the only way to get followers to perform. Probably the best way to inspire performance is to make sure your followers enjoy doing the jobs you assign them and to make sure that you give your followers the training and other support they need to do their jobs properly. This results in your followers working well because they want to, which is far more compelling than doing a job because the leader says so, or to gain rewards or avoid unpleasantness. (If you want to find out more about how to get followers to perform well, see Chapter 10.)

Here's an important point about power: Just as in physics, where for every action there is a reaction, power is most effective when it is in balance. Once you use power, especially against another person, power gets out of balance and people automatically try to restore it.

Building your personal power base

Power and influence build gradually, along with your track record for being a leader who is reliable, who achieves results and who is useful to know. Here are some ways to speed up the process:

- Be approachable.
- Be fair dinkum because truth is a two-way street.
- Be honest, sincere and supportive in your feedback.
- Be informed and share information with your followers.
- Bring competent followers on board, know their strengths and weaknesses, keep training them and acknowledge good work.
- Do as you say and practise what you believe in.
- Don't make enemies.
- Don't whine, complain or criticise.
- Enjoy your followers' company.
- Know that any comment you make may be repeated.
- Look after your followers' physical environment, tools and equipment.
- Make other people look good.
- Respect your followers (treat each follower as a VIP).
- Stay professional and cultivate a positive, accurate image.

Appreciating the Principles of Politics

Do you think politicking is dirty and you don't need to stoop to taking part? In some organisations, politics is very dirty, but hopefully not in yours. (When you encounter dirty politics in an organisation, my advice is simply to get out.)

Politics is not really an adversarial sport. If you expect to persuade and influence your followers and others in your organisation to get the results you need, then you have to understand how to play the game of politics. Political savvy is the icing on the cake of your leadership competence. Political savvy helps you avoid being shafted and enables you to make the best possible contribution to your team of followers and to your organisation.

Still not sure? Politics is nothing more than the relationships formed between people in order to get the job done and achieve goals. After all, no-one operates in a vacuum. Research shows that the quality of leaders' relationships is central to getting results that matter. To produce quality results, leaders must first produce quality relationships.

The first three ingredients to being taken seriously as a leader are

- Earning a reputation for being a sensible, responsible leader
- Knowing and networking with a variety of people (especially the right people — those with power and influence)
- Understanding and fitting into your organisation's culture

These ingredients earn you the right to wield a bit of influence around the place.

Here are some other qualities that leaders can develop:

- Be visible and, without boasting, talk about what you do. Don't expect people to recognise what a great job you and your followers are doing when you never mention your achievements. Keep your leader posted on your progress and what you and your followers have accomplished. Make your team's successes known and talked about throughout the organisation, giving full credit where credit is due. Providing progress reports, attending functions, being active in industry associations and networking are all ways to increase your visibility without coming across to others as a braggart. Avoid empty publicity that you cannot back up with solid achievement, however.
- Consider the impact of your actions and inactions on others. Have plans to improve systems and procedures, and discuss these plans with people who may be affected by them or who may be able to offer some helpful ideas and perspectives.

✔ Gain access to — or better still, take control of — scarce or sought-after resources, knowledge and expertise. Access to desirable resources increases your value to others and allows you to bestow favours (and receive favours in return).

✔ Find out what people are good at and praise them liberally, because people who feel liked and understood are more open to persuasion and influence. Don't underestimate the value of a simple thankyou, of asking after someone's family or how their weekend went, or expressing appreciation for what your supporters do in a task.

✔ Hang around with high achievers and build alliances with influential and respected people. Demonstrate, by word and deed, your loyalty and commitment to your job and your organisation, because being well known and considered trustworthy, enthusiastic and dedicated is important. Even if a course of action is in your own interests, speak and persuade people in terms of the benefits to the organisation or — when only your own followers are involved — the benefits to the team.

✔ Help others get to know you. Find common interests with your followers, your own leader and other leaders. The better you know people, the better you understand not just what they want but why they want it, their hopes, fears and constraints. Then you can make sure everybody wins, not just you.

✔ Help your own leader succeed, and you also shine by association. The same holds true for special projects and committees to which you may contribute. The more you're associated with success, the greater political standing you attain.

Spend enough time politicking to achieve your leadership aims but not so much time that you don't get any work done. Over-politicking (rightfully) earns you a reputation as a do-nothing vessel of hot air! Think about building effective relationships, rather than being seen.

Part III
The Science and Art of Leadership

Glenn Lumsden

*'In my experience, I've found the carrot to be
a lot more effective than the stick.'*

In this part ...

Welcome to the realities of leadership. This part concentrates on how to make the most of your followers' skills. I show you how to figure out what you expect of your followers and what your followers, your own leader and other important people expect of you.

I describe precisely how to bring out the best in your followers and how to identify and untangle problems, fix problems and make sure they stay fixed. Then, in case you're wondering how you can ever find the time to do all this work, I show you how to spread the workload and assign work, not just to get a job done but to develop your followers' skills and keep them interested and energised. Finally, you find out how to lead worthwhile meetings that followers are happy to attend.

Chapter 9

Managing Expectations

*B*ecause leaders and followers work in partnership, they need to know they can depend on each other to carry out their duties and meet their responsibilities to each other and the organisation. This shared confidence can't happen without mutual respect, trust and understanding, and a bit of leeway and compromise to fit in with each other's personalities and working styles.

Underpinning the partnerships between leaders and followers are the expectations they hold of each other. Allowing expectations to be informal and imprecise — inferred from people's actions, from what has happened in the past and from statements made, for example, during recruitment — is a mistake. Even when expectations aren't discussed openly, followers and leaders actually see them more as obligations than expectations, which means that tension and conflict result and performance suffers when people don't live up to unofficial deals and promises.

As a leader, you need to make your own expectations and your organisation's expectations clear to your followers. And you need to understand your follower's expectations so that you can make sure they're realistic and that they enhance the organisation's and your team's vision and purpose. You also need to know what your own leader expects from you, and fulfil those expectations in order to build a strong relationship, live up to your responsibilities and be appreciated for your efforts.

This chapter explains how to build strong links with your co-workers, based on ascertaining and meeting their expectations and making your own expectations clear. I describe how to work well with your own leader (and with everyone else), how to work with difficult leaders, and how to get your ideas implemented.

Mapping Out Your Expectations

When leaders and followers honour each other's expectations, a sense of fairness and trust builds, increasing commitment, satisfaction and willingness to cooperate and do your best. But living up to expectations is hard to accomplish when you're working in the dark. Guessing what people want and need from you leads to all sorts of misunderstandings and hard feelings.

Be explicit about the performance levels, behaviours and attitudes you expect from your followers. Discussing your expectations openly and frankly is essential so that each of your followers and your team as a whole understands exactly what you expect.

Explaining the job

The first and most obvious discussion needs to revolve around your expectations about the tasks your followers are to perform and the results they need to attain. This explanation forms a large part of every introductory discussion with a new follower, and reviewing your expectations at subsequent performance discussions is a good idea. 'This is what I need from you' or 'This is what I expect from you' are efficient ways to start performance conversations with new followers. (You can find more information on this aspect of leadership in Chapters 10 and 19.)

If you're a new leader to an established team, avoid making sudden changes. Meet with each follower individually and ask each person to describe to you exactly how they see the job they do. Ask what each person sees as their key result areas (KRAs) and what their overall job purpose is. From these discussions, you can get an accurate feel for how your team operates before you start making changes. (For more on key result areas and job purpose, see Chapters 4 and 10.)

Explaining the organisation's expectations

Most leaders make expectations concerning an organisation's values and ways of working clear to new followers who join their team. For example, followers are advised to:

- Act with integrity.
- Ask for guidance when in doubt.
- Be at work on time.
- Contribute to decision making, problem solving and improvement.
- Maintain confidences.

Explaining cultural expectations

Many leaders may not actually state other expectations because they're assumed as part of the widely held Australian work ethic. For example:

- Behave in a courteous, cooperative and friendly way to the people around you.
- Demonstrate loyalty to your leader, team and organisation.
- Develop new skills and update old ones.
- Help your team-mates out when they need help.
- Uphold the organisation's (and your leader's) reputation.
- Work hard and carry out your tasks responsibly, honestly and dependably.

Just to make sure, though, I recommend that you discuss cultural expectations like those listed previously with your new team of followers and with new followers who join your team. Phrases such as 'In this team, we . . .', 'We like to . . .' and 'It's important that . . .' are three friendly ways to explain expectations that may otherwise go unsaid and may never be fully clear to new followers.

Explaining your personal expectations

Most leaders also have expectations based more on their own personal beliefs and working styles. These expectations often concern matters such as how leaders want their followers to

- Go about their business
- Dress on the job
- Keep their work areas tidy
- Practise work habits — for example, encouraging followers to finish one task before moving on to another task
- Show initiative

When you're a new leader to a team and when new followers join your team, discuss your personal expectations up front, using opening lines such as 'I'm a real stickler for . . .' and 'I'd like to outline a few guidelines that are really important to me about the way I want us to work together'.

Determining your own expectations

Not every leader has the same expectations as every other leader, which is why knowing what your expectations are and making them clear to your followers is very important. If you don't make your expectations clear, tensions are bound to build and bad feelings escalate simply because followers don't realise you expect them to behave in particular ways. The more clearly you discuss your expectations with your followers, the more likely your expectations are to be met, which makes everyone happy.

To find out your own particular expectations of your followers, grab a blank sheet of paper and do a 'brain dump', answering these questions:

- How do you want to work with your followers?
- How do you want your followers to work together?
- How do you want your followers to treat each other, you and people outside your group?
- How much fun and energy do you want to see and hear?
- What do you want to feel and think when you stand quietly and observe your team of followers?
- What do you want to see and hear as you look at your followers and watch them go about their business to confirm your team is meeting your expectations?

Start writing now. When you think you're finished, just sit and wait to allow more ideas to come to you. When you really finish, look over what you wrote and identify key themes. Then think about how you can explain these themes to your followers if they're not meeting some of your expectations. When you're finished, save yourself from having to reinvent the wheel by filing your list of ideas in a general induction file. Use this list to guide your 'expectations explanation' with new followers who join your team.

Understanding Your Team's Expectations

Followers have expectations of their leaders. Some typical expectations of leaders are that they

- Ask followers for opinions and listen to their ideas
- Be approachable
- Be available to listen and help followers
- Coordinate resources and work flows
- Coach followers and offer feedback to build their skills
- Ensure followers receive fair pay
- Give recognition for innovation and ideas
- Keep calm in emergencies
- Keep followers updated on relevant organisation information
- Liaise with other departments on behalf of followers
- Obtain and maintain needed resources and organise the use of those resources efficiently
- Provide guidance as needed
- Provide opportunities for training and development
- Support their followers
- Treat followers fairly, impartially and consistently
- Treat followers with respect and consideration

(To find out more about generational differences in expectations of leaders, see Chapter 17.)

Followers also expect that when they behave in particular ways, certain outcomes are more likely. For example, most followers expect more interesting or challenging tasks or greater flexibility in taking breaks in return for good performance. These expectations about what followers genuinely believe they can get in return for what they give are seldom explicit. However, these expectations are real and followers feel cheated when these expectations are not fulfilled. The result is that followers can quickly withdraw their goodwill.

You may occasionally need to initiate a difficult conversation about expectations with followers when you sense that their expectations are not realistic or that their expectations are counter to the norms you want your group to follow. If that happens, see Chapter 18 for ways to lead these discussions.

Understanding Your Own Leader's Expectations

Meeting your leader's expectations of you is an important part of your role as a follower. Apart from ensuring you agree on your key result areas and main goals, finding out and meeting any unspoken expectations your leader may have of you wins your leader's trust and may help you move into the inner circle by becoming more valuable.

One fact is certain: Your leader doesn't want 'yes' men and women. Here are the eight most important expectations your leader is likely to have of you:

- **Accept duties outside the confines of your job description.** Be willing to take on new challenges; don't ignore problems just because they're not your responsibility and never say 'That's not my job'.
- **Adjust the way you work to fit in with your leader's working style.**
- **Behave honestly, reliably and cooperatively.** This way your leader knows you're reliable.
- **Fix your mistakes.** When a mistake is serious and your leader needs to know, explain the situation (no excuses or blame — take responsibility) and explain how you plan to make sure you don't repeat the mistake.
- **Follow through.** When you say you're going to do something, do it.
- **Listen and act.** Respond to any tips your leader gives you about how you can better perform your role.
- **Take the initiative.** Don't wait to be asked or told to do a task.
- **Understand your leader's objectives, priorities and constraints.** Make your leader's goals important to you too. The better you understand what your leader wants done, the better you can help your leader.

It's a seller's market

People join organisations but they leave leaders. Research shows that as many as 80 per cent of resignations are related to unsatisfactory relationships with leaders. Resignations are costly and damaging because efficient followers are scarce, and replacing efficient followers is difficult and expensive. Finding out and meeting your followers' expectations is extremely important.

Understanding your leader's working style

People work in different ways. For example, maybe you're a person who likes to talk situations, plans and ideas through but your leader needs to read information in order to understand it. In that case, stop talking and get used to writing clear reports and memos. Otherwise, your way of working jars with your leader's way, your relationship suffers and you find yourself in trouble.

To work well with your leader, find the answers to these questions as they apply to your particular situation and adjust your style to suit:

- ✔ Does your leader need all the details of the work you and your team are doing or just a broad-brush overview?

- ✔ Does your leader prefer to be involved in every decision and problem that arises or expect to hear about only major decisions or problems?

- ✔ Does your leader prefer verbal briefings followed up with a memo or a memo followed by a discussion?

- ✔ Is your leader's approach formal or informal?

- ✔ How does your leader prefer to receive information — through memos, formal meetings with set agendas, phone calls, emails or informal discussions?

- ✔ How much information does your leader need to know about what you're doing to feel comfortable?

You can ask your leader the questions above. If your leader isn't clear on his or her own working style (many people aren't), use your observation skills to work out the answers for yourself. Watch and notice when your leader responds best or seems most relaxed and comfortable. Watch who your leader seems to enjoy working with. (See the section 'Working Well with Everyone' later in this chapter for more information on working styles.)

Asking for feedback

If you don't have any feedback on how well you're meeting your leader's needs, you're working blind and depending on guesses and assumptions. Major misunderstandings are almost inevitable.

Look for signals about what your leader appreciates and what irritates. Check out your assumptions. Ask your leader to give you feedback and ask questions when you're not clear about the feedback; and make sure you act on it. Here are some specific questions to which you need to know the answers:

- ✔ What are you doing well?
- ✔ What are you doing that your leader may not want you to do?
- ✔ What are you not doing that your leader may want you to do?
- ✔ What can you do to improve?
- ✔ What guidelines does your leader want you to follow?

The answers to these questions may change as your leader's own goals, priorities and constraints change. Keep the communication channels open if you expect to have a good relationship with your leader and meet each other's expectations.

When you and your leader are new to each other, keep checking that you are meeting needs and expectations. When you hand in work, check the work is what your leader wanted and expected and whether your leader would appreciate your doing something differently. Ask — don't wait to be told. Similarly, take extra care to give similar feedback to new followers so that they understand what you expect.

Other groups have expectations, too

As a leader, you also have to meet the expectations of five other important groups of people who are key stakeholders, of one type or another, in your organisation's operations.

- ✔ Customers or clients
- ✔ Owners (shareholders when the organisation is a company); tax payers (when

the organisation is a government enterprise); people who donate to and benefit (when the organisation is a not-for-profit organisation)

- ✔ Suppliers
- ✔ The closer community
- ✔ The wider community

Working Well with Your Leader

Working well with your leader is a high priority. Your job isn't only to make your team and organisation more successful. Your job is also to make your own leader more successful.

Working smoothly with your leader simplifies your own job and eliminates potentially big problems. Finding the answers to these significant questions about your leader helps you avoid trouble:

- ✔ **What are your leader's aspirations?** Help your leader reach aspirations as well as goals.

- ✔ **What are your leader's concerns?** Address any concerns ahead of time so your leader knows you're reliable and alert.

- ✔ **What are your leader's pressures?** Understand the pressures so you can relieve them when possible. Try to understand the background when your leader makes a decision or request that seems odd. And don't add to your leader's pressures.

- ✔ **What tasks does your leader dislike?** Volunteer to take on those tasks to help your leader whenever you can.

Help your leader think through how to resolve problems by asking relevant questions. Try to do this in a way that makes it clear that you're not questioning your leader's capabilities or judgement. Instead, you're helping your leader look at all the angles and viewpoints in order to obtain the best possible outcome.

Using your leader's time and resources selectively

Your leader is probably as limited for time, energy and influence as you are, so be careful how you draw on these valuable resources. For example:

- ✔ Don't ask a question unless you're really sure you can't find the answer yourself.

- ✔ Don't flag a problem without also suggesting a couple of possible solutions or, failing that, offer something positive, such as how fixing the problem can benefit your leader.

- ✔ Don't take up your leader's time with any unimportant issues.

- ✔ Don't whinge and whine — choose the battles that are worth fighting and discard the rest.

Keeping your leader informed — no surprises — inspires trust. Pass on any interesting bits of information you hear and update your leader on current news in the workplace, including the bad news. When you need to alert your leader to a problem, here's a good approach:

- Analyse the information in one paragraph or provide up to ten bullet points so you can present the information succinctly.
- Detail what you want the solution to the problem to achieve.
- Present a minimum of two, preferably three or four options (depending on how complex the problem is) to resolve the problem.

Being led by a poor leader

Wouldn't it be nice to be led by a great leader? Someone who helps you grow and builds your skills and your confidence, who's enjoyable to be around, who appreciates your input, who sets a good example, makes sound decisions — you know, someone who is the sort of leader you are or are soon going to be. Yes, some leaders are revered leaders; sadly some leaders are reviled.

While expecting your leader to be perfect is unreasonable — no leaders are — some leaders prove that boss can be a four-letter word. The following sections examine the most difficult types of leaders, the kinds you want to stay away from, and give some tips on what to do when you can't avoid them. I begin with a relatively easy type of poor leader to deal with and move gradually on to the worst-case scenario. (If reading about one of these leaders is a bit like looking in the mirror — you can't say you haven't been warned!)

The distracted leader

Some leaders are so wrapped up in their own thoughts and projects that they seem to hardly know you exist. If your leader interrupts you, looks around the room or off into the distance when you're talking, carries on with other work or responds to your comments superficially, you may have a *distracted leader*. Try saying something like this:

- Can we arrange a time to meet to discuss this situation when you're not so busy?
- This information is really important because . . . so I'd appreciate your full attention. Can I start again from the beginning?
- This situation is quite serious so can we please put our heads together and see whether we can find a solution?

Of course, it's possible your leader isn't distracted but simply prefers to read memos or emails than talk to you. When that's the case, try presenting information and asking for information in writing.

The control freak

Any time is never too soon to start worrying; never too late to check, recheck and check again; or review all details — yet again. *Control freaks* display an attention to detail that can be mind-numbing, especially if you aren't detail oriented yourself. These anxious leaders plan every action to the finest detail and keep the panic button close at hand. Nothing is left to chance and you're never safe to relax.

The always-looking-over-your-shoulder leader can be irritating. The early morning email is the giveaway: 'I've been thinking a bit about this and I want to discuss it some more', your leader writes. Becoming dependent on these leaders is easy because they do all your thinking for you.

Calm their qualms by providing plenty of information, even when you think so much information is overkill. Establish priorities. (Doing this may not be easy because to many control freaks, every task is an 'A' priority and these leaders give the same attention to trivial matters as to critical matters.) Stay on top of details and deadlines and build trust with regular progress reports. Hopefully you can help your control-freak leader gradually to come to understand that you're dependable and able to produce the right results without their continual input. Find out if your leader gives anyone else more leeway. Watch how that person operates and try to figure out why they're more trusted than you seem to be.

Always understand that nothing can ever be good enough for a control-freak leader — and that includes you. Don't allow the control freak to erode your self-confidence — the problem lies with your leader, not with you. However, if you can cope with being controlled, you can find an advantage in this behaviour. Your control freak's zeal for perfection can teach you how to think clearly and prevent projects from going off the rails. Also, you can shine in the reflected light of your leader's successes.

The dictator

Dictators take leading from the front to a new level (refer to Chapter 2 for more on leading from the front). Dictators take no questions and give no explanations. These leaders issue orders and tell you what to do even when you don't need instructions. Dictators keep information to themselves, solve your problems and everyone else's and make all decisions themselves — even those their followers can help them make.

Dictators enjoy the sounds of their own voices. Often they're driven by an inability to trust other people — in this case, their followers, even though the followers may be trustworthy. Dictators believe they have no other choice but to drive their followers to achieve goals.

Followers can become dependent on dictators. Keep your head down, do your work, look for a new leader and don't let the dictator style of leadership rub off on you.

The hollow superstar

Hollow superstars are the publicity hounds with the big reputation, the smooth-talking, high-profile networkers extraordinaire. These leaders are pretty much sole operators who offer no support or guidance because they're too busy advancing their own interests and preening in the mirror. People who don't need to follow these leaders often think they do a great job. People who do need to follow these hollow superstars usually have little praise for them.

The followers of these leaders are the ones left to make their leaders' grandiose promises work in the real world, to write their fabulous speeches and to stand in the shadows while the leaders take all the glory — except when their schemes go awry. At this stage, these leaders are quick to stand back and push a follower forward to take the blame.

When you are led by an empty superstar type of leader, find out your leader's plans, help make those plans happen, become indispensable to your leader and have a fun ride on your leader's coat-tails.

The wily politician

Leaders who behave like *wily politicians* extol the advantages of whatever is the current trend in an organisation. Next month, when that trend changes, their exhortations change too, with the grace and speed of a verbal contortionist. These leaders rush towards power like iron filings to a magnet and their sole goal is to survive and thrive — whatever that takes. Their political skills are awesome.

Wily politicians are excellent barometers of the prevailing mood and can even predict changes of direction. But their gaze is always directed upwards, towards senior leaders rather than level to their leader peers or, heaven forbid, downwards to their followers. The only value followers have to wily politicians is how effectively they help the wily politicians look good and how quickly the followers can respond to their leaders' frequent contortions.

When wily politicians are also able to deliver at least minimal results, you can benefit from being part of their highly thought of team and, when you can offer something solid in return, you may even be admitted to their circle of power and influence.

The narcissist

Narcissists are leaders who can 'rally the troops' and engage people's hearts and minds but they also have ego problems. These leaders adore the sound of their own voice and tend to dominate meetings. Narcissists are terrible coaches and mentors because they indoctrinate rather than teach and they can be emotionally isolated, distrustful of others, self-involved and unpredictable. To top it off, narcissists are often convinced of their own infallibility, which can lead to reckless risk-taking and the ability to hear only what they want to hear.

Disagree with a self-centred self-admirer at your peril! Take care not to burst the narcissist's inflated self-image bubble. Show how well you understand these leaders' feelings, praise them like mad and don't let them destroy your self-confidence. Communicate your information in terms of your narcissistic leader's own best interest. These leaders like to take all the credit for your ideas and hard work.

The drowning flounderer

Drowning flounderers aren't waving, they're drowning. These leaders are out of their depth and prove the accuracy of the *Peter Principle* — leaders keep rising until they reach their personal level of incompetence. The truth is that drowning flounderers are more likely to have been put into their leadership position because they're so likeable. These leaders may even have been wily politicians before they attained their current level of leadership incompetence.

If you're stuck with a drowning flounderer for a leader, remember the words of German writer Johann Wolfgang von Goethe:

> Against stupidity, even the gods themselves struggle in vain.

Find a new leader before the flounderer drowns you too.

The bully

Bullies don't mind when people hate them — in fact, being hated rather pleases them. Bullies pick on one or two of their weaker followers and entertain themselves by abusing, belittling and berating these followers, assigning them impossible tasks with ridiculous time constraints and generally setting them up to fail. To everyone else, bullies are charming. In fact, others find it hard to believe that a bully leader really does intimidate, terrorise and persecute some people.

Stay out of the way of bully leaders. Find another leader — and quickly. When you're the victim of a bully leader, guard against believing that you're the failure your leader is making you out to be and, until you can find another leader, keep a record of the bullying treatment you receive (dates, times, locations, what was said, who was present). Keeping records can help you see, objectively, that you're not to blame and you may be able to use your records as proof of your leader's toxic behaviour towards you.

Find a leader who inspires you and helps you achieve feats you never knew you could achieve — a leader who is talented and has high yet realistic standards. Find a leader who gives you constructive feedback, sets challenging targets and expects a lot of work from you — and who makes you feel energised and confident. (And make sure your own followers describe you as this type of leader.)

Getting your ideas implemented

As a leader, your ideas need to be well thought through and practical and those ideas need to benefit the organisation more than they cost in financial terms. However, meeting these criteria doesn't guarantee automatic acceptance of your ideas.

You need to convince people to listen to your ideas and you need to convince people that your ideas are worth trying. That means laying the groundwork, building a framework strong enough to support various interests, building a coalition of supporters, selling your ideas to the decision makers and making sure your ideas can stand up to use.

Plan your ideas

First, know specifically what results your ideas can produce and how those results benefit your organisation and the key people inside it (refer to Chapter 8 when you need to know how to find out who the key people are in your organisation). If your idea only furthers your own goals, then your idea is going to be a non starter. Then identify your idea's possible key supporters and knockers — potentially everyone who your idea affects.

Think about

- ✔ **Identifying which people and groups stand to gain and lose from your idea.** Consider your ideas from everyone's perspective. Your ideas probably have a different impact on each individual and group. For example, your idea may make more work for some people, siphon resources from another group and make some people more visible and others less so.

- ✔ **Knowing the main goals of the potential key supporters and knockers and how they are similar to or different from what your idea can achieve.**

- ✔ **Recognising the ways in which each potential supporter and knocker could support you or sabotage you.**

- ✔ **Turning your idea into a winner, or at least neutralising your idea for those who stand to lose.**

Then get to work at building the benefits and removing or reducing the downsides. After giving your idea time to mature in your own mind, test your idea on a few people you trust to help you uncover any concerns, questions or flaws you may have overlooked.

Assemble your supporters

Now that you know who you need to bring onside, you can start building your coalition slowly but surely. Concentrate on people whose buy-in to your idea is crucial. Think about the best order to approach these people in order to enlist their support — generally you approach the most influential people first so that you can say, 'I've floated the idea by Joan and she thought it would work really well; what are your thoughts?' Think about how to best explain your idea to each potential supporter to make your idea persuasive — for example, some want all the details and some prefer an overview, some respond best to an informal chat and some prefer ideas in writing.

Position your idea so that everyone wins from your plan and sell it softly without downplaying its benefits. Pay attention to the body language of the people you're meeting, as well as their tone of voice and look for other clues as you float your idea. Expect some resistance — don't take resistance personally and don't become defensive. Listen to any criticism and try to understand the significance of the criticism so that you can figure out how to use that criticism to make your idea more palatable.

Ask for the thoughts and advice of the people whose support you seek. Stay flexible and amend your ideas as you gather suggestions and different opinions. Incorporating people's ideas and including them in devising your strategy are great ways for those people to share ownership of the idea with you — earning people's support is easier when 'my idea' becomes 'our idea'.

Spend time with your supporters. Pick up the phone, go to lunch, drop by for a quick chat and include them in relevant emails. As your supporters hear about and discuss your proposal, their familiarity with your idea adds to the comfort level. (Review Chapter 7 to make sure you take your best shot; and when you want to know more about who to bring onto your side, turn to Chapter 8.)

Encourage your supporters to make public commitments supporting your ideas. Public backing is more durable and reliable than private backing and several people who actively advocate an idea exert more influence than a lone advocate.

Pitch your ideas

The best packaged and presented proposals are usually the ones that get the nod. Once you have gauged reactions to your idea, build a coalition of supporters and work out how to appeal to those your proposal affects. Now the time has come to put forward your plan for formal acceptance. A good pitch contains

- ✔ A clear overall aim of your idea, emphasising what is most important to the decision makers — the bottom line, the effect on morale, public image and so on.
- ✔ An outline of your idea, showing how your proposal fits in with the organisation's values and mission.
- ✔ The advantages of implementing your idea, how it benefits the organisation and the people it most directly affects. Go with the three strongest benefits because if you list them all, the knockers may leap to the weakest and pull your idea apart.
- ✔ The costs of implementing your idea.
- ✔ The potential difficulties of implementing your idea and how those difficulties can be avoided or made manageable.

You may also want to explain the consequences of not acting on your idea. People often forget that sticking with the status quo is also a decision. Would they choose the status quo if it were not already in place?

Express your ideas clearly and your colleagues are more likely to take your ideas seriously. Avoid over explaining — too much explanation detracts from the detail of your idea. Share the credit — when a lot of people are involved in and support your idea, rejecting the idea becomes more difficult.

You also need a plan to ensure that your idea, once implemented, continues to operate and that the easy option of reverting to the status quo won't be taken. This is your keep-it-in-place strategy. Even when you don't include this strategy in your pitch, you need to know how to protect your idea and keep your idea working, not only in case you're asked to implement your idea but also to make sure your idea works long term (for more on this subject, refer to Chapter 5).

Working Well with Everyone

Without wishing to pigeonhole people, you can describe people's personalities in many different ways. The system in the following sections looks at four main personality styles based on whether people attend more to the task or more to other people, and whether people are more outgoing or more inward looking. (If you want to find out more about concentrating on the task or people, you can find information in Chapter 3.)

Understanding your own, your leader's and your followers' personality styles gives you a good understanding of how to lead and be led more comfortably and effectively.

Most people don't fit *perfectly* into a style but they fit one description better than another. As you read through the styles in the next sections, think about your leader and the people you lead and decide which styles best describe them. Notice which styles sound most like you and which sound most like the other leaders in your organisation.

Dominant directors

Dominant directors pay attention to the task before people and are outgoing, results-oriented, strong-willed, competitive people who take charge easily and express themselves clearly (sometimes too clearly). In fact, dominant directors can seem blunt, pushy and impatient. Try to avoid telling dominant directors what to do; stick with suggestions or provide recommendations or options they can choose.

If a dominant director leads you, give this person all the respect they know they deserve. Turn in quality work that's practical and demonstrates results and never try the patience of dominant directors with abstract ideas or too much attention to 'fluffy' people issues. Don't burden dominant directors with details. Be brief, accurate and to the point because dominant directors hate waffling, bluffing and rambling.

If any of your followers exhibit the characteristics of a dominant director, be aware that these people tend to resist authority. Give dominant director followers as much leeway to make decisions as you can.

Energetic socialisers

Energetic socialisers are friendly, outgoing, optimistic, talkative people, the types who bring life and fun to a group (although sometimes these socialisers can overdo their enthusiasm). Energetic socialisers are generally informal, filled with energy and clever at coming up with ideas and influencing people. But ask energetic socialisers to work on a task that involves a lot of detail and their souls shrivel. They're much better working on expansive, creative projects that require a fast pace of work. Energetic socialisers are often excitable, disorganised and inattentive to detail, and can be undisciplined and manipulative.

Whether you're leading or following energetic socialisers, get into the habit of beginning conversations with phrases such as 'How are you?', always explaining the overall goal and bringing in only those details that you absolutely must. Be enthusiastic, especially about their ideas, let them know you appreciate their efforts and contributions and keep detailed work away from them as much as you can. If you lead energetic socialisers, encourage them to plan and follow through with the tasks they do.

Quiet team players

Quiet team players are the reliable, steady leaders and followers who achieve goals because they work hard and consistently. Quiet team players dislike conflict and prefer a familiar routine to the untried and untested. These people are helpful, quiet, consistent, reliable, loyal, supportive and patient. Quiet team players are deep thinkers and patient listeners. However, to some people, these steady players can appear to be unsure, indecisive, awkward and insecure conformists.

When your leader is a quiet team player, take a slow and steady approach when presenting information — and don't be too loud, pushy or abrupt, either. Suggest rather than insist, and remember to seek the opinion of quiet team players because they're unlikely to offer it otherwise. Take the time to become better acquainted and build trust with quiet team players or they won't enjoy leading you or want to be led by you.

As a leader, be sure to let your followers who are quiet team players know how they're doing and don't forget to say thanks. Overlooking or taking quiet team players for granted is easy because they're so dependable and prepared to work in the background. When a quiet team player is your leader, inform them of your progress so they won't worry and have to keep asking how your work is going.

Conscientious detailers

Conscientious detailers are high-achieving perfectionists. When they can't do a task correctly, they prefer not to do the task at all. These people are orderly, systematic, attentive to detail and accurate. Conscientious detailers are also logical and clever at weighing up alternatives. They love to analyse and pull apart thorny problems and puzzles. Conscientious detailers can also be judgemental, critical and slow at making decisions.

Conscientious detailers don't like sudden changes, so don't spring surprises on them. If you need to change procedures, assignments or even the way the workspace is set out, explain the changes clearly, make room for questions and give conscientious detailers time to adjust to changes.

 Give conscientious detailers who follow you the detailed work that dominant directors and energetic socialisers so dislike (and are so poor at completing well). When you work for a conscientious detailer, don't even think about turning in sloppy work. Prepare thoroughly for meetings and have the facts and figures at your fingertips. Explain slowly and carefully, pause often to let conscientious detailers think through what you're saying and include the details these people crave. Be professional, courteous, and correct with conscientious detailers and stick to established procedures and precedents. One more suggestion — don't make silly jokes. Conscientious detailers are pretty serious people.

Chapter 10

Bringing Out the Best in Your Followers

*F*ollowers generally start a new task with great hopes about enjoying their jobs and doing their jobs well. But frequently problems arise. Maybe no-one explains exactly how to do the job, maybe the system sabotages their efforts and slowly grinds down their enthusiasm or maybe the other team members or their leader fail them. Too often, followers end up going through the motions, doing the minimum amount of work and not fulfilling their own or their leader's expectations. Such a waste.

In my 30 years of consulting to (mostly) wonderful organisations around the world and working with (mostly) wonderful leaders, I looked, listened and learned a lot. One puzzle that intrigues me is why some organisations and teams disappoint whereas other organisations and teams always delight. Well, I have cracked the conundrum.

I isolated the drivers of peak performance and grouped them into five key enablers that, together, unlock productivity and allow people's capabilities to flourish. I have named them the five keys to make them easy to remember and, therefore, easy to use:

✔ What to

✔ How to

✔ Want to

✔ Chance to

✔ Led to

These five keys are simple — but not simplistic. And I can tell you this fact for sure: You cannot bring out the best in your followers without turning all five keys to open those five doors to success.

If any one of these essential keys (or part of a key) is missing, performance begins to crumble. This chapter gives you the tools to make sure your followers' initial high hopes don't collapse and turn to dust. I explain how to use the five essential keys to build a highly efficient, highly motivated, highly productive group of followers in a way that brings out the best in everyone.

Key 1: Ensuring Followers Know What to Do

Have you heard of Sisyphus? The gods condemned him to endlessly roll a boulder up to the top of a mountain, only to have it fall back down, at which point he had to start rolling the boulder up the mountain again. Nothing is more hellish than pointless work.

Whenever you ask a follower to take on a task without explaining clearly what you want done, why the task needs to be done, where the task fits into the business and why the task is considered important, the likelihood that your follower tackles that task with enthusiasm is remote indeed. That's what the *What to* key prevents.

Building a solid framework

To avoid pointless work that's a series of meaningless tasks, explain clearly what you expect from your followers by giving them an overall 'framework' to guide their efforts. This framework is made up of each follower's task, as follows:

- **Job purpose:** Make a succinct statement of why the follower's role exists.
- **Key result areas:** Each follower needs five to seven main areas of accountability and responsibility.
- **Main measures of success:** Be sure followers can easily track these measures as they do their work.

A clear overall job purpose supports followers' efforts and shows why each follower's task is important. Key result areas put individual tasks into context, and measures of success give followers goals to pursue and allow the followers to measure their achievements, which motivates and encourages individual accountability.

This framework gives each follower a structure upon which to base their efforts and attention. (If you need help to write a job purpose or determine key result areas, refer to Chapter 4; you can find all you need to know about measures of success in Chapter 12.)

Making your expectations clear

While the three-point framework in the previous section deals mostly with performance, *expectations* deal mostly with behaviour. Making your expectations — or non-task goals — clear is important. Expectations include

- ✔ Being cooperative, friendly and helpful to colleagues and customers
- ✔ Keeping your work area tidy
- ✔ Looking for more efficient ways to complete tasks

(To brush up on your expectations of your followers, refer to Chapter 9.)

Using the hot-stove principle

The *hot-stove principle* is about rules and regulations that aren't negotiable — such as following safety procedures, following standard operating procedures and following customer-service procedures. Flag these rules in advance so that every follower knows the rules and knows that these rules must be followed without exception.

Just as you warn a person when a nearby stove is hot, so you can warn your followers to comply with hot-stove rules and the penalties that apply to people who break the rules. When a follower does break one of these rules, step in quickly. Make sure your action is:

- ✔ **Consistent:** Just as you're burnt every time you touch a hot stove, reinforce the fact that these rules apply to everyone all the time.
- ✔ **Immediate:** Just as you're burnt straight away when you touch a hot stove, deal with infringements of your rules immediately.
- ✔ **Impartial:** Just as a hot stove burns every person who touches it, don't play favourites with rule breakers. The rules apply to everyone — no excuses or exceptions.

Key 2: Ensuring Followers Know How to Do a Job

Followers can only do their jobs when they know how to do those jobs and that's where the *How to* key — that deals with training and experience — comes into play. Develop your followers both *formally* (through in-house and external training programs) and *informally* (through coaching, experience and special assignments that build their skills).

Another important aspect of the How to key is the learning environment you build, where followers can extend their skills, share their knowledge with each other and continually find better and more effective ways to achieve results. Learning environments also provide plenty of feedback, formally and informally, to help followers to continually assess progress and find ways to improve their performances. (You can find more about being a coach and developing followers by giving them special assignments in Chapter 12.)

Thirty years ago, plant and equipment made up about 80 per cent of a company's assets, and the knowledge of its employees made up approximately 20 per cent. Today, the reverse is true — the knowledge of the people inside an organisation and how well they use it is now the principle asset of most Australian organisations.

Key 3: Ensuring Followers Want to Do a Job

A leader's perennial question is: How can I motivate my followers? The fact is, you can't motivate anyone. Motivation is an inside job. The *Want to* key isn't about lighting fires under your followers — the Want to key is about lighting fires within each follower and then fanning the flames.

Helping your followers find motivation basically boils down to this line:

If you want people to do a good job, give them a job they want to do.

Nothing is worse than having to do a boring, repetitive task, or having to do a task you dislike.

Taking a stick to fear

You probably know the old chestnut about the carrot and the stick — enticing followers with a carrot and scaring them with a big stick. This assumes followers are donkeys.

Followers are not donkeys (at least, the vast majority of followers don't behave like asses). The time has come to dispel that offensive myth.

While fear can motivate people for short periods, fear certainly does not bring out the best in people — fear merely produces compliance. And after people have experienced fear, most people adapt and so the fear loses its power. Long term, fear doesn't work. Short term, fear produces only the bare minimum of effort.

Finding out what makes followers want to do a good job

When you ask people what their main motivator is, the first answer that generally pops out of their mouths is — money.

Sure, money motivates, but motivation includes far more than merely the money you're paid for doing a job. If money were the only motivator, people would never do more than scrape along, doing just enough work to pick up their pay cheques.

In fact, money can be described as the base line of motivation. Without money as a reward, most followers wouldn't bother to turn up for work (volunteers excepted, making the following information extra relevant when you lead volunteers).

What really motivates people are intangibles that don't pay the bills but satisfy the soul — psychological rewards. Studies show that psychological rewards act as strong motivators for Australians. These rewards that motivate include

- ✔ Achieving goals
- ✔ Contributing to team efforts
- ✔ Developing skills
- ✔ Doing new tasks
- ✔ Enjoying the work

✔ Feeling responsible

✔ Gaining respect from others for skills and contributions

✔ Gaining self-respect from a job well done

✔ Having clear goals

✔ Participating in decisions

✔ Receiving praise and recognition from a leader

✔ Rising to challenges

✔ Seeing the results of your efforts

✔ Working with friendly, competent people

Give followers your attention and time. Get to know your followers and what makes them tick. You can then figure out which of these common motivators appeal most to which followers, and allocate assignments that satisfy those needs. But first, make sure your followers have a good job to do.

Giving followers a good job to do

A challenging job provides followers with the three Es — Enrichment, Enlargement and Empowerment.

A great way to keep followers interested and fulfilled is to keep increasing their challenges and responsibilities. Don't expect performances from your followers that are unrealistically high. But keep tweaking up the standards just enough to make their jobs rich and to keep followers involved, energised and engaged. *Enrichment* — keeping up the challenge — also increases followers' skills and usefulness. (See Chapter 12 to find out more about enriching your followers' jobs through delegation.)

A second way to give followers rewarding jobs is to ensure those jobs contain a variety of tasks — known as *enlargement* — so that the work doesn't become too repetitive.

The third aspect of a fulfilling job is *empowerment* — allowing people to apply flexibility and discretion to how they undertake tasks and allowing your followers to make decisions in their areas of responsibility. Showing that you trust your followers increases their commitment and motivation and further develops their skills, making your followers more valuable to your team and to the organisation.

Merely adding new duties and responsibilities to followers' workloads is not empowerment — just more work. Real empowerment takes time to develop and you need to provide the right climate and, particularly, the right resources, information and authority to support your followers.

Enrichment, enlargement and empowerment result in well-designed jobs made up of an interesting and challenging set of tasks that followers want to complete — provided they enjoy doing those types of tasks.

Putting the right follower in the right role

On the first Tuesday of November, Australians are reminded that every horse runs better on some courses than on other courses. Just as trainers take care to race their horses on the tracks that give those horses the best chances of winning, leaders take care to assign to followers work that gives them the best chances of succeeding at the tasks they're performing. That's called correct *job placement* — work that followers actually enjoy doing and that draws on their skills, experiences and aptitudes. Putting the right followers in the right roles increases the followers' commitment to you and to the organisation.

Although no-one loves *every* aspect of their job — all people have tasks they prefer not to do — try to ensure that, overall, your followers enjoy most aspects of their jobs. This gives your followers (and you) the best odds of winning in the peak performance stakes.

Key 4: Giving Followers a Chance to Do a Job

Here's a question that stumps most leaders at first: When a follower knows what to do in a job, how to do the job and wants to do the job well, and then doesn't do the job well, what is the problem? The answer is that something is wrong with the person's work environment.

Even when you have the right followers for a particular job, those followers won't be able to be as productive as they can be, need to be and want to be when their work environment doesn't offer them the *Chance to* key to enable them to do a good job. A work environment isn't neutral. The environment either supports performance or smothers performance. The Chance to key opens up a support system for followers while they do their jobs, removing the frustrations and obstacles that may trip them up. The Chance to key is about giving your followers a sporting chance to do a good job.

Supplying the right tools for the job

Poor workers blame their tools but, the truth is, doing a satisfactory job with poor, faulty, badly designed, badly maintained or outdated equipment is difficult. Eventually you give up and just go through the motions of completing the job.

Make sure your followers have the tools and equipment they need to do their jobs efficiently and make sure their tools and equipment are regularly maintained.

Designing helpful systems and procedures

The way people undertake particular tasks evolves over time. Before you know it, work systems and procedures collect unnecessary steps, introduce unnecessary backtracking, develop bottlenecks and begin using materials and other resources that really are not needed. What started as a simple job can become awkward and cumbersome. And you and your team members are so busy following your procedures that you seldom find time to step back and see all the unnecessary moss your stones have gathered.

Unnecessary work causes frustration and shackles productivity. With all the good will in the world, even the best followers can't win against an inefficient system.

Show your followers how to step back and examine how a job is being carried out. Make it easy for your followers to come up with ideas and suggestions for improvement. Make sure each step in a process flows logically and easily into the next step so that your followers aren't obstructed on their way to achieving your goals.

Supplying the right resources

Thanks mainly to over-zealous downsizing, many organisations have gone beyond *lean and mean* and have become *anorexic and angry*. As a result, many followers are doing the jobs that two or even three people once performed. So overburdened are these followers that they no longer have the time to do every task they want to do or they no longer have the time to do tasks properly. The result is that some tasks have to be performed a second and sometimes third time because the followers were not able to complete the tasks properly the first time. Some Australian studies estimate that people can save 13 hours every week by eliminating rework. Imagine what a great job your followers could do if they each had 13 hours extra each week to do their work.

Along with corporate budgets, access to the supplies followers need to do a job properly is tending to shrivel. Budget cuts and staff cuts mean people are trying to 'do more with less' and are now so busy that they don't have time to share or pass on information to team-mates who need that information to do their jobs efficiently. Lack of time also prevents many followers from building the congenial relationships that make workplaces run much more smoothly.

As a leader, your job is to obtain the scarce resources your followers need to do their jobs. How? Carefully plan strategies that can win you what you need for your followers. Make sure your followers' working spaces are well laid out, inviting and conducive to getting the job done efficiently. If you don't support your followers in these ways, your followers are bound to give up, shrug their shoulders and go for the 'She'll be right, mate' option, which is never the best option.

Resources aren't always expensive or difficult to obtain, such as a brand new IT system or brand new machinery. In fact, the stumbling blocks tripping up your followers are far more likely to be the little, everyday resource needs. That saying, 'Nobody trips over mountains; the small pebbles are what cause people to stumble' often applies to resources that are lacking. By keeping up the supply of smaller resources and smoothing out work procedures to make them more efficient, your followers have accessed two important parts of the Chance to key.

Building a talented team

Teams don't work like well-oiled machines without a little (actually a lot of) oil — I mean help, mostly from the team leader. How well the followers in your team work together has a big influence on how effectively your followers perform.

Lack of coordination, poor internal relationships, unclear expectations and badly designed work areas can cause team members to work poorly together and make work unnecessarily difficult. These conditions can prevent followers from performing well — individually and as a unit. A disagreeable and unfavourable environment of poor relationships and unsuitable surroundings can grind down followers so they lose their willingness to put in the effort required.

Build your followers into a cohesive team where each follower understands what all the other followers are trying to achieve, where followers share common goals and purposes and where each can support and value the efforts of the others. This type of team achieves far more than single followers working alone ever can. (For tips on building a successful team, go to Chapters 15 and 16.)

Not sweating the small stuff

When your followers can't use the Chance to key and open up the opportunities described in the previous sections, then you have the reason for poor performance 85 per cent of the time. The other 15 per cent of the time, disappointing performance is due to what is called 'Acts of God' — situations that leaders can't predict or avoid. For example, a flu epidemic may cut the staff to half normal levels, or a flood may destroy equipment or damage the work environment.

Similarly, when a follower is going through a messy personal situation (such as a divorce), has lost a loved one, or perhaps is planning a wedding, then that follower may not be able to give full attention to the job and performance may drop temporarily. And everyone — including you — has the occasional 'bad hair' day.

Because you can't really do much to deal with problems that arise by chance, and since personal issues are unavoidable, and because together they cause only a small per cent of under-performance overall, you don't need to be too concerned about their impact on performance. Instead, concentrate on the first four aspects of the Chance to key described above — that's where you get the biggest pay-off for your efforts.

Guard against self-fulfilling prophecies

The human brain works in strange ways. When you believe that a fact is true, you can find plenty of evidence to verify the fact.

If a leader sincerely believes one or all followers are lazy and irresponsible, the evidence to confirm that belief is everywhere, and vice versa. Sooner or later, followers come to live down (or up) to their leader's expectations of them (or they find a new leader). In any case, their responses prove the leader's belief as correct. The truth is irrelevant.

Because of this tendency for a leader's perceptions to reflect on followers, leaders are wise to move very slowly — very, very slowly — to label any followers as lazy or irresponsible. However, leaders need to be very quick — very, very quick — to label followers hard-working and reliable. Work with your followers to make the hard-working and reliable label a reality. After all, what leader wants to be saddled with a poorly performing follower?

Key 5 — the Ultimate Key: Knowing How You Can Lead to Peak Performance

You probably are aware that your followers watch everything you do and talk about you when you're not around. Outsiders also watch an organisation's leaders and form strong impressions about the organisation from what the leaders say and do.

As a leader, you hold the *Led to* key that enables you to set the pace and the overall standard of your team's approach and results. I can't overemphasise the importance of you, as a leader, knowing your own values and consistently leading your followers to live up to those values and the values of the organisation. (For more on values, refer to Chapters 3 and 5.)

You and the other leaders in your organisation are critical to the performance standards of your followers because you

- ✔ Are the important role models that your followers follow
- ✔ Build a working climate that encourages people to keep learning and keep finding ways to do things easier, better, cheaper and faster
- ✔ Delegate work and assign the special projects that develop people's skills and keep them interested and engaged
- ✔ Establish and maintain the kind of culture your organisation needs and that followers want to join and remain in

✔ Hold the authority to make sure the day-to-day operational systems and procedures help people to do their jobs, rather than make doing their jobs difficult

✔ Provide the coaching and feedback that helps followers build their knowledge and performance

✔ Represent your organisation to people outside the organisation

✔ Set clear goals and develop your organisation's talent

In fact, your leadership is a critical element of the *What to*, *How to*, *Want to* and *Chance to* keys that bring out followers' best efforts and enable them to achieve the results you need them to achieve.

Polishing the gold

On 17 May 1848, a 12-year-old boy sailed with his parents and younger brother from Glasgow to New York City. He arrived with no money and no education, yet he became the wealthiest man in the United States of America — and also in the world. His name was Andrew Carnegie.

At one point, Carnegie had 43 millionaires working for him (and $1 million then was worth a lot more than $1 million today — about 27 times more). These followers of Carnegie's didn't start out as millionaires but became millionaires working for him.

A journalist asked Carnegie how he trained his followers so that each became worth such a large salary. Carnegie replied, 'Men are developed the same way gold is mined. Several tons of dirt must be moved to get one ounce of gold. But one doesn't go into the mine looking for the dirt. One goes in looking for the gold.'

Andrew Carnegie's words remind leaders to look for gold — not dirt — and polish that gold like crazy. Just looking for gold isn't enough, though. You also need to use the five keys I describe in this chapter to unlock the conditions that support your followers as they go about their tasks and that make your followers' superior performance easy.

Chapter 11

Removing Obstacles and Making Decisions

*L*eaders sometimes feel pressured to act quickly, yet you and I know that haste makes waste. And certainly, when it comes to tackling problems and making decisions, no matter how pressured you feel, taking your time and thinking through problems and decisions properly is almost always going to be your best option.

In this chapter, I fill you in on why leaders involve followers as much as they can in solving problems and making decisions. I explain how your brain can sabotage your best efforts and how to guard against that happening. And I outline the six straightforward steps that leaders use to solve problems. You also find out how to make a good decision, what to do when your decision is unpopular and what to do after you make a poor decision. Finally, you find out how to keep getting better and better at solving problems and making decisions.

Enlisting More Brains for Better Results

Successful leaders know the benefits of involving followers in solving problems and making decisions. These benefits include followers

- Being more committed to making a solution or decision work because of their involvement in the projects
- Developing more and better options resulting from a range of experiences and knowledge and the opportunity to build on each other's ideas
- Gaining valuable experience and training
- Generating enthusiasm by people working together to reach a decision or resolve a problem
- Understanding the courses of action chosen and why those courses were selected and others rejected

In fact, research shows that people working together make better decisions than even the brightest individual in a group does alone — provided the team members apply the six important steps to solving problems and reaching decisions that I describe in the section 'Using the Six Straightforward Steps to Solving Problems' later in this chapter.

You won't always need to involve your followers in problems and decisions. When the answer is obvious and when a decision or problem has no real effect on your followers, involving your followers is pointless. In other situations, try to involve followers, especially when your followers

- Are affected by a decision or solution
- Are involved in implementing a decision or solution
- Need to understand and accept a decision or solution
- Want to be involved or can benefit from the experiences making a decision can offer

Here are some tips to help you when you involve followers in solving problems and making decisions:

- Don't vote — voting only produces winners and losers.
- Encourage creativity.
- Encourage followers to take ownership of the whole problem-solving process.

✔ Find consensus. Consensus is beneficial — unless consensus is achieved too easily.

✔ Keep the attention of all team members on the objectives of the resolution or decision, on the future and on solving the problem.

✔ Never involve followers only to get their agreement to your decision — followers spot shams straight away.

✔ Welcome differences of opinion as a way to gather additional information, to clarify issues and to force you to seek better information.

Avoiding Brain Sabotage

Most of the time, your brain goes all out to help you. Sometimes, though, for the best of reasons, your brain can hinder you, particularly when you're dealing with complex or confusing issues or information. Just when you need to consider, weigh up and balance contradictory information, your brain automatically steps in and applies a thinking routine or shortcut. These mental shortcuts are called *heuristics*. This process protects you from *cognitive dissonance*, the brain pain that comes from too much contradictory or confusing information.

These mental shortcuts are designed to help you find your way quickly and easily through the mire of too much complex and contradictory information. Often, heuristics work for you. However, these mental shortcuts can also sabotage you when you're not careful. Fortunately, forewarned is forearmed. You need to look out for potential brain tricks, described in the following sections, and compensate for these traps when you spot them.

Looking out for selective vision

Your brain is wired to seek evidence that confirms and supports your point of view or preferred course of action. Your brain is also wired to avoid information that contradicts what you already 'know' — or believe to be so. This selective vision, which psychologists call *confirmation bias*, can be so strong that sometimes you can't even see information that's right in front of your nose.

Seeing what you want to see affects where you go to collect information, how you interpret that information and to whom you listen. Confirmation bias causes you to put too much weight on information that supports your thinking and too little weight on information that challenges your thinking.

To figure out what's really going on in a situation, apply these rules:

- ✔ Don't accept confirming evidence without question.
- ✔ Don't make a decision and then figure out how to justify it.
- ✔ Don't undermine the real facts with your own expectations and biases.

Instead, you can follow this advice:

- ✔ Be aware of your opinion and admit that you may be inclined to think a certain way so that you can consciously open your mind to other ways.
- ✔ Find someone to play devil's advocate and argue against your opinions and conclusions.

Many assumptions people hold are so entrenched they don't even realise they're making assumptions and they behave as though those assumptions were really true. Think about the assumptions you may be making and examine your assumptions to make sure they are correct.

Avoiding anchoring

You go into a shop to buy something — say a pair of shoes, and spot a nice pair straight away, but think, 'Oh, I'll just have a quick check and see what else is here.' Then you spend the next half hour looking around only to end up buying the first pair you saw. That's anchoring in action.

Anchoring means giving too much weight to what you see or hear *first* and *last* — whether you're dealing with something to purchase, information, evidence, opinions, estimates or ideas — and ignoring information and thoughts that come in between. Not considering *in between* information is dangerous — who's to say that the first and last is best or better than the middle bits? Thinking the 'middle bits' aren't as good doesn't apply to information and ideas any more than it does to chocolates.

Avoid anchoring by

- ✔ Being cautious about your first and last impressions and information
- ✔ Making an effort to give fair weight to what you see and learn in between
- ✔ Not automatically sticking with whatever idea or solution occurs to you first

Be careful of anchoring your followers with your opinions, too. Wait until you hear their ideas and suggestions before giving them your own ideas and suggestions.

Side-stepping the status quo

The conventional wisdom of the sayings 'Leave well enough alone' and 'Let sleeping dogs lie', are warnings not to take action that's radical or even that's different. Doing nothing — maintaining the *status quo* — can often be easier than making an effort to change a situation. On top of that is the niggling feeling that the less action you take, the less open you are to criticism. Yes, inertia can be temptingly safe.

Maintaining the status quo may be a good choice but keeping a situation the same just because taking no action to change it seems to be safe and easy is poor leadership. Instead:

- Ask yourself whether you would select the status quo if it were just another alternative.
- Think about what you want to achieve and consider whether the current situation does that well enough or whether another alternative would be better.

Cutting your losses

Setting aside a previous choice is hard to do when that choice isn't working, but sticking with a mistake rather than cutting your losses and changing course only compounds an error.

Don't threaten your chances of success by hanging onto a bad decision or a failed solution in a vain attempt to recover your investment in time, money and effort. And don't try to turn a poor decision into a good decision. When your previous decision or solution isn't working, set that aside and try a new decision or solution.

Changing your direction

Your *framing* of a problem or decision colours the way you set about working with that problem or decision. Framing guides you down one path or down another and points you towards certain actions and away from others.

To avoid being unconsciously pushed in one direction or pulled in another, follow this advice:

- ✔ Change how you word problems and decision criteria to look at them differently.

- ✔ Don't automatically accept the way a problem or decision is worded when it's presented to you. State the problem or decision in your own words so that you can think about the issues differently.

- ✔ Look for distortions that could be caused by the way problems and decision criteria are stated.

- ✔ State problems and decision criteria in neutral ways that reflect different reference points.

Opening up your brain filters

Your brain filters and directs the flow of information in your mind. You gather some of these *filters* from your organisation, some from the group you're leading and some from your very own personal filters. Your followers have their own personal filters, too. Unless you're vigilant, you may not realise when your filters are snapping into action.

Filters sort information and decide what data to allow through and what data can be ignored. Watch for these important filters:

- ✔ **Contextual filters:** These filters enable you to reject the significance of your surroundings, preventing you from tuning into important signals. Contextual filters can also prevent you from respecting cultural expectations, leading you to a wrong decision or course of action. And these filters can prevent you from being influenced by the expectations of important people (refer to Chapter 8 to find out more about deciding to whom to listen; and Chapters 4, 8 and 15 for more information on cultural influences).

- ✔ **Self knowledge:** Failure to understand what drives you to do what you do blinds you to information that is blindingly obvious to others, and allows you to ignore important information and misinterpret meaningful information — leading you in the wrong direction or towards a poor course of action.

- ✔ **Social filters:** These enable you to ignore information based on its source. Whatever the reason — perhaps you don't rate the source highly or perhaps you want to block out bad news — these filters can fool you into deciding on a poor course of action.

Guarding against groupthink

Another important decision trap, called *groupthink*, comes from our natural desire to be part of a group that gets along well. Groupthink can appear any time you're working with your followers to solve a problem or reach a decision, especially when you're under pressure to make a good decision. The sad result, though, is that groupthink can lead you to reach an unwise or even dangerous decision — the safety-in-numbers effect can make people more willing to reach riskier decisions as a group than each may have done when reaching a decision alone.

When a strong team spirit exists, team members may be reluctant to point out the downsides to a decision or to disagree with what seems to be the majority view. Here are the main signs that alert you to the presence of groupthink:

- ✔ A strong sense of 'us' and 'them'
- ✔ Assuming the group is right and ignoring ethical consequences or other side effects of decisions
- ✔ Complacency
- ✔ Considering only a few alternatives and reaching a decision or course of action very quickly
- ✔ Excessive optimism
- ✔ Ignoring or rationalising warning signs or contrary information
- ✔ Overconfidence
- ✔ Reluctance to raise new information or contrary evidence
- ✔ Strong pressure to conform and agree with the majority view

Now that you know how to recognise groupthink, here are some ways to head off groupthink before poor or dangerous decisions occur:

- ✔ Actively look for the weak points in your decision or solution.
- ✔ Appoint one or two followers to be devil's advocates to spot flaws in thinking.
- ✔ Ask questions such as 'What makes you uncomfortable with this idea?' or 'On a 1–10 scale, how confident are you that this solution can work?' or 'Do you see any flaws in this?' or 'Have I missed anything?'
- ✔ Be suspicious when agreement comes too quickly or too easily or when followers seem to be avoiding conflict.

✔ Develop an atmosphere of open inquiry by actively seeking alternatives; and an atmosphere of careful consideration by seeking different opinions, exploring them and searching for the pros and cons of your alternatives.

✔ Invite experts and outsiders to review and contribute to your team's thoughts and ideas.

Solving Pesky Problems and Momentous Decisions

Organisations are becoming *flatter* as layers of management disappear. As a result, leaders at every remaining level are called upon to take stock, draw on their own and their followers' experiences, think through decisions and work out answers to all sorts of predicaments. As a leader, your good judgement and unflappability have never been more important. Some other abilities you need to solve problems and make the right decisions include the following (with some extra reading if you want to know more):

✔ Anticipating others' reactions to decisions (you can find more on this in Chapters 7 and 8)

✔ Developing a workable plan and harnessing enough resources — but not so many as to be wasteful (refer to Chapter 5 for the guff on planning)

✔ Having forbearance and restraint to think through decisions, combined with an action-oriented approach that gets a job done (check out Chapter 3 for information on the mindsets that can help you)

✔ Political understanding (for more on this subject, take a look at to Chapter 8)

✔ Setting and sticking to priorities (refer to Chapter 6 for this subject)

Ignore the conventional wisdom

The cholera outbreak of 1854 in London's Soho district was believed to have been spread through the air. But physician John Snow marked the locations of each death on a map and found the deaths were concentrated around a water pump on Broad Street, indicating that water from the pump may have been the source of the deadly disease. Snow presented his evidence to the council, which removed the pump's handle so that the pump couldn't be used, stopping the spread of the epidemic and saving many lives.

The next time you have a problem that lingers on despite your best attempts, try ignoring widespread beliefs and deal with the facts.

Investing the right amount of time

Some predicaments are quite straightforward and pop up often enough that you can save reinventing the wheel by simply automating the response. Agree with your followers on the best way to handle a situation and put a system, policy or practice in place — a *standard operating procedure* — for followers to use every time a particular situation arises.

Before getting to work on the rest of the problems and decisions that arise, work out how much time, effort and trouble each one is worth. That way, you can invest your time, effort and other resources accordingly. At one end of the scale are insignificant and inconsequential predicaments that don't deserve much time or energy. At the other end are complex, momentous dilemmas that deserve all the time, effort and creativity you can muster.

To figure out where a problem or decision is on that scale, consider these conditions:

- Risk involved
- Potential consequences of reaching the wrong or right decision
- Effects on other people
- Effects of taking no action
- Resource costs — money, time, goodwill and so on — of either ignoring the problem or fixing the problem

---

Tips for better brainstorming

Brainstorming is a tried and tested way to develop lots of ideas quickly. It's a great place to begin when you need to develop options or ideas and don't know where to start. You can brainstorm by yourself, with a sheet of paper to collect your thoughts. Better still, begin a group problem-solving or decision-making session by brainstorming, collecting everyone's ideas on a big flip chart where they can be seen (and spark other ideas). Here are some tips:

- Address a specific topic or goal.
- Don't criticise — not even a raised eyebrow is allowed.

- Don't edit or 'improve' while you're writing down ideas.
- Don't judge ideas; let them emerge and grow before evaluating them.
- Go for ideas only, and quantity not quality (you can fix them up later).
- Have fun — laughter encourages creativity.
- Write down everything, even silly ideas because silly ideas may spark seriously good ideas.

Think of Goldilocks. Make decisions and problems as simple as you can (but no simpler) and invest just the right amount of time, effort and energy in a problem or decision that it deserves. Agonising over small matters at the expense of more important matters is silly and so is making an important decision in haste, only to repent the decision later.

After you assess how much attention and effort to bestow on a decision or problem, figure out whether to use total rationality and logic, gut instinct, intuition, creativity, or a mixture of all of these to reach your goal. (The mixture is often your better choice.) Then think about whether or not to involve others to achieve better results.

Rousing your creativity

The world is changing so fast that fresh and useful ideas are mandatory for survival. This means that resourceful, inventive leaders are becoming increasingly precious resources.

Great ideas are often the product of sudden 'Ah ha!' moments. Those moments can slip away because of a fear of sounding silly or not daring to think or try something unusual. Coming up with creative ideas often means extracting information that is already there — simmering away in your subconscious — by relaxing enough to let those new ideas float to the surface of your mind. Here are some guidelines to help your creative thinking powers emerge:

- Approach problems and decisions from various points of view.
- Have fun.
- Listen to your subconscious to allow creative ideas to 'bubble up'.

Using the Six Straightforward Steps to Solving Problems

If gardens only produced sweet-smelling flowers and delicious, vitamin-packed vegies, gardeners wouldn't be able to find work. The weeds are what cause the bother. And choosing the wrong weedkiller can do more harm than good. Leaders have weeds to ward off too. And, as with the weeds in your garden, eliminating bothersome problems and reaching the right decisions are essential when you don't want to do more harm than good.

Sleeping on a problem

You probably notice that your creative ideas, intuitions and insights often appear out of nowhere, when you're thinking about something else, daydreaming or even sleeping — provided you're relaxed enough to be able to allow your subconscious to percolate the ideas through to your conscious mind.

You can use a technique called *incubating* to draw on the vast powerhouse of knowledge and wisdom in your subconscious. As you're falling asleep, review what you know about a problem that you're trying to solve, a decision that you need to make or a situation that's puzzling you. Now think what you want to happen or to find out. Then go to sleep and let your subconscious get to work.

Eight out of ten times, providing the skill and knowledge is in your mind for your subconscious to draw on, your creative subconscious provides an answer within three nights of incubation.

Follow these principles for keeping weeds, and problems, at bay:

- ✔ Avoid quick fixes because they seldom work and the problem just keeps recurring.
- ✔ Know where problems are likely to arise and be sensitive to early warning signs.
- ✔ When you spot a problem, start solving the problem quickly, before the problem causes too much harm, or festers and becomes a crisis.

Problem solving and decision making overlap but not all decision making is the result of a problem — some decisions start out as decisions. Whenever you are faced with either, a thorough, systematic approach is your best course of action. Here are the six steps to follow when you want to eliminate a problem properly. If you don't have a problem and just need to make a good decision, you can skip Step 3.

Step 1: Defining the problem

You need to know that a problem exists and you need to know precisely what the problem is before you can solve it. Write a clear, short statement of what the problem is or what the decision is about. This single sentence frames your problem, acting as the mental window through which you view the problem and therefore how you attempt to deal with it. Finding the right form of words is critical because the right words can prevent you from wasting time, effort and other resources by solving a problem in the wrong way.

If you can't say what the problem is in one breath, then your problem is too long. You might be describing more than one problem or you may be trying to decide too much at once. If the words include 'and', you're almost certainly describing more than one problem and you can divide them and consider each problem separately. Never attempt to solve multiple problems — this just won't work. If you have several problems, prioritise them and work on them one at a time.

If you're stuck with how to solve a problem, state the problem as a 'How to' question. For example, 'The equipment is breaking down too often' becomes 'How can the equipment be kept running properly?' Another example: 'I keep running out of time to finish X and it's always late' becomes 'How do I make enough time to finish X properly and on time?'

Step 2: Spelling out your aim

You need to know clearly what you want to happen instead of what is happening or what you want the decision to do for you. List your goal or goals, factoring in any constraints you must include, for example, time or finances, to make sure your aim is realistic. If the situation is complex, divide your criteria into *musts* and *wants* — What your solution *must* do for you and, ideally, what you *want* your solution to do for you.

Once you have a clear picture of what you want to happen, develop some measures of success so you know your solution is working (refer to Chapter 5 to find out more about success measures).

Preventing potential problems

Leaders aim to spend more time preventing problems than dealing with them. Identifying, assessing and managing risks or unintended consequences, whether positive, negative or neutral, are part of both problem solving and decision making. Your goal is to minimise negative outcomes and make the most of opportunities in two areas:

✔ From your own activities

✔ From your environment

Tighten up with circles

Use the *circling technique* to make sure you know exactly what solution you're aiming at. Write your problem statement down and then circle the key words. For example:

How do I keep the equipment running properly?

The words to circle are *keep* and *equipment running properly*. Here's how to define the words in this example:

✔ **Keep:** This can mean forever more, between biannual services or for the next six months when replacement is due.

✔ **Equipment:** You specify which particular equipment because different equipment probably needs different types of attention and has different ways and cycles of not working properly.

✔ **Running:** This can mean in perfect working order or with only minor adjustments that every follower can perform.

✔ **Properly:** This can mean without a single hitch between services, with minor maintenance between major services by your team members or with a bit of attention from maintenance people.

Step 3: Analysing the problem and finding the chief cause

Perhaps you have heard the cautionary tale about taking an aspirin for a headache when the real problem is eye strain. If you're not thinking clearly and carefully, confusing a symptom with a problem is easy. Symptoms result from problems, and fixing symptoms won't fix a problem. If all you 'solve' is a symptom, you end up 'fixing' the same problem over and over again and often create new problems in the process. Most leaders can't afford to waste precious time and effort solving a symptom and leaving the real problem untouched, to discover it keeps returning. The only way to fix a problem is to find its cause and fix or remove the cause.

To do that, you need to invest some time investigating the problem from all angles. A double benefit is that often, once you begin untangling a problem and examining it carefully, the solution becomes remarkably obvious.

The questions you need to know about a problem are

✔ **Who**

- Is affected?
- Is involved?

✔ **What**

- Are people's feelings and opinions about the problem?
- Equipment is involved?
- Else is going on when the problem occurs?
- Facts do you have readily available?
- Facts do you need as well as those you already have?
- Has changed?
- Is the problem (refer to the earlier section, 'Step 1: Defining the problem') and what it is not?
- Is the specific nature of the problem?
- May cause the problem (not to fix blame but to get to the primary cause so you can eliminate it)?

✔ **When**

- Did the problem first occur?
- Does the problem occur?
- Doesn't the problem occur?

✔ **Where**

- Does the problem occur?
- Doesn't the problem occur?

✔ **How**

- Does the problem affect other parts of the organisation or your customers?
- Does the problem affect other people?
- Many times has the problem occurred?
- Often does the problem occur?
- Serious is the problem?

Looking at the extent of a problem is also important. For example, find out whether a problem is getting worse and, if so, how quickly it is getting worse.

Time exists to be taken. Don't rush the important step of thoroughly analysing your problem. Collect facts and opinions, challenge assumptions, open up your brain filters. Without being glacially slow, take time to ponder. Once you understand the problem well, you can brainstorm possible causes.

The ultimate question you are seeking to answer is: Why? You want to know precisely *why* you have this problem or *why* the problem occurs. Keep working at your analysis until you find the real cause, not just a symptom. When you know that, you know the problem's cause and you can move on to thinking about how to deal with the problem.

Step 4: Working out your options

After you discover the most likely cause of a problem, you can start thinking up ways to fix or remove the cause. Unless the solution is staring you in the face, the more options you can find, the merrier.

Brainstorming for options is a good way to begin. Once you have a feast of reasonable and feasible ideas, you can choose the best idea (or combination of ideas) to put into action.

Step 5: Selecting the best option

Use the aim you settled on in Step 2 as your decision criteria to evaluate your options and select the one that best meets your criteria. If you have sorted your criteria into *musts* and *wants*, discard any alternatives that don't meet all your *musts*. From those that are left, go with the solution that meets most of your *wants* or your most important *wants*.

Training your followers

If you often deal with emergencies and problems your followers bring to you, build their skills in identifying, preventing and dealing with these problems themselves. Ask your followers these questions, in this order:

- What, precisely, is the problem?
- What is your goal in solving this problem?
- What have you tried already?
- What do you see as your options?

- What do you recommend?
- What do you think the first step could be?

If your followers seem reluctant to tackle the problem, coach them to think through all aspects of the problem with these questions:

- What end result do you want?
- What could help you achieve that result?
- What do you need to do to make your solution happen?

Be sure to avoid the following two false solutions:

- **Patches:** When you put a 'she'll be right' bandage on a problem, you're likely to end up creating even more problems.
- **Quick fixes:** When you can't fix the problem properly now, wait until you can.

When you decide what to do: Stop. Take a step back and be a pessimist for a minute. Look for the weak points in your solution. You need to know about any fatal flaws and you need to work out any kinks before these can cause damage. Think through the implications of your decision on other parts of the organisation. Then you can put a plan into action with confidence.

Sometimes no perfect solution to a problem is possible. The best you can do with some problems is not solve them, but rather sort them out in the best way possible. Decisions that make everyone happy are few and far between.

Step 6: Planning and implementing your solution or decision

By Step 6, most of your thinking work is over — you now only need to develop a plan to put your solution or decision into place and make sure your plan works. (Refer to Chapter 5 to check the best way to develop a workable plan.)

Life on Mars

If you're stuck on how to solve a problem, look at it from a different angle. For years, NASA engineers kept trying to figure out how to get the Rover to land on Mars and kept asking, 'How do we keep the rocket from crashing?' The engineers were fixed on thinking the rocket would crash and so came up with strategies to slow down the rocket and protect it from disintegrating on impact.

Then they switched to a different question: 'How do we land the rocket?' That generated a wider range of creative ideas, including circling the rocket with airbags so it could bounce safely, which proved a much simpler and cheaper solution.

The moral of this story is: Challenge your stereotypes and look at problems, decisions and options through different frames.

Ambiguity is the enemy of a successful plan. Make everyone's responsibilities and accountabilities clear. Once you know who's responsible for doing what, where and when, how you can track your solution, how well your solution or decision is working and how to recognise if your plan is going off track, you're nearly home and hosed — unless your solution isn't working. If that's the case, remove the solution entirely and find a better plan. Leaving a failed solution in place only causes you more problems.

Making the solution stick

Once your solution is in place, you're still not finished. Here are some important actions to take to ensure your solution or decision isn't glossed over or passed by:

- Discuss how the solution is working at team meetings and how the solution could be improved or refined.
- Make the solution part of a regular training or induction program.
- Make the solution or decision part of normal procedure. If the solution entails a change to procedures, post the new routine where followers can easily see the details as a reminder until they get used to incorporating the new solution.
- Refine your solution so that it continues to improve.

Summing Up Leadership Decisions

Your first decision, when you need to make one, is to decide whether the situation merits your involvement. When it does, your next decision is whether to deal with the situation now or later. The answer depends on the implications of the decision. If the situation is no big deal, don't turn it into one by searching for every last (unnecessary) detail or asking every Tom, Dick and Harriet for their opinion. Some problems go away when you leave them alone. But don't use that as an excuse not to act.

If you're tempted to defer a decision, ask yourself what you may know tomorrow or next week that you don't know today. If the answer is 'Nothing much', then act now. Sitting and wishing doesn't solve problems that won't change — decisions and actions are what make a difference.

Whenever a decision has potentially serious repercussions, deal with that decision as a matter of priority and spend the time on it that it deserves. Always follow Steps 1, 2, 4, 5 and 6 in the section 'Using the Six Straightforward Steps to Solving Problems' earlier in this chapter.

When a decision is unpopular

Leadership isn't a popularity contest and leaders understand that best when they make a decision they know won't be well received. When you square up to this hurdle, engage your ethics and values and use all your leadership muscles (refer to Chapter 5 for more information on strengthening your leadership muscles). Think about how your decision affects people and why they may feel reluctant to accept it.

Use your understanding of how others may receive your decision and why to explain (not excuse) your decision. Aim to communicate each decision you make as carefully and tactfully as possible. And never blame anyone else for your decision.

The next time you need to make and explain an unpopular decision, think about how the best leader you know goes about explaining decisions. Use that leader as your role model.

Being RAPT with your plans

Use the RAPT formula to implement the solution you select to solve a problem:

✔ **Results:** Step 2 tells you the results you're after.

✔ **Activities:** These are the activities you complete to get your results.

✔ **Period of time:** This the time each activity takes.

✔ **Timetable:** Note when each activity is to be done and who is to do the activity so no activities can be overlooked.

Note: RAPT works for any type of plan — try RAPT for planning your weekly schedules.

When you've made a poor decision

The best way never to make a bad decision is never to make any decisions at all. But that's not what leadership is about. Face it — not every decision is going to be a wise one. Leaders know how to recognise and rectify poor decisions and, just as importantly, how to learn the lessons they teach.

Don't ignore, cover up, make excuses or find someone to blame. Analyse what went wrong and decide what to do. Then do it.

Figure out what went wrong. Get some advice from others with similar experiences. Think about what you could have considered and didn't; what you could have done but didn't. Think back through the steps in the section 'Using the Six Straightforward Steps to Solving Problems' earlier in this chapter. Did you omit any steps? The more you understand where you went wrong, the less likely you are to make the same mistake twice.

Diagnosing your decisions

Leaders habitually review just about everything they do, including the decisions they make, to see how they can improve their performances. Here are the main areas to review:

- ✔ **Appropriateness:** Think about how right your decision was, whether it was based on the right facts and opinions, and whether it suited the people and the situation.

- ✔ **Execution:** Think through how well your decision was implemented, whether responsibilities and timelines were clear and what may have made your decision roll out more smoothly.

- ✔ **People:** Think about whether you involved the right people and whether you brought them in too soon or not soon enough and whether you involved them in the right way.

- ✔ **Speed:** Evaluate whether your decision was made too hastily, before all the relevant facts and opinions were in, or too slowly, forcing people to deal with a poor situation longer than they needed to do so.

Keep a decision file, electronically or in a little notebook, of the main experiences you gather. Review these experiences once in a while when you have a few spare minutes and whenever you need to make an important decision.

Taking the high road

Every leader can think of examples when the easy option is not the ethical option. If you're tempted to take an easier road than the right road, think again. Make sure:

✔ Reasonable people can agree with your decision.

✔ The decision doesn't compromise you or your reputation, either personally or professionally.

✔ You can morally defend your decision.

Chapter 12

Spreading the Workload

. . . .

. . . .

*P*erhaps you're lucky enough to have worked with a leader who set challenging goals that stretched but didn't break you, who trusted you to achieve those goals and gave you the support and encouragement you needed. Perhaps you're lucky enough to work with a leader like that now.

Leaders who help develop the skills of their followers don't mollycoddle followers by doing their jobs for them or by giving followers tasks that are too easy for them. These leaders guide followers to achieve results that the followers never thought possible.

In this chapter, you find out how assigning work and delegating duties allows leaders to fulfil two vital responsibilities — getting the right results and developing followers' potential. You discover how to assign work and set goals that your followers are happy to achieve and you discover which tasks to delegate and which not to delegate. I explain the four easy steps of delegation and what to do when followers don't get the job quite right. I also alert you to the dangers of *upward delegation* — when followers want to delegate their jobs to you as their leader — and how to prevent that happening.

Assigning Work

Assigning the right duty to the right follower in the right way is a skill that leaders use every day. When leaders assign work properly, followers feel committed to achieving results and work wholeheartedly towards achieving those results. If you assign work incorrectly or assign work to the wrong follower, followers merely comply and you get only half-hearted effort.

Following these four important principles ensures that your followers commit to assignments and complete those tasks to the best of their ability:

✔ Assign tasks that reward followers.

✔ Establish a task's importance and how the task fits into the project.

✔ Explain clear measures of success.

✔ Recognise the efforts your followers make and the results your followers achieve.

Assigning horses to courses

A good match between followers and assignments rewards you with energised followers who get results. When you ask followers to take on a responsibility, make sure the task is the type of work they

✔ Are trained to do

✔ Enjoy

✔ Have a natural aptitude for

✔ Want to learn to do

If you're not sure which of your followers may enjoy a task or has a flair for it, find out who

✔ Enjoys repetitive work and who prefers variety

✔ Has a good eye for detail and who is better at broad-brush overviews

✔ Is better at 'thinking' and who is better at 'doing'

✔ Likes to interact with others and who is better working on their own

✔ Likes to move around a bit and who prefers to stay put

✔ Prefers a stable routine and who is flexible enough to handle the unexpected

Now match the types of tasks with your followers. Think about the task and then ask who

- ✔ Can add the task to their other duties without becoming overwhelmed with work?
- ✔ Can do the task now?
- ✔ Has the skills or attributes the task needs?
- ✔ Is interested in the task?
- ✔ Wants to learn the task?

(For more information on assigning work to suit people, refer to Chapters 3, 9 and 15.)

As much as you can, apply *cross-skilling* to your followers — that is, train your followers to do each other's jobs. That way, when people take leave (or leave the job), the work still gets done and you can shift duties around to increase job interest.

Explaining the overall project

Tasks seen in isolation seem meaningless and destroy enthusiasm. Prevent this by explaining to your followers why tasks are important and how particular tasks fit into and contribute to the wider work of the team, department or organisation. A task may add to

- ✔ Cost reduction
- ✔ Improved customer service
- ✔ Improved organisation or department image
- ✔ Market leadership
- ✔ Organisation improvement
- ✔ Productivity
- ✔ Profitability
- ✔ Quality

A task's contributions may be direct or indirect, but followers need to feel that their input supports a worthwhile cause. You can explain how an assignment adds value in many ways. Here are a few suggestions:

- ✔ Before this task comes to you, it has been ...
- ✔ Doing this task correctly is important because ...
- ✔ Pay attention when you do this task because ...

✔ This task is important because ...

✔ This task is worth doing well because ...

✔ When you complete this task, the results go to ... for ... so that ...

Productivity suffers when followers feel overwhelmed. Don't pile so much work on that they feel out of control and over-stretched. Your job isn't to push your followers to work harder or faster but to help make their work go more smoothly.

Setting clear success measures

Followers also need to know the precise results you expect. Give your followers a clear target at which to direct their efforts and attention, with clear measures of success or *key performance indicators*. (Refer to Chapters 5 and 10 for more information on measures of success.)

Good goals motivate. In fact, goals are essential to establishing a peak performance culture that gets results. Research shows that goals increase performance in terms of both quality and quantity more than any other technique — including pay rises. Never underestimate the power of a well thought out and clearly expressed goal.

A goal is not a goal unless it has a deadline. Research shows that leaders setting deadlines is better than followers setting them, perhaps because the latter may make the deadlines seem less important. Research also shows that the way to keep followers on track with complex duties and projects is to set interim deadlines, or milestones. If the goal is big, break it down so followers won't become despondent and give up trying.

If a follower has a tendency to procrastinate, talk about beginning a task, rather than talking about finishing the task. Instead of saying, 'And I'd like the report finished by the end of the month,' say 'I'd like you to get started on a rough outline some time today and show me your final outline on Thursday.'

The power of goal setting

Thomas Edison was a master at setting explicit goals. When he set up a scientific village in New Jersey, his goal was to make one minor invention every ten days and a 'big trick' every six months.

Before long, he was applying for 400 patents a year. His crystal-clear and challenging goals propelled him and his team into action.

When explaining the results you expect, think in terms of

- Accuracy
- Cost
- Quality
- Quantity
- Safety
- Service levels
- Time frames

When followers respond tentatively (for example, by saying, 'I think I understand', or 'I'm sure I can figure it out'), they probably mean, 'I don't understand but I'm not game to say so'. Go over the assignment again or ask what other information or clarification you can offer the follower.

Set goals that are ambitious but achievable. When reaching a goal is an impossible or highly unlikely challenge, only the most gullible followers even bother to try. The rest of the followers say, 'Yeah, right', and carry on as normal.

How to set a great goal

You don't 'do' a goal — you achieve a goal. Effective goals identify an outcome. When followers 'go for' results, they know what they're after and why.

Be sure to state your goals in positive terms — say what you want to achieve, not what you want to avoid. For example, measure the number of satisfied customers, not the number of customers who complain; measure the number of loaves of bread baked within specifications, not the number of loaves rejected.

Great goals are also SMARTT:

- **S:** Specific — the goals mean the same to everyone.

- **M:** Measurable — everyone is clear about whether the goals are achieved.

- **A:** Ambitious — yet achievable.

- **R:** Related to the organisation's vision, mission, strategy and your team's purpose (that is, achieving the goals takes you even closer to realising the organisation's overall goals and your team's purpose).

- **T:** Trackable — goals make assessing progress easy.

- **T:** Time-framed — you have a specific completion date.

Don't set too many goals because your followers won't be able to remember them. Choose a few important goals that really track success and that you and your followers can keep 'front of mind'. Go for goals that help you track your progress — knowing how you're *going* is far more valuable than how you *went*. (Refer to Chapter 5 for more information on setting clear and useful measures of success using lead indicators.)

The first two letters of goal spell 'go' — goals are about going for results. But don't just set goals and then forget them in the rush of the work. Track your progress throughout the course of the job.

Appreciating effort and results

Be liberal with your praise. While followers remember the sting of criticism four times longer than the balm of praise, they respond to praise better. What gets rewarded gets repeated. You don't need to use money, bribes or gifts — words are best.

Making clear that you attach importance to what your followers are doing prevents your followers feeling that they're working in a vacuum. Acknowledgement prevents your followers thinking you're not noticing or appreciating their energy and efforts. But don't just say 'Thanks — great job'. Be specific about what you appreciate so they know what to keep doing.

(For more information on types of feedback and how to give useful feedback, see Chapter 15.)

Delegating Special Duties

You can't ever find enough hours in a day to do everything you want done — especially if you try to do all the work yourself. Trying to do every job yourself leaves you feeling pushed and pulled in all directions. Here are some excuses that people use to avoid delegating tasks:

- Doing the job myself is quicker or easier (that may be true initially, but not long term).
- Doing the job myself means getting the job done properly (when you don't trust your ability to train your followers, find out how to train them).

✔ I don't want to lose control of the job (you won't lose control of the job if you monitor key success measures to check the job's progress).

✔ Training followers to do my job makes me less valuable to the organisation (on the contrary, training people makes you far more valuable and available for promotion).

Prioritising is one answer to the leader's perennial lack-of-time problem. (Refer to Chapter 6 to find out how to set priorities.) Another answer is delegation. Prioritising and delegating work together to allow you to perform your duties as a leader.

Ways to assign work

You can assign work to your followers in many different ways. Here are some ways to choose:

✔ **Precise instructions:** In addition to explaining the job to your followers and the results you require, explain exactly what you want done, how to do the job and when and where to do the job in the following circumstances:

- In emergency situations

- To inexperienced, careless or reluctant followers

- When certain procedures must be followed for safety or quality reasons (back them up by posting written step-by-step instructions)

- When time is of the essence

✔ **Outcome assignments:** When followers are skilled and assume responsibility easily, explain the result you're after for a particular task (as well as the bigger picture, if they don't already know it) and then leave your followers to get on with the job.

✔ **Requests:** 'Would you please ...' 'Could you ...' and 'Would you mind ...' are courteous and considerate ways to assign work and enlist cooperation. Requests that start with these words work with most followers.

✔ **Implied requests:** 'We need to ...' is a less direct request that works well when you're looking for an end result but are willing to leave the details of doing the job up to the follower. Implied requests draw out ideas and cooperation, so they are particularly suited to skilled and experienced followers who know the ropes.

✔ **Calls for volunteers:** Stating what is needed and why, without asking anyone in particular, gives followers the choice to volunteer for a particular job. Call for volunteers when you don't want to play favourites by assigning a popular job to a particular person and when a job is unpopular or may be beyond the call of duty.

Passing on instructions

Saying 'He told me ...' or 'They want ...' when passing on instructions from your own leader sounds like you're dodging responsibility and lowers your prestige in the eyes of your followers. Accept responsibility and see that your instructions are carried out by using 'We' or 'I', which shows you have confidence in the request.

Delegating in four short steps

Feeling overworked while your followers feel unchallenged and unfulfilled is silly. Doing work that can be done just as well by a follower is also silly. Completing tasks at the least expensive level adds up to cost effectiveness and effective time management. Delegation also

- ✔ Can be a great motivator because delegation can make followers' duties more interesting and varied (refer to Chapter 10 for more information about how assignments can motivate)
- ✔ Develops and extends valuable skills and experience and builds on followers' talents
- ✔ Frees up your valuable time for other important leadership activities, increasing the value you can add to your leadership
- ✔ Helps your followers identify and harness their unique strengths

Don't get so carried away freeing up your own time through delegation that you overburden your followers. Before passing on tasks, think about the followers' current workloads. And don't keep shovelling additional work onto the most skilled or obliging followers. Evenly distribute work and the opportunity to experience new tasks by taking the steps in the following sections.

Step 1: Deciding what to delegate

To select which tasks to delegate, list your recurring duties — those duties you do regularly, whether daily, weekly or monthly. Then list tasks you do occasionally. Now cross out any task that is

- ✔ A planning or monitoring activity
- ✔ Boring
- ✔ Confidential (for example, to do with pay, performance feedback or appraisals)

- Dangerous
- Disagreeable
- High cost
- High risk
- Mundane
- Politically sensitive
- Related to security or policy
- Urgent

You now have a list of tasks that are suitable for delegation. Transfer each task to a separate piece of paper and list the standards to which the task must be done. Think in terms of time, cost, quality, accuracy, quantity, safety and service levels. (You can find more information on this subject in Chapter 5.)

Now list any constraints associated with each of these tasks, particularly time, quality and cost constraints. Balance these constraints with the resources that are available, such as people, equipment, information and written procedures.

Suitable tasks to hand over

Successful leaders recognise that a lot of their tasks and duties are suitable to delegate to followers. Here are tasks that practically cry out for delegation:

- Any tasks that don't require your personal input

- Detailed work and information gathering (leaders can't afford to get bogged down in details or researching facts and information)

- One-off tasks

- Portions of projects where assistance is helpful

- Recurring duties and tasks

- Tasks that increase the number of people who can perform critical assignments

- Tasks that need a special skill or aptitude that you don't have but some followers do have

- Tasks that some followers are already able to do

- Tasks you do that would make an ideal development opportunity for followers and add variety to their routine work — client visits, making presentations, conference calls, attending meetings on your behalf and so on

Now you're ready to decide which tasks to delegate first. Keep them handy so you can start delegating them and file the rest away in case you decide to delegate them later.

When new work arrives on your desk, think about whether that work is suitable to delegate. Table 12-1 helps you to choose which jobs to delegate.

Table 12-1	Recognising Which Jobs to Delegate
Don't delegate based on	*Do delegate based on*
I enjoy this job so I'll hang onto it	This is a perfect task for building someone's skills
This job is easy — I'll keep it	Delegating this task can free up a lot of my time
I hate this job so I'll dump it	This is a task outside my skill area so I'll give it to a follower who does this type of job well

Step 2: Selecting a delegate

Now decide which follower is the most suited to pick up each task you decided to delegate. Don't delegate

- ✔ Tasks well beyond a follower's training or experience
- ✔ To the same followers all the time
- ✔ The best tasks to your favourite followers (don't have favourites)

Step 3: Delegating

When you meet with the *delegate* — the follower to whom you're delegating a job — provide the following information, in this order:

- ✔ The importance of the task you're delegating and how that task fits into an overall plan (for example, the work of your department or how that task can help achieve an important organisational goal)
- ✔ Your reason for selecting this follower (for example, to develop the follower's skills, to provide an assignment the follower may find interesting or because the follower has a flair for this type of task)
- ✔ A clear description of the task, the end result or the end product and the standards you expect, including the expected start and completion times and any other constraints (refer to Chapter 5 for more about setting standards)

> ✔ The resources available to help complete the task; for example, people who can assist, funds, equipment, information and access to areas or people the delegate doesn't normally encounter (and let those people know your delegate may be in contact)
>
> ✔ The options open to the delegate when help is needed

Set up some meetings to discuss progress and log the agreed follow-up dates, electronically or in your diary. Ask the delegate to do the same. Before you part, check that you have explained clearly what you need done.

Unless delegates don't know how to do the task and you're still training them, emphasise results rather than details by delegating the *what* about the job, not the *how*. When you need to train delegates to do a task, take them through the task slowly, step by step, and give them a checklist to refer to until they're comfortable with the job.

Step 4: Keeping tabs

The sink-or-swim approach is no way to delegate — you're still accountable for a delegated task's correct completion and you need to see that results are up to scratch. Check in with delegates to ask whether they need any help from you and to find out whether the tasks are being completed correctly. This doesn't mean doing tasks for delegates or breathing down their necks. Rather it means checking back often enough so that if anything is going wrong, you're around to spot the problem and help resolve it. Use your diary to follow-up dates as your monitoring plan.

If you haven't delegated much work before and have now delegated several tasks, you may want to keep a delegation log in a special file in your electronic task manager or in a special section of your To Do list. This file takes a load off your mind because you can rest easy knowing you don't have to remember every detail or what you've delegated to which follower.

Here are five levels of expertise to help you monitor work you delegate, based on the delegate's experience and expertise:

> ✔ **Level 1: Go for it!** Use this level with delegates who know how to do the job and are keen to get on with it. Put a few warning signals in place to alert you to any potential problems.
>
> ✔ **Level 2: Keep me informed.** With delegates who are slightly less skilled and experienced, but keen, ask them to carry on but to update you at certain key points or with certain key information so that you can satisfy yourself that the delegated task is progressing well.

✔ **Level 3: Check back first.** Ask delegates who aren't fully up to speed to check with you before proceeding at certain key junctures, so you can satisfy yourself that they're on the right track.

✔ **Level 4: Let's talk it through.** This level of monitoring is for delegates who know how to do the job but haven't done it often. Support them as they gain competence and confidence by asking them to talk their approach through with you before acting, which gives you a chance to assess their progress and coach them if they need coaching.

✔ **Level 5: Let me walk you through it.** Carefully train delegates who are new to a task and give them time to build their skills, moving up the levels of monitoring as they gain experience and confidence.

Respecting your delegates

Give plenty of positive, specific and helpful feedback to delegates. When they do a good job, say so. If they think you haven't noticed, they think you don't care and that the job isn't important after all. If that's the case, why would they bother to keep doing it well?

Don't overmonitor your followers — overmonitoring takes up nearly as much of your time as doing the task yourself. If a delegate is new to the task, plan the delegate's training carefully and be ready to offer support or delegate the task to someone better able to do it.

When your leader delegates to you

When your leader delegates a job to you, ask enough questions to make sure you understand the assignment fully. You need to know

✔ How extensive your authority is to make decisions and which decisions to refer to your leader for approval

✔ How your leader wants you to report progress (for example, how much or how little detail, in writing or verbally and how regularly)

✔ The resources available to you

✔ What priority the task has — not just its importance to the organisation but also to your leader

✔ What the ideal outcome of the task is in terms of quality, time frame, accuracy and other measures of success

Summarise your understanding in a memo, which gives you a record of what you are trying to achieve in case the project goes pear shaped.

Be honest when you feel you need some training or coaching and ask whether your leader is willing to coach you or can nominate someone else to help you.

Keeping Your Standards High

Don't confuse *differently* with *poorly*. Delegates probably won't do a task exactly as you do, but that's generally okay. People often change a bit here and add a bit there. Wanting to put your own stamp on a task is natural — people need to be creatively involved in their work. So unless there is a strong reason to carry out a task in a particular way, successful leaders enable followers to use their own initiative and methods.

But everyone gets a job wrong sometimes and when the work isn't being carried out to the standard you requested, you need to step in, find out why and help the follower do the job correctly. Unless you gave the job to the wrong person, taking a task back after you delegate it can seriously dent the delegate's self-confidence and deprive that person of an opportunity to gain new skills.

Selecting the best course of action

Followers underperform and make mistakes for different reasons. Before you can help followers improve their performances, you need to know the causes of poor performances. The main reasons for underperformance are that the follower is

- ✔ Not willing and not skilled and you may have assigned the task to the wrong person or you may have a more serious problem (if the latter is the case, Chapters 18 and 19 can help you with this problem)

- ✔ Skilled but not willing, so you need to work on building confidence and supporting the follower as the follower gains experience on that particular task; or you may need to work on the follower's motivation if lack of willingness is a general problem (Chapters 18 and 19 can help you when a follower lacks motivation for more than just this one task)

- ✔ Willing and skilled, so the problem lies in the work environment or in the supply of resources (Chapter 10 offers solutions when this is the problem)

- ✔ Willing but not sufficiently skilled at the task, so requires more training

When you delegate, you also delegate the right to make mistakes and to learn — getting the job done isn't your only important goal. Developing followers' skills and extending their experience is also important, even when a task isn't done quickly, efficiently or perfectly at first.

Improving performance

You may be lucky and find that every follower performs every duty perfectly, first time and every time. Bunyips roam the outback, too. The truth is, people make mistakes — both leaders and followers. You may be in a hurry and not explain what you want clearly enough, to later hear the words, 'I didn't realise that was what you wanted'. Those words show you need to always find the time to explain properly. Or you may mistake willingness for skill and fail to provide enough training or time to build experience and confidence while you play backup.

If and when work is not up to your standard, respond calmly and investigate to see what both you and your follower can do to improve the results. Have a chat in private, review the results and find out what lies at the heart of the problem — skills, confidence or a problem in the work situation, such as cumbersome systems, substandard equipment or lack of time — and fix it.

Ask for your follower's suggestions on getting the task back on track and how to prevent it slipping off track next time. If your follower is at a loss for ideas, switch to coaching. Don't dwell on past mistakes. Concentrate on future performance. Use phrases such as, 'Next time . . .' and 'From now on . . .' That way, your comments are positive and helpful — provided your tone of voice is calm and your demeanour shows you want to help, not hurt.

Never criticise or remark on people's personalities or personal qualities. Provide constructive information and helpful improvement suggestions by talking about what you do want (not what you don't want) and explaining what can be done or what should be done (not what your follower is doing wrong). If your follower needs more support, provide more support. Table 12-2 shows some ways to turn criticisms into helpful comments.

Table 12-2	Making Negatives Positive
Leaders don't say	*Leaders do say*
No, that's wrong; do it this way	That's not quite right; let me show you
You forgot to . . .	Remember to . . .
Why can't you . . .	How about . . .
I've told you before to . . .	From now on, remember to . . .

Rather than waiting for followers to complete a task perfectly, you can encourage your followers while they're making progress. If you don't show you're noticing their work, followers may well stop trying. (Refer to Chapter 19 for more on appreciating your followers' work.)

Helping Followers Do Their Own Work

Followers often go to their leaders with problems and difficult tasks. Don't fall for what's called *upward delegation* and say something like: 'Leave it with me and I'll sort it out' or 'Let me think about it and get back to you' or 'Okay, I'll see what I can do'. Taking your followers' problems and work onto your own shoulders is a bad habit to get into because you end up doing your followers' work for them.

Unless your followers are incompetent or untrustworthy, don't solve their problems or do their jobs for them. When they're incompetent, organise training sessions for them. When they're untrainable or untrustworthy, then the time has come to share your doubts with them candidly and tactfully (see Chapters 18 and 19 for more on how to deal with these types of followers).

Followers often know what to do but need a bit of reassurance. Spend a few minutes chatting through what they can do and when you're satisfied they're thinking along the right lines, let them know that you're confident in their abilities.

Phrases to lead by

Being able to nudge followers' performance in the right direction is easier when you're being helpful. Here are some phrases that work:

- From now on . . .

- Here's another thought . . .

- I'll know you're doing a good job when . . .

- Next time . . .

- That disappointed me because . . .

- That was good and you could also . . .

- That was great and another thing you could do is . . .

- Try it this way . . .

- Would you please . . .

If followers don't know what to do, help them think through their options. Thinking through the matter with you builds their confidence and skills because you're helping them to think for themselves. Turn their questions around and ask them to suggest solutions. For example:

- ✔ Do you need any more information?
- ✔ How about developing a plan of action and then chatting through your plan with me?
- ✔ I don't have time to write the report for you but I'd be happy to check your report for accuracy.
- ✔ That's an interesting problem. What do you suggest?
- ✔ What exactly is the problem? Can you explain it to me in one thorough, objective statement?
- ✔ What have you thought about doing?
- ✔ What have you tried so far?
- ✔ When did you first notice this problem? Does it seem to be getting worse?

Falling into the trap of doing your followers' work and solving their problems for them leaves you little time left to attend to your own responsibilities. Help your followers think for themselves by asking them to include a recommended-actions section in their progress reports.

Chapter 13

Making Meetings Work

Some people love meetings because they can sit back and relax, spruik their achievements or get away from the real world where they actually need to do some real work. Meetings can waste enormous amounts of time and that applies particularly to meetings that aren't well planned, well led and well followed up. Meetings like these generally end up with nothing more to show for them than a roomful of warm, stale air and dented morale. But meetings need not be that way.

You can use meetings to reinforce your position as your group's leader and to strengthen the group — sometimes the only time individual followers actually come together as a group is for a meeting. Meetings can help followers understand their shared aims, create commitments and even generate enthusiasm. Meetings also help groups revise, update and add to their shared knowledge and understandings. And meetings are a great way to keep followers informed, gather followers' ideas, air problems and plan ways to solve problems.

This chapter looks at how to plan and lead meetings. You find out when to call a meeting (and when not to), what types of meetings to call and how to plan and lead meetings. I explain how to lead discussions that stay on track, how to keep good meeting notes, how to deal with awkward attendees and how to make sure the next meeting you lead is even better. I also run through how to be a valued and valuable meeting participant.

To Meet or Not to Meet, That Is the Question

Meetings are expensive. If you don't believe me, multiply how long the last meeting you led or attended lasted by the average hourly pay of the people attending the meeting and you see what I mean. For example, calling together six followers who earn $100 an hour to discuss a proposal for an hour costs $600 plus your own hourly earnings.

Before calling a meeting, check that the meeting is really necessary. A meeting is necessary when you

- ✔ Can say no better or less expensive way exists to achieve the result (for example, a telephone call, memo or email exchange).
- ✔ Need other people's help to solve problems, reach a consensus or develop a plan.
- ✔ Want to gather or exchange information or opinions.
- ✔ Want to generate discussion and ideas.
- ✔ Want to pass on, explain or 'sell' a decision, plan or information personally — for example, because the subject is complex or controversial or has major implications for the attendees. You may believe that giving the information personally has symbolic value or you may believe the information warrants discussion or other types of information exchange.
- ✔ Want to present information quickly and you don't want to use email, SMS or memos.

If you want to call your followers together but everyone is busy and you shudder at the expense, buy lunch — gourmet food-filled rolls or yummy pizzas — and hold the meeting in the lunch hour. Your followers are unlikely to mind giving up their lunch hour when they're getting good nosh and a worthwhile get-together in return. (Sound out a few followers first to check the idea is popular and give a few days warning so your followers don't make other plans.)

Skip meetings when

- ✔ Involving other people in a decision complicates the situation.
- ✔ Nothing specific needs to be discussed.
- ✔ The meeting is merely a substitute for 'real work' or an excuse for a get together.
- ✔ You already made the decision.
- ✔ You don't need anyone else's input.

Planning a Magnificent Meeting

Nothing destroys credibility like a badly planned meeting. Your first decision is what you want the meeting to achieve. The goal may be to reach consensus on a course of action, to identify and prioritise problems or to update followers on the performance of the organisation or department.

Once you know your goal, you know what type of meeting to call, how long the meeting should last and even how to seat people. Leaders plan and lead these major types of meetings:

- **General catch-up meetings:** In addition to regular one-on-one meetings with each follower, most leaders hold short team meetings fortnightly or monthly to keep followers up to date on team and organisation events. I like to begin these meetings by asking each follower to provide a two-minute report on what they achieved since the last meeting and what goals they set themselves for the next period. This report helps keep open the channels of communication and strengthens working relationships and team performance. Limit the meeting to 30 minutes (or 40 max.) and email or post an agenda on the noticeboard when you're covering several topics.

- **Information-exchange and ideas-gathering meetings:** Gathering people together to work creatively and combine and build on each other's knowledge, experience and ideas is a great way to harvest good ideas and develop new concepts and procedures. Techniques such as brainstorming (refer to Chapter 11 for some tips on brainstorming) help participants at a meeting develop ideas, options and solutions.

- **Information-giving meetings:** When you need to provide a lot of information quickly and when the information is straightforward, posting a notice or sending an email is fine. But when the information is complex or controversial, and when the information directly affects your followers, then you are better to deliver the information in person. Similarly, when the information can benefit from some discussion or a question-and-answer session, call your people together in a meeting.

  You can say exactly what you mean and present the information clearly by following these guidelines:

  - Avoid long words and terms that may be unfamiliar to attendees.

  - Don't ramble or repeat yourself.

  - Emphasise key points by slowing down, saying them more softly or loudly, repeating them or making an analogy. (Use all of those techniques, not just one, to avoid being boringly predictable.)

- Keep your sentences short enough so that you can say them in one breath.

- Pause for three to five seconds after you make a key point to allow the meaning to sink in.

You could use PowerPoint to reinforce your message but be very careful how you use this technology. (To find out more on how to make presentations and use PowerPoint effectively, refer to Chapter 7.)

✔ **Introducing change meetings:** Change is occurring faster than ever, so you need to be comfortable leading meetings that introduce change to help followers understand the reasons for change and to gain the support of your followers. Explain the change fully and clearly, explain why change is needed and answer, acknowledge and respect questions and concerns. (See Chapter 14 for more information on introducing and leading change.)

✔ **Planning meetings:** When you want to develop a plan to accomplish a desired outcome or goal, invite the people who are to implement the plan to a meeting to help develop the plan. Guide these team members to set priorities, decide who does what, when and how, and establish monitoring and follow-up procedures. (Refer to Chapter 5 for more information on how to develop a workable plan.)

✔ **Problem-solving and decision-making meetings:** Enlist your followers and sometimes experts from outside your team to solve problems and make decisions, particularly when your followers are directly affected by a solution or decision or are involved in implementing a decision. Guiding team members at a meeting to explore, develop and evaluate possible solutions or options and selecting the best result may take one meeting or several, depending on the complexity of the problem or decision. Problem-solving and decision-making meetings are often followed by a planning meeting. (Refer to Chapter 11 for more information on how to solve problems and make decisions.)

✔ **Quality- and service-improvement meetings:** Quality- and service-improvement meetings combine idea gathering, problem solving, decision making and planning meetings to identify and resolve problems and find ways to improve productivity, quality and service. Drawing on your followers' knowledge, skills and experience is a smart move because your followers are the people who best know the problems and can see the solutions most easily. Like problem-solving and decision-making meetings, you may need several meetings to complete a quality- and service- improvement cycle.

✔ **Team briefings:** Team briefings are a special type of meeting that spreads information like a cascade through an organisation to keep everyone up to date on what's happening and help them feel involved and valued. Team briefings also prevent guesswork and rumour-mongering and strangle grapevine gossip.

To kick off the team briefing meetings, the most senior leader — for example, the chief executive officer — holds the first meeting and briefs the senior team, and then those leaders brief their teams. The information cascades through the organisation as the next level of attendees brief their followers and so on.

Team briefings cover topics such as the following (and generally in this order):

- **Progress:** How the organisation has performed against its key success measures

- **People:** New appointments, visitors, news about people in the organisation

- **Policy:** Any new or altered policies or procedures or reinforcing existing policies and procedures

- **Points for action:** Priorities over the coming month for the team and the organisation

Time for general information is usually left until the end, along with time for questions and suggestions so that team member involvement and contributions can be fed back up to senior leaders.

Seating significance

When you want people to participate — for example, in problem solving, information exchange, ideas gathering and quality-improvement or service-improvement meetings — seat people in a circle. Rectangles also encourage participation but put more attention on the leader, which helps you facilitate, direct and moderate discussion. Rectangular seating works well for decision-making and planning meetings. (Have plenty of paper on hand or an electronic whiteboard with a copying function to capture ideas and important information from these meetings.)

To keep the attention on you and to limit discussion, for example, in team briefings and information-giving meetings, opt for theatre-style seating in rows or a semicircle. When you want to keep the meeting short, sharp and shiny, ask followers to gather around the water cooler or in your office.

When you want merely to announce a change, give followers time to mull over the change and then regroup to discuss the implications of the change. In this situation, seat people as for an information-giving meeting. Explain why you're using this seating and explain that you set time aside later to ask questions and clear up any concerns. Otherwise, seat people in a rectangle so they can ask questions and discuss the change.

Benefiting from an action-packed agenda

Agendas list the discussion topics in the order they are dealt with. Agendas also show the date, start and finish times and place of the meeting. I recommend showing either a start and finish time for each topic or an indication of how much time is allowed for each item.

Write an action agenda by beginning each point with a verb: Decide, Plan, Review and so on. This structure enables people to concentrate on the outcome, guides the discussion by showing what contributions are (and are not) relevant and provides a sense of direction. (Avoid beginning an agenda item with the verb 'Discuss', because this word can lead to a lot of talk that goes nowhere. Discussions need a purpose. Instead of 'Discuss' choose a verb that suits the purpose.)

Put the most important items high up on the agenda to encourage participants to arrive on time to deal with these subjects while the participants are still fresh. Here are some other ways to structure the sequence of topics on an agenda:

- From the most to the least urgent
- Logically, so that topics can build on each other
- So the most interesting items come up about 20 minutes after the meeting begins, when energy often flags

Try to finish a meeting with a feel-good topic or a topic that achieves a positive result.

Try not to have so many items on your agenda that the meeting runs longer than one hour (30 to 45 minutes is even better). If you can't manage that time, hold short stand-up-and-stretch breaks every 40 minutes or so or hold two separate meetings.

In informal team meetings, post the agenda on the noticeboard or email the agenda to all participants, asking that they respond with any requests for other items to add to the agenda. When you use a noticeboard, leave space at the bottom for participants to write suggestions for other topics. When the meeting is more formal, send the agenda out at least a week in advance, along with any background information or supporting documents.

Thinking through the logistics

When you're calling the meeting just to give information or brief your team, numbers don't matter that much. When you want to encourage a free-flowing discussion, try to keep numbers below 12 to help keep everyone's attention on the topic; having smaller numbers of participants also encourages people to speak more freely. When you have more than 12 followers, you can hold more than one meeting or invite representatives from different areas to keep the numbers down.

If your meeting includes people other than your followers, decide who should attend by using the *Two-Thirds Rule* — each participant can contribute to two out of every three agenda items. When this doesn't apply to one or two of the people you want to invite — and these people can usefully contribute to one or two agenda items or need to be present for another reason — consider inviting these people into the meeting for only the items relevant to them.

Hold the meeting during normal hours, at a time convenient to everyone. If some of your followers are remote (for example, home or part-time workers), make special arrangements for them to attend. (See Chapter 16 for more information on leading meetings for mixed teams and virtual teams.)

Think about the best place to hold your meeting — a neutral conference room in your building that you can book, a conference room in a hotel or conference centre that you can hire or, less formally, your office or even gathered around the café bar or a lunch table. The appropriate setting depends on the type of meeting and the atmosphere you want to create. You may want to welcome participants with coffee on arrival and, when the meeting takes longer than an hour, you may want to have coffee and fruit and biscuits brought in at half time.

Wherever you decide to hold the meeting, minimise interruptions and ensure attendees' comfort. Think about temperature and ventilation and, when the meeting must be longer than an hour, think about people's backsides. 'Ouch! I can't move' is not the standard of attention you're seeking.

Don't hold so many meetings that followers get sick and tired of meetings. Aim for just often enough so they feel part of a group, well informed and able to contribute.

Leading Productive Meetings

When you lead a meeting effectively by building a positive atmosphere and keeping attendees' attention directed at results, participants feel relaxed and free to communicate openly, making achieving your meeting's goals easier. Get ready to draw on your strong people and communication skills to create the right atmosphere.

Here are some tips to help meeting members work well together to achieve your meeting's aims:

- ✔ Have the purpose of the meeting and each agenda topic clear to everyone.
- ✔ Keep to the agenda and keep discussions directed at the topic under discussion.
- ✔ Pose questions to clarify when someone's point isn't clear.
- ✔ Help meeting members build on each other's ideas, knowledge and experience.
- ✔ Gather facts, opinions and ideas from all meeting members.
- ✔ Help meeting members explore issues fully before reaching a decision.
- ✔ Summarise progress often.
- ✔ Record all decisions, agreements and actions to be taken.

Here are some tips to building an atmosphere that helps people work well together at a meeting:

- ✔ Begin meetings by welcoming people, thanking them for attending and saying a few words about what you hope the meeting can achieve.
- ✔ Give meeting members some time to get to know each other when they don't know each other well, or give them time to catch up when they don't see each other regularly. Ask members to arrive 15 or 20 minutes before the official start of the meeting and welcome them with coffee and fresh fruit.
- ✔ Have clear ground rules for how to behave and stick to the rules.
- ✔ Lighten up the atmosphere with some humour.
- ✔ Use disagreements and differences of opinions as opportunities to explore ideas in more depth.
- ✔ Value people's contributions.
- ✔ Wind up the meeting positively by summarising what you achieved together and thanking people for their time.

Opening the meeting with panache

Plan your opening comments to set the scene and create the tone you want your meeting to have. Think about how to introduce each topic on the agenda. Introducing topics needn't take long, but unless you're a highly experienced meeting leader, or born with a silver tongue, you can't expect to turn up and have the right words magically spout from your mouth.

Think about any difficult meeting participants who may be there and how to handle them. Also, think about any questions you may be asked, especially difficult questions, so you can think your answers through and won't be caught unawares or at a loss for words.

Set the scene and establish a friendly atmosphere by arriving at the venue first so you can greet people when they arrive. (Don't even *think* about breezing in after people are seated, twiddling their thumbs and awaiting their illustrious leader.)

Don't penalise those who are on time and reward the latecomers by waiting to begin until everyone has arrived. Start on time, even when all the participants aren't there. This establishes the rules for 'next time' and teaches people to turn up or miss out.

Setting ground rules and sticking to the agenda

When you're leading a meeting with a group of participants for the first time, explain your ground rules and check everyone agrees to them. When the meeting is with your own team and you're leading the first of what are to be regular meetings, agree the ground rules together and post them at every meeting. (Agreeing the ground rules may be a meeting in itself.) Here are some common ground rules for participants to follow:

- ✔ Acknowledge contributions.
- ✔ Arrive on time.
- ✔ Be factual (not personal).
- ✔ Check you understand correctly when you're not sure.
- ✔ Have fun.
- ✔ Listen.
- ✔ No interrupting — only one person at a time to speak.

✔ Recognise that team time belongs to the team.

✔ Speak up.

✔ Stick to the topic under discussion.

✔ Treat each other with respect.

✔ Value differences in personal style.

As you introduce each agenda item, briefly review the item so that everyone understands the topic and the purpose of discussing it. This also encourages people not to drift from the topic. When people do drift on to other subjects, bring the discussion back on track — no rambling shop talk, red herrings or soap boxes allowed.

In decision-making meetings, tell participants how the final decision is to be made to prevent adverse reactions. For example, when meeting members believe they're to make the decision through consensus, they get a nasty surprise when they find out at the end of the meeting that you only want to sound out their opinions.

People in a meeting watch the leader and follow the leader so mind your manners and your body language and respect the ground rules as you expect the others to respect them.

Encouraging a good discussion

You're after a wide-ranging but goal-oriented discussion with each meeting member contributing. Asking open-ended questions is the easiest way to achieve this outcome. You may need to keep talkative participants' inputs succinct and on the topic without cutting off the speaker. You may also need to invite contributions from quiet participants. You may even need to go around the table asking each person for their thoughts.

The role of the meeting leader is not to dominate a meeting but to guide the meeting along. Unless you need to provide information, stick to introducing agenda items, briefly summarising at intervals, asking questions to clarify and giving the floor to participants who have information or ideas to contribute. Limit the rest of your input to one comment or question at a time. Generally, putting your ideas forward last is a good move. That way, participants don't feel compelled to adopt your ideas.

Learn to be a great listener. Listening alerts you to digressions, repetition of ground already covered and irrelevancies and allows you to summarise properly and at the right time. If a discussion wanders, steer it in the right direction with a question such as, 'Who has more information to add on the topic?' or review your objectives for the agenda item.

Here are three other ways to get a discussion back on track:

- ✔ Redefine the subject to look at it from a different angle.
- ✔ Summarise progress.
- ✔ Take a short break.

Treat everyone equally. Don't say 'Good idea' or 'Good point' to some and not others. Ideas and contributions — not the individuals who offer the ideas — are what count.

Most people have short attention spans (less than ten minutes, in fact) so summarise frequently to help participants stay on track and keep the meeting moving along. If you can see people's minds are wandering, suggest a five-minute break and let people get up and move around.

If an issue is contentious, give all sides equal 'air time'. Use differences of opinion as opportunities to explore issues in more depth. Don't let people masquerade their opinions as facts and don't argue over facts — delay the discussion until the next meeting when you can gather the facts or ask someone to go and check the facts when they can get that information quickly. When you form a working party or subcommittee to find those facts or work on a project, appoint one person to convene the committee and report back on its behalf by a certain date.

Don't vote — voting only gives you 'winners' and 'losers' and creates factions. Keep discussing items until you reach consensus or, when you need to prioritise or choose between a large number of items, give everyone three votes. This system shows the group's choice without creating winners and losers.

Stay sensitive to sensibilities

Research has shown that gender and culture can influence meeting behaviour. For example, male meeting participants tend to dominate discussions and interrupt more often and hold the floor for longer while women tend to wait their turn and contribute only when they have a helpful comment to add. People from polite Asian cultures, whether male or female, avoid interrupting and speaking unless they're directly called upon to speak.

When consensus is reached quickly, be alert for the possibility of groupthink (refer to Chapter 11 for more information on groupthink). Don't assume silence means agreement. Go around the table and ask people for their thoughts when some participants haven't clearly concurred.

When energy wanes and enthusiasm wilts, promise a quick finish in return for action: 'We can wrap up in ten minutes if we can reach consensus on this', or 'All that's needed is just a few more ideas to take forward and then we can call it quits for today.'

Wrap up a discussion when

- ✔ Events are changing rapidly and are likely to alter the basis of the discussion.
- ✔ Not enough time exists to complete the discussion properly (in which case, reschedule the item for the following meeting).
- ✔ Meeting members need more time to think or discuss a subject with people who are not present.
- ✔ The meeting has reached consensus.
- ✔ Two or three people can settle the matter themselves, without taking up everyone else's time.
- ✔ You need more facts before you can make further progress.

Don't leave a discussion unfinished. Reach a conclusion, even if only to suspend the discussion until the next meeting. Then summarise the main points discussed and agreed and review the next steps or agreed actions.

When meeting members develop a plan, reach a decision or agree a solution to a problem, ask: 'How can we know if this is going wrong?' This alerts meeting members to areas they may have overlooked.

Keeping notes

When the meeting is very informal, make a few notes of what was discussed and agreed and any action items and distribute them to your team or post them on a noticeboard. Alternatively, ask someone to keep notes of what is said (or to keep minutes when the meeting is more formal) and to type them and post the minutes on the noticeboard or email or post them to participants.

Unless you have appointed a permanent meeting secretary to take and distribute meeting notes or minutes, I suggest you rotate this responsibility among meeting members. Think about asking members to write the minutes on a flip chart or electronic whiteboard as the meeting progresses so that everyone can see them; that way, people needn't worry that a point they made has been missed and feel compelled to repeat it.

Here's how to keep good notes that don't get in the way of listening:

- ✔ Listen for key points.
- ✔ Put any personal comments in brackets so you don't confuse them with the speaker's comments.
- ✔ Put a question mark if you miss something; someone can fill you in later.
- ✔ Skip examples unless you need them to clarify or illustrate a point.
- ✔ Use abbreviations.
- ✔ Write down formulas, dates and numbers.
- ✔ Write in short phrases.

You don't need a lot of details — just the facts, key points, agreed actions and important decisions. My favourite headings for writing up notes are (in this order)

- ✔ Item discussed
- ✔ Information shared
- ✔ Decisions made
- ✔ Actions to be taken (include the agreed date)
- ✔ Pending issues

A list of headings like this one makes scanning the minutes or finding what they're most interested in easier for participants.

Add the action items for which you accepted responsibility, with the target date, to your To Do list as soon as possible after the meeting (or during it, when that's feasible). Tick off those action items on your copy of the minutes as soon as you complete them.

Closing the meeting

Before sending meeting members off on their merry way, review who is responsible for doing what by when, and double check that all decisions and actions to be taken have been noted by the minute taker. When a lot of action items exist, distribute a list of who is to do what by when soon after the meeting ends.

Don't ask, 'Do any other matters need to be covered?' This may invite the meeting to drag on. Instead, ask 'Do any items need to be put on the agenda for our next meeting?'

Confirm or agree the date, time and location of the next meeting. Then — very important — end on a positive note by

- ✔ Commenting briefly on how well the meeting went
- ✔ Summarising what you accomplished together
- ✔ Thanking those who attend for their time and participation

Keep a paper or electronic file of agendas, minutes and background documents sent with the agenda for every meeting you lead (or attend) regularly, even your informal team meetings.

Dealing with disruptive and difficult participants

Some meeting participants are prone to behaviours that get in the way of achieving the meeting's aims and can even annoy other participants (not to mention the leader). When you don't deal with their behaviours, the meeting can struggle and, eventually, completely derail.

Here are some common troublesome meeting behaviours and suggestions for stopping them quickly:

- ✔ **Grandstanding:** Attention seekers generally just want their cleverness and heroism to be acknowledged, so briefly summarise and thank them for their comments.

✔ **Holding side conversations:** When a meaningful 'look' doesn't stop the big mates from chatting, ask the chatterers to share their comments with the rest of the meeting. If they don't take the hint and continue to chat, instruct side talkers to take their conversation outside the meeting room if their discussion is urgent or to postpone their conversation until after the meeting. Be sure to keep your tone of voice neutral and non judgemental — embarrassing them can result in other meeting members sympathising with them and costing you their goodwill.

✔ **Interrupting:** Give people who interrupt a 'look' that says, 'Wait until the speaker has finished — then I'll call on you'. If necessary, hold up your hand. When necessary, put your look in words and say, 'Hang on — Frank hasn't finished', or 'Philippa, you were starting to explain something; would you like to finish please?'

✔ **Not contributing:** Some participants are naturally quiet and need to be invited to speak; watch their body language for hints that they have a contribution to make and ask them for their thoughts. Don't let anyone interrupt them when they do speak and thank them for their comments when they finish. Warn them that you plan to direct a specific question to them: 'Jim, I'd like to ask you your thoughts on this in a minute, after we've heard from Sue'. (If Sue's a bit of a yabberer, this also warns her to limit her comments.) After the meeting, you may even want to reinforce in private how helpful the quiet participant's contributions were to encourage them to speak at the next meeting.

✔ **Slating:** Thank critics for their comments and ask what they *do* like about an idea, how they think the idea may be improved or how their objections could be overcome; try rephrasing their comments to make the comments more acceptable. When knockers suffer from a chronic condition and can't stop themselves commenting, you may need to have a quiet word with them outside of the meeting and explain you expect them to balance their negative comments with positive ones.

✔ **Unprepared:** When you sense a participant may arrive unprepared, make contact before the meeting with a reminder to prepare and complete their action items; explain that your reminder is a one-off and, from now on, all meeting participants are responsible for honouring their commitments without being reminded. If the participant turns up at future meetings unprepared, discuss whether they may prefer to withdraw from future meetings. (See Chapters 18 and 19 to find out how to lead such a discussion.)

✔ **Waffling:** When wafflers draw breath, thank them for their input, summarise the points they make to show the point has been made and ask for input from others. Then move on to the next person who has indicated they have something to say. Try to seat long-winded wafflers at your extreme left (when you're right-handed, or your extreme right when you're left-handed) to make catching your eye and capturing the floor difficult for them.

✔ **Wandering:** Some people have a knack for swerving the discussion off course. Channel the meeting back on course with one of the following approaches:

- Drawing — tactfully — the wanderer's attention to the agenda

- Suggesting that you postpone the wanderer's points until the next meeting, when you can put the topic on the agenda and deal with it properly

- Summarising where the discussion is

- Tying the wanderer's comments to the topic at hand (when you can)

When participants are really disruptive, have a quiet word in private before your next meeting, explaining the behaviour you expect and that you expect their cooperation in making the meeting work.

Holding a post-meeting-mortem

After the meeting, think through how the meeting went — what helped the meeting to achieve its aims and what held it back. That way, you can lead the next meeting even more effectively.

While you think through the meeting, check whether any of these problem situations emerged and, if so, make a note to avoid them next time:

✔ Cliques and factions forming and asserting their own goals, or *hidden agendas*

✔ Differences of opinion escalating into arguments and confrontations

✔ One or two people dominating the meeting

✔ Participants arguing without really listening to each other

✔ Power struggles developing

✔ Railroading the meeting with your own ideas and opinions

✔ Some people not getting a chance to air their views

If you recognise any of the following good deeds, congratulate yourself and keep doing them:

✔ Enabling some laughter and light moments

✔ Ensuring everyone is heard and their contributions respected

✔ Establishing a friendly and receptive atmosphere

✔ Listening carefully, asking good questions and summarising well

When you have an opportunity to attend other meetings as a participant, observe the leader and see what you can learn in terms of dos and don'ts for the meetings you lead.

To find out how to lead virtual meetings, such as teleconferences, videoconferences and multimedia conferences, see Chapter 16; and to find out more about leading cross-cultural meetings, see Chapter 17.

Being an Effective Meeting Participant

Most leaders also attend meetings as participants and the way they present and conduct themselves helps the meeting succeed and builds and reinforces their images and reputations.

The first rule is to prepare for a meeting. This may be by reading relevant documents and working through the agenda, thinking about the contents and considering the contributions you can make on the various items. As well, you can collect information you may need to offer the meeting (for example, to back the points you intend to make). Or you may need to make sure you complete assigned tasks from the previous meeting. Whatever the preparation you need, never tarnish your image by turning up unprepared.

Don't damage your reputation by disrespecting other participants and the meeting leader and wasting everyone's valuable — and expensive — time by arriving late or distracting other participants with side conversations, irrelevant comments and so on.

Speak up when you can contribute but don't take up more than your fair share of the speaking time or waste time with personal stories, jokes or anecdotes unless they make a point. Organise your thoughts before you speak by jotting down a few key words to remind you of the main points you want to make. Look around the table as you speak, making a few seconds eye contact with each person. If you're asked to comment but have no useful information or thoughts to add, say so rather than spout hot air.

If people have a habit of talking over you, you can pre-empt this with comments such as 'I have two points I'd like to make about this'. You can keep the floor by saying 'I haven't quite finished, Sam', and continue with what you're saying.

If you want to disagree with or build on an idea someone else has offered, briefly summarise the earlier comments to show you heard and understood the idea. Don't play devil's advocate for the sake of creating opposition and try not to disagree unless you have an alternative idea to offer. Phrase your concerns, reservations or confusion tactfully and in a way that shows you're open to hearing the answer.

Don't dump data on a meeting. When you have statistics that can help make a point, draw up a graph or two and distribute copies to everyone or offer to provide statistics after you verbally summarise what the numbers indicate. When people ask for more detailed information, you can provide that information then.

Beware open-ended meetings with no specified finishing time on the agenda. Ask how long the meeting leader intends the meeting to take, explaining you want to set enough time aside for the meeting and plan your day accordingly.

Part IV
Building and Leading a Winning Team

Glenn Lumsden

'The workers are miserable, conditions are disgraceful and morale is at an all-time low. Well done, team.'

In this part . . .

Teams, if properly led, can produce great results. This part is about one of your most important duties as a leader — achieving goals through others. I begin by explaining the tried-and-tested ways that leaders introduce and lead the inevitable and continuous changes, large and small, that are part of life in modern organisations. Then you find out about the power of many and how to grow a gaggle of individual followers into a team that produces impressive results.

In this part, you also see why involving people is better than the old-fashioned 'command and control' style of leadership (even though involving followers takes quite a few more skills and a bit more work and self-mastery than commanding and controlling them). As well, I run through how to lead the new styles of teams — virtual teams, temporary teams, merged teams and teams of mixed followers, some working part time, others full time, speckled with temporary followers, casual followers and contractors. You find out how to lead teams filled with youngsters, oldsters and in-between-sters and how to lead followers from different backgrounds and different cultures.

Chapter 14

Leading in an Age of Never-Ending Change

*L*ife is awash in change. Massive technological and societal change, emerging biotechnology and nanotechnology and increasing globalisation mean that change is occurring at a very fast rate in all areas of our lives.

Change is a normal part of life. Civilisations and organisations grow, prosper, plateau and fade because of change — and sometimes make great leaps forward. The same is true of living organisms — when people and animals aren't developing and changing, they're dead or dying. Organisations and the people who lead them need to change too or they may be left behind by their competitors.

So that change doesn't faze you or your followers, this chapter examines how to build a bridge of change and take your followers across that bridge in phases. When change is major, the bridge is precarious, so give each of these phases generous time, care and attention. A bridge of minor change is less wobbly, but you still need to cross that bridge in the series of phases I describe in this chapter.

I also explain how to enlist and engage your followers in the changes you introduce and take them gracefully from the now to the new. Finally, you find out what to do when your efforts to change grind to a halt, how to deal with followers who don't want change and how to make changes that last.

Phase 1: Getting the Change Clear in Your Mind

The more a change affects the way followers go about their routines and the ways they work with each other, the less you can expect your followers to welcome change.

To avoid frightening your followers into finding ways to sabotage and to stall change, put yourself in their places and think about how change affects them. That helps you decide how to introduce the change, how to implement change and how to make the changes last.

To successfully effect change, carefully think through the change first, considering the following questions in this order:

✔ What is the change intended to achieve?

✔ What is going to be different once the change is up and running?

✔ What questions are your followers likely to ask?

✔ What does the change means for your followers — who stands to lose out and who stands to benefit, how are their relationships affected, what does the change mean for their workload?

✔ Who is likely to support the change and who is likely to resist it, and why?

✔ What factors can you expect to push the change forward and what factors can you expect to push against the change?

✔ How much time is available to get the change up and running?

✔ How are you going to measure how successfully the change is working?

✔ What do you need your followers to do to make the change work?

✔ How can you recognise and reward followers for adopting the change?

Thinking through a change like this helps you avoid nasty surprises and allows you to work out how to explain the change in a way that creates a common vision and sense of purpose so that your followers understand, accept and even embrace the change.

Next, assemble an alliance of people to support the change. Include other leaders and influential people in other parts of your organisation as well as your most influential followers to help get the change going and keep it moving. Trail blazers are essential to show the others the way ahead. (To find out more about how to build a coalition of supporters, refer to Chapter 8.)

Phase 2: Painting a Clear Picture

The known is predictable and comfortable while the unknown is often frightening and threatening. In fact, some say that even the certainty of misery is better than the misery of uncertainty. Therefore, when you're leading followers into uncharted territory, make that territory clear and inviting.

Here's where change is like a bridge. You're at one end of the bridge and you're asking your followers to step out of their comfort zones onto the bridge of change and cross over to the other side, where unknown dangers lurk. And why do you think they want to do that?

Changing from the old ways is hard enough — and well nigh impossible when you don't know where you're going. When you seriously expect followers to cross a bridge with you, painting a clear picture of life on the other side is essential. This vision is your followers' lifejacket to make them feel secure while they cross the bridge. (To find out more about creating a compelling vision, refer to Chapter 5.)

When change just causes your followers more work, you can anticipate strong resistance. Explain how a change can benefit them. That doesn't mean you're shying away from difficulties. While you want to convey optimism, avoiding false spin is important. Trust your followers to handle the truth.

Forecasting a pleasant change

Change in the workplace is a bit like a change in the weather — it can blow hot or cold. The difference is that in the workplace you can control the temperature and you can influence people's responses to the change. To effect the best possible results from change, ensure your followers

✔ Have the resources they need (training, time to prepare and so on)

✔ Know precisely what they each are expected to do to achieve the change

✔ Share the same understanding of how to achieve the change

✔ Share the same view of the future and are personally committed to the change

---

Even when you don't know all the details, say what you do know. Some of the information your followers want to know includes

- ✔ How the change affects them as individuals and as a group.
- ✔ What is the goal of the change and why the goal is important.
- ✔ What the change can achieve.
- ✔ What you expect from your followers, individually and as a group, as they implement the change and make it work.
- ✔ What won't change.
- ✔ Why the change is needed (and what might happen if the situation isn't changed).

Expect your followers' minds to be filled with questions. If they need to learn new skills or follow new procedures, for example, they want to know how they are to be trained and how much time they are to be given to build their skills and confidence or to become used to the new procedures. Answer all their questions fully and honestly; when you don't know an answer, say so and tell them you intend to find out the answer for them.

Create a climate of certainty because when followers resist change, generally they're resisting because of the sense of insecurity that the change brings. To supply some certainty, stability and routine, explain what won't change. Give your followers a clear picture of what awaits them on the other side of the bridge so they see and sense clearly where they're headed.

Phase 3: Communicating Constantly

Followers are especially hungry for information during times of change and they look to their leader to supply that information. Followers also look to you for positive energy, optimism and confidence when they're thrown off balance by a major upheaval. If you let them down, the grapevine fills the void and probably with a negative spin that only increases people's discomfort and resistance, making your task even harder.

Counter this negativity by communicating as much as you can and as often as you can. Continually spreading your message increases its 'stickiness'. Don't worry about information overload when you're chatting through change. Explaining once is never enough. Keep communicating, even when you repeat an important message and even when the message may change. When you think you're communicating enough, communicate some more.

Help followers across the bridge

Change is about communication — about how clearly you explain every aspect of a change to your followers. Following these steps from the now into the new helps ease the way:

✔ **From the now:** Recognise the sense of loss that many followers feel. Changing from the old ways is difficult when followers identify with those ways or feel a sense of self or purpose with their routines. As well, asking people to do jobs differently, or having changes take place around them also implies that what they do — and have done for a long time — is wrong. Make clear that the methods of the past suited the conditions at the time — now new and improved methods are needed.

✔ **Halfway there:** After followers have placed their trust in you and stepped onto the bridge, despite their fears and doubts, feeling disoriented is normal. They haven't completely crossed the bridge yet and the comfort zone of the past that they're leaving behind seems to be crumbling. This time is tough for many followers but eventually, as they near the other side of the bridge, they see what's on the other side more clearly and they see that the change may not be so bad after all. This discovery helps your followers take the final step off the bridge and into the new.

✔ **Into the new:** Although followers seldom step off the bridge into the new ways of working in unison, most eventually step into the new and gradually invest energy and effort to make the change work.

Make all your messages — verbal and non verbal — clear, consistent and positive, but don't sugar-coat them. Communicating is more than sharing information; communicating is also about building trust. Convey a clear and positive vision and remember that followers listen closely to everything you say and do (and everything you don't say and do) and then put their own slant on your messages.

Making your messages stick

Talking about change provides a sense of familiarity and helps followers feel more comfortable with the change. Supplying the right information at the right time to the right follower can be quite an art form. You can provide the right information in these stages:

1. **So, what's happening?** At first, your followers just want to hear about what's happening in general terms.

2. **How does the change affect me?** Next, followers want to know how the change affects them personally, particularly in their daily routine.

3. **What exactly do I need to do?** After that, followers begin wondering what they need to do and what resources they need to make the change work; they want to know the specific behaviours, time frames and measurable outcomes they need to meet and what support you plan to give them.

4. **How is it for you?** Once the change has been running for a while, followers want to make sure people, such as customers and other teams, are benefiting from the change. Help your followers find out so they know their efforts have been worthwhile.

Followers reach these stages at different times, so what one follower needs to hear isn't the same as what another follower needs to hear. Listen to their comments and questions to suss out which stage they're in so you can provide the information they really need.

Listening is an important part of communicating. Listen to your followers' comments and questions and to what they say and don't say about the change. The more you know about what's going on in their minds, the more you can take their perspectives into account and help them cross the bridge of change and enter the future. (Refer to Chapter 7 for more ideas about communication.)

Here are some smart ways to make your messages hit home:

- **Be specific and positive.** Say what you do want, not what you don't want because the human brain is inclined to ignore the negative in an instruction.

- **Practise what you preach.** 'Do as I say, not as I do' may have worked 50 years ago, but that rule seldom works today. Stay visible, set a good example and do what you say.

- **Repeat your message frequently.** Repetition helps the message get home and stay there. The more followers hear your message, the more your message sticks.

- **Say why your message is important.** If your followers understand the purpose behind what you're asking, they're much more likely to cooperate. This also helps turn chores into worthwhile tasks.

- **Show followers that you notice.** When followers are doing what you want them to do, ignoring their efforts sends a clear message that their efforts don't matter. When you offer *positive reinforcement* — that is, when you commend good deeds — followers repeat them.

When the news is bad

Some change, such as closures, layoffs and takeovers, just can't be couched in positive terms. The more people identify with what they're losing, the more their responses resemble grief rather than regret or resistance.

When informing your followers of unpleasant changes, avoid blaming anyone or anything and avoid cheerily urging your followers to see the benefits to the organisation. Understand how they're seeing the situation and be as empathetic and supportive as you can be. Offer whatever assistance you can on behalf of the organisation (counselling, outplacement consulting, further training and so on). Now is the time to offer a formal closure to help them break with the past and move on with some positive energy. (See Chapter 20 if you need more information on how to deliver bad news.)

Addressing followers' concerns

Although change is normal, change is seldom comfortable so you can expect some resistance. After all, the *status quo* (no change) is easier than the effort of making a change.

Ignoring, smothering or glossing over opposition only strengthens the problem and allows problems to grow, fester and eventually erupt. Use the SHEER (Surface, Honour, Explore, Explain, Re-check) change memory jogger to bring your followers' concerns into the open so you can discuss and resolve their qualms:

- ✔ **Surface:** Ask questions to bring any concerns and questions followers may have into the open. Draw out your followers' thoughts so that you can deal with them.

- ✔ **Honour:** Always honour your followers' reservations. Don't brush aside any concerns as wrong or silly or consider the follower as just being difficult. To people facing change, concerns aren't silly at all — they're very real.

- ✔ **Explore:** Always explore concerns. Ask a few questions to find out what causes followers to feel the way they do and what lies at the heart of their hesitation.

- ✔ **Explain:** Answer questions as fully as you can. Review why the change is needed and what the organisation and your followers stand to gain from the change in a way that addresses your followers' concerns, not as a rebuttal but in the spirit of sharing information.

- ✔ **Re-check:** Make sure you have provided the information your followers want and addressed questions and concerns fully.

Why change is challenging

An older, relatively primitive part of the brain, called the *basal ganglia*, takes charge when you follow a familiar routine. But when you do something that is difficult or different, you need to pay attention because a more sophisticated part of the brain, the *prefrontal cortex*, takes over. This part of the brain uses more energy than the *basal ganglia*, which is why doing a new task or doing an old task in a new way can seem like hard work.

Comfort yourself and your followers with this good news: When you're learning and changing, you're building new connections in your brain and, as a result, improving your ability to think and lifting your intelligence. Research also shows that you're also warding off brain diseases, such as Alzheimer's disease.

Phase 4: Deciding the Details

In Phase 1, you paint a clear picture for the future. You won't get there overnight, though, so developing a transition plan is important. Recruit followers to help make the change work, not just to help soothe their uncertainties, fears and doubts, but also to give them a sense of ownership in the change — people support what they have a hand in designing.

Involving followers also ensures they understand what they need to do and why and gives them a chance to work together to test the change out in their own minds. Involving followers in this way helps them develop the new ways of thinking and working that change often requires.

Followers need to know precisely what they need to do to make the change happen. Once you agree on your measures of success and work out who needs to do what and when, post the plan in a place where everyone can see it. Agree on short-term goals for your followers to work toward to provide a sense of achievement as they reach goals.

Creating a visual map reminds people what to do and allows progress to be ticked off, creating a sense of advancement and achievement. Check that your change plan is complete and covers *contingencies*, or events that can prevent your plan from working as expected. (Refer to Chapter 5 to find out more about developing a workable plan, and Chapters 5 and 10 for more about measures of success.)

Hold a ceremony to allow followers to find *closure* — that is, to leave behind the old ways so they can begin the new ways of doing their jobs. A small ritual to formally close the door to the past is a powerful and satisfying way to stop followers from yearning for the good old days and never fully accepting the change. The ceremony can be tongue in cheek and fun, short and simple, or serious, depending on the nature of the change.

Phase 5: Keeping up the Momentum

The tendency to revert to the old ways is strong. Failing to keep the change on the move invites followers to return to the past. Go for a few small wins early on to build momentum for the change and allow followers to feel a sense of achievement.

A lull often occurs halfway through a change. Followers can become despondent at this stage and begin to believe that the process of change is failing. To avoid this pause in your progress

- ✔ Celebrate each step forward.
- ✔ Deal with any unexpected obstacles that get in your followers' way.
- ✔ Provide enough time and other resources to implement the change.
- ✔ Provide plenty of individual and group feedback about how the change is progressing and how your followers' support is helping.
- ✔ Provide the necessary training.

 Be sure to do as you ask your followers to do if you don't want to drag cynical and distrustful followers behind you. To lead a change and carry it through to success, you must be personally credible.

Avoiding fizzle, fatigue and false starts

When change is introduced like a sparkler — with a lot of flash and flare — it usually splutters and fades just as quickly. Successful change is introduced consistently with realistic goals, a clear plan and constant communication.

 Speed is disorienting and tiring, and too much change too quickly unsettles followers and wears them out. Counteract change fatigue by taking one step at a time and allowing plenty of discussion. Give followers time to pause, catch up and adapt — moving too fast can kill enthusiasm just as much as moving too slowly.

Conversely, when change moves too slowly, attention wanders; followers end up disillusioned and moaning about false promises. Make the change not too fast, not too slow, but just right — fast enough to give a sense of progress but not so fast that followers can't absorb it. Prevent the three steps forward and two steps back syndrome with a clear vision, plenty of communication and planning.

Keeping the focus and rewarding the supporters

Resistance mushrooms in a leadership vacuum, so stay right out there, communicating and leading the change. Don't give the organisation's grapevine a chance to kick in — aim always to be your followers' primary source of information. Even at points where you haven't much to say, your followers still need to hear from you. Give progress reports, reiterate the goals and vision for the future that are part of the plan of change and give followers a clear path to follow.

Continue to champion and promote the change. Chat about the change with your followers and find out how the plan for change is progressing from their points of view — what has surprised them, what's working for them, what needs to work better and how they think the change can be improved. Be alert for any remaining reservations and do what you can to ease those reservations (refer to the SHEER change formula in the section 'Addressing followers' concerns' earlier in this chapter).

Don't beat yourself up over hiccups as the change rolls out — you probably haven't been down this track before, so you and your followers are unlikely to introduce change without a hitch. Fix the hitches and move on.

Make sure followers understand the benefits the change offers. Rewarding those who make the change shows the laggers that benefits from change do exist. Because what is rewarded is repeated, supporting the supporters also ensures their continued support for the change. (Refer to Chapter 10 for information on how to reward followers and the range of unofficial rewards you can use.)

When followers begin looking for ways to make the change work more smoothly and then to make improvements to the change itself, you know you're leading the plan for change well. Take the time to acknowledge and thank your followers for their efforts and support.

Phase 6: Anchoring the Change

Change needs to sink deeply into followers' normal routines and become the normal way of doing a job. But don't assume success too soon. Followers can slip easily back into the old ways if you don't provide an incentive to stick with the new ways.

Find ways to consolidate and institutionalise the change. Work with your followers to integrate the change into the rest of the systems and procedures they use and help them to continue improving and modifying the change in the light of experience.

Then comes the day when you and your team look back and see the bridge in the far distance behind you. The change has become a habit and soon the time is coming when you can lead a new plan for change across a new bridge.

Chapter 15

Building a Team with Muscles

The benefits of people working well together are extensive. In fact, you can rely on an effective team to perform better than the strongest individual in it. When people pool their talents, skills and knowledge, they spark the energy, enthusiasm and ideas that can achieve challenging goals, solve tricky problems, reach difficult decisions and develop complex plans. And they have fun and fulfilment doing it.

Building up a burly team isn't easy, but it is rewarding. This chapter explains how to decide who is best to have on your team and how to turn a group of individuals into a team of people working towards the same goals, working well together, communicating openly with each other, helping each other out and sharing their knowledge with each other. I explain how teams grow, the inner workings of teams and how to build a robust team through special team training and daily nourishment. Finally, I describe how to use feedback to build your team's muscles and get the results you all want to achieve.

Finding the Right Followers

Your team is only as strong as the people in it. Successful teams are made up of people who are able to contribute skills, knowledge and the ways of working that a team needs to achieve its goals. Teams also need people who can deal with a variety of challenging situations. When you're looking for people to join your team, your instincts may help you recognise these positive contributors, but alone your instincts aren't enough.

You also need to know how to

- Attract potentially good team members to your team
- Ask questions that give you the information you need to decide whether a candidate is suited to your team and which candidate is the best suited
- Decide what types of team members you need
- Help new followers find their team feet quickly when they join

Inviting a team member on board who isn't right for your team damages the way your team operates and its ability to get results and costs you untold heartache.

Deciding what types of followers you need

You're not looking for the best person but the person who best meets your team's needs. To find that person, be clear about the particular skills, knowledge and attributes you're seeking. Think your way logically through these important points:

- **What tasks you expect the team member to do.** Even when you're replacing a team member who's leaving, don't automatically assign all the departing follower's duties to the new team member. Try *cross-skilling* and *multi-skilling* — using the opportunity to rotate tasks among other followers to provide more job interest and allow people to learn new skills.

- **The type of person who can do the tasks best.** For example, you may choose someone who

  - Copes with being in one place for long periods
  - Prefers repetitive work or needs variety to remain enthusiastic
  - Wants to move about a lot
  - Works best with equipment, details or ideas, numbers or words

- **The environment the team member is to work in.** The environment tells you a lot about the type of follower you need. You may need someone who

  - Is able to think clearly under pressure
  - Works best in a formal environment or a relaxed environment
  - Works best in a structured or an unstructured environment
  - Works best on their own or as part of a tightly knit team

✔ **What approach to work you want the team member to take.** Think about the ideal team member in this role. You may need someone who

- Is conscientious and who fulfils their duties correctly and on time

- Is neat and tidy

- Is reliable and can work without a lot of direction from you

- Is willing to find work without being told

Now that you can easily recognise the right team member, you can meet with candidates and find out how they work best and what skills, knowledge and attributes they can bring to your team. (Refer to Chapters 3, 9 and 12 for more information on personality styles and working styles.)

If you're still not sure that you can recognise the right person, think about your best team members and what makes them so important to have around. Perhaps they're energetic, self-motivated, friendly and helpful and keen to learn. That may also be what you want your new team member to be like. Think about the skills they need to have and what they need to know or understand, too.

Asking the right questions

The best predictor of future behaviour is past behaviour. Some people are just naturally more gregarious than others, some are naturally more thorough than others, some are better time-keepers than others, and so on. Unless a major and traumatic event occurs to alter the way they think, work and behave, people tend to carry on thinking, working and behaving in their own characteristic ways.

To find out how well an aspiring team member meets your needs, ask a lot of investigative questions. Suss out the working styles and personality styles of the people you're considering inviting into your team so you know how well they can fit in with and complement the other team members, contribute to the team and enjoy doing the work you offer. Ask your potential new followers to tell you about

✔ A difficult team-mate they encountered and how they handled the problem

✔ A problem they recently solved and how they went about solving the problem

✔ A typical day in their working life

✔ The best team they worked in and their role in that team

✔ The most difficult aspect of their current role

✔ The most rewarding part of their current role

✔ Their proudest achievement so far

Now here are some questions that help you probe for more information:

✔ What made you decide to ...?

✔ What led to that?

✔ Could you tell me more about that?

✔ Earlier you mentioned that ... Can you give me an example?

Selling your team

Aim to get potential team members talking for about 70 to 80 per cent of the time you meet with them, which is generally about 45 minutes to an hour. Look and listen carefully (and show that you're listening by leaning slightly forward and responding with appropriate murmurs or expressions). Note areas where the potential team member does and doesn't meet your needs. Jot down a few reminder notes to flesh out later so that you don't spend valuable time taking such detailed notes that you miss what the potential team member is (and isn't) saying.

Questions that waste your time

Some questions don't help you learn anything accurate or useful about the person you're interviewing. Here are some examples of the types of questions to avoid:

✔ Asking more than one question at a time (for example: What are your main responsibilities and what you like most and least about them, and whether you have any specific targets to meet? And how do you get on with your team-mates?)

✔ 'Either ... or' questions (for example: Are you good at teamwork or do you prefer to work on your own?)

✔ Hypothetical, or 'what if' questions (for example: If a team member were rude to you, how would you respond?)

✔ Questions that can be answered with a 'Yes', 'No' or a straightforward fact because they go nowhere (for example: Do you enjoy those types of tasks?)

✔ Questions that indicate the answer you're expecting (for example: You enjoy working in a team environment, don't you?)

✔ Unclear and general questions

Use the remaining 20 to 30 per cent of the time to briefly explain the role you expect the team member to fulfil and to talk about the organisation. Then talk about your team; explain the team's purpose and what being a part of the team involves. Be truthful and inviting. With the declining birth rate and the high number of retirements among the baby-boomer (post World War II) generation in Australia and New Zealand, even the best leaders are experiencing difficulties in finding enough of the right followers. Potential team members no longer have to sell themselves to the leader as much as the leader has to sell the tasks, the team and the organisation to them.

Don't oversell. If you oversell, the new team member may soon be out the door and you can find yourself starting the interview process all over again.

Diversifying for success

A team made up of *homogeneous* (like-minded or similar) team members operates more like a club. A team of like-minded *clones* (people who offer no individual differences) may be predictable and comfortable but the team is also weak because of the limited experiences, backgrounds and points of view.

Teams need all types of members to be strong. Teams that are made up from an assortment of *heterogeneous* followers from various backgrounds and cultures and with different experiences, skills, abilities, work preferences, ways of working and personality styles are well rounded and able to deal with different issues and unexpected situations.

Bring in followers who round out your team so that between them they can do everything that needs doing — and more. Know what areas in your team may be weak so that you can find one follower or more with solid strengths in those areas to compensate. (For more information on working to your strengths and knowing your weak areas, refer to Chapter 4; for more information on building a diverse team, refer to Chapter 3. Chapter 9 explores how to work well with everyone and Chapter 12 deals with assigning the right work to the right people.)

Helping new followers fit in

New team members can't be fully productive until they're integrated into the team so the more quickly you and the team help them in this regard, the better for everyone. Before a new follower even joins your team, send an information pack about the organisation with a couple of its most recent newsletters, important policies, its values, vision and mission statement and so on. That way whenever new team members turn up on that first day, they already feel some familiarity. Be sure they already know where to park their cars, where to come and what time to arrive, too.

First impressions count, so be there to greet your new followers on their first days (and when that's not possible, appoint a team member to meet them and offer your apologies for being absent). Give your new team members an outline of what information you plan to cover over the next few weeks and a small notebook to jot down reminders, questions, observations and so on. Have their workspaces ready, waiting and welcoming. Make new team members feel welcome with a 'Welcome to the Team' lunch on their first day; lay on some nice sandwiches and fruit and give the team members a chance to get acquainted with their new colleagues.

Get right down to the basics on the first day. New followers want to know where to park, where the amenities are (toilets, water cooler, café bar, kitchen and so on) and where the nearest shops and nicest walks for lunch breaks are. Introduce them to their team-mates and explain your standards regarding matters such as time-keeping and tidiness. Give them a tour of your team's territory, including the location of fire escapes and fire equipment and where to find supplies. Go over the team's purpose, talk about your expectations regarding working habits and outline the new team members' duties, stressing how they contribute to the team. (For more information on explaining your expectations, refer to Chapter 9.)

People can't absorb too much new information at once, so deliver important information in small doses over several days. Give new team members an overview of the organisation and show them around the building, explaining how the team fits into the wider organisation. Once new followers are feeling more comfortable, familiarise them further with the organisation — who's who, who does what and where, and so on. Introduce them to other leaders and key people in other teams and explain the organisation's important policies (health, safety and welfare, diversity and so on).

New followers struggle to fit into the team's accepted ways of doing particular tasks and can unintentionally disrupt them, even reversing the team's progress. To help them fit in more painlessly and quickly, explain the expected behaviours in your group and in the wider organisation (refer to Chapters 4 and 8 for more information on norms and culture).

Growing a Mighty Team

Teams, like people, go through a life cycle from birth to death. But the life cycle of a team has nothing to do with how 'old' the team is or how long its members have been together as a team. This life cycle has to do with how effective the team is at its tasks, how well the members understand the team's purpose, goals and measures of success and how well the team members work together to achieve their goals.

As a team matures, it becomes able to take on more complex tasks. If you know where your team is in its life cycle, you can help your team grow to its full potential more quickly (provided the team has the right resources and support — for information on providing a team with the resources and support it needs, refer to Chapter 10). Here are the phases a team passes through as it matures.

- **Birth:** When a group of individuals first come together, they go through a polite getting-to-know-you stage, finding out about their team-mates and what each can contribute, sorting out what is their joint purpose and what are their individual roles and responsibilities. The rules of how to behave haven't been established yet and people are cautious and watch for clues about what is expected of them.

    Give a new team time for its members to get to know each other and provide a clear purpose, goals and measures of success. Explain your vision and how you want people to work together to achieve it. (Refer to Chapter 5 for information on how to point followers in the same direction; and refer to Chapter 9 for information on how to explain your expectations.)

A new team depends on its leader for guidance and direction, so lead from the front with strong direction and support (refer to Chapter 2 for more on leading from the front).

- **Teething troubles:** After a while, differences in values, working styles, personalities and so on emerge. Conflict and in-fighting erupt as team members jostle for their places in the pecking order and their roles in the team. The discord may be obvious (making it easier to resolve) or the friction may bubble away under the surface.

    Not surprisingly, task achievement levels are low during this stage so help followers through this stage as quickly as you can by clarifying the team's goals and helping team members work through their difficulties openly and honestly. Demonstrate the behaviours and types of communication that you want team members to adopt (see the section 'Strengthening communication' later in this chapter).

- **Adolescence:** Like teenagers everywhere, life for team members at this stage is about conforming to what have become the accepted codes and customs of how their team operates. Team members know where they stand and what is expected of them. They have settled into ways of working together and feel committed to the team and its goals and are depending less on you.

Now is the time to begin gradually leading from the centre (refer to Chapter 2 for more on leading from the centre). Continue to guide the team and ensure that helpful norms are developing (see the section 'Teams have habits' later in this chapter). Give feedback against the team's success measures and the progress the team is making towards its goals. Make the work visible and document progress so the team can feel proud of its achievements. Establish a climate where team members aren't afraid to share bad news and concerns.

Keep your eyes open for cliques developing among your team members. These teams within teams are coalitions of people who like and respect each other and share similar ideas, values and so on. However, these alliances can wield a lot of influence, either sabotaging or supporting the team you're trying to build.

- **Coming of age:** At some point, well-led teams perform to the max, working like a well-oiled engine, and output, energy and enjoyment are high. Team-mates can work singly, in sub groups or all together. Team members don't think: 'That's her problem and she's got to fix it' but 'That's our problem — how can we fix it?'. Team members are proud to be part of their team and team spirit is high. Teams that have come of age are a leader's dream come true.

By now, you're probably leading from the back (refer to Chapter 2 for more on leading from the back), encouraging *empowerment* in your followers so they can find problems and solve them, make decisions and allocate tasks among themselves. You are now the team's chief supporter and chief resource for providing general guidance and helping them obtain the resources they need to achieve their goals.

A team's growth needs to be cultivated carefully. Coming of age is the result of a long process of preparing followers to accept responsibility, training them and building their skills as team members, problem solvers and decision makers, getting the climate just right and providing the resources, information, authority and tools the team and its members need to get the job done.

Leading a team through tough times

If you're leading a team that's going through significant change or facing uncertainty, rapid growth, extremely difficult issues or challenges, such as severe budget cuts, provide plenty of support by leading from underneath (refer to Chapter 2 for more on leading from underneath). Have a short get together every morning. Go around all team members and give them a chance to raise an issue, concern or discussion topic so issues and problems are aired quickly, before they fester and become difficult to resolve. If some team members are part-time workers or work on the road, ask them to join in on the telephone.

✔ **Saying goodbye:** Teams disband for happy reasons and for sad reasons. Sometimes a team member leaves and the team members feel as though the team they knew is coming to an end. Sometimes the temporary project team you lead has completed its project and members say goodbye to each other, at least as team-mates. Sadly, sometimes teams disband due to closures of branches, outsourcing, corporate restructuring or corporate takeovers. In strong teams, members feel a sense of emptiness, sadness and loss when the team is disbanded or members leave.

Help the team through this period by holding a formal ceremony — a special morning tea or team lunch, with small gifts or awards and invite a speech or two — to mark the end and let team members say farewell. If one team member is leaving, set time aside to discuss how the departure affects the rest of the team members and their ability to achieve the team's goals. Discuss any projects or tasks that may be particularly vulnerable and how to protect them. And plan, together when possible, how to cover the departing team member's responsibilities until a new member joins. Now is the time to discuss whether reallocating any duties or altering the work flow is desirable (refer to the section 'Deciding what types of followers you need' earlier in this chapter).

Teams are always changing and growing and no two teams are ever identical. Teams seldom, if ever, go straight through the life cycle from birth to saying goodbye but move back and forth as team membership and even team leadership changes, and as the resources the team has at its disposal become more limited or more abundant. Stay aware of what part of its life cycle your team seems to be in and help your followers move forward when they seem to slip backward.

Promoting a winning team

If the conditions are right, involvement grows into empowerment as confidence builds. Here are some ways to help your team come of age:

✔ Be a good role model.

✔ Develop followers' and the team's task and process skills.

✔ Give the team and individual members responsibility and accountability for achieving results.

✔ Help people think for themselves.

✔ Make decisions with your team (not for them) as much as possible.

✔ Make the team feel like a winning team and proud of its accomplishments.

✔ Provide plenty of coaching and feedback.

✔ Remove the obstacles that prevent the team from achieving results (refer to Chapter 10 for more on how to do this).

✔ Set time aside for team planning and problem-solving meetings.

✔ Share information.

Understanding What Goes On Inside a Team

The purpose of a team is to achieve a goal — this is known as the team's *task*. The way a team goes about achieving its task — this is known as the team's *process* — makes all the difference to how easily and how effectively it achieves its task. (Refer to Chapter 13 for more on task and process issues in a team.) In short: Leaders who build teams with strong and healthy internal processes, or ways of working together, enable their teams to achieve their task far more easily and far more pleasurably than teams with poor internal workings.

Factors that affect how well team members work together to achieve a task include

✔ How effectively the team is led

✔ The culture of the wider organisation

✔ The level of interpersonal skills of the team members

✔ Whether a team has enough of the right resources

(Refer to Chapter 10 to find out what else followers need to achieve their goals.)

These four factors largely determine the patterns and forms of interactions between team members, their relationships with each other and their leader and the way team members go about their duties.

Teams reflect their leaders

They say that a fish rots from the head down. The same applies to teams. (If you want to find out more about being a strong leader worthy of your followers, refer to Chapter 3.)

Similarly, if you have ever watched any of the forensic crime shows on TV, you know that every contact leaves a trace; every contact a leader has with a follower leaves its trace, too. For good or ill, followers learn from their leaders and try to be like them.

Teams reach for their purpose

The collective hands, hearts and heads of teams can achieve great feats when they have clear goals to work towards and a compelling team purpose that explains what the team members do and why they do their jobs.

Bond your followers together by involving them in crafting a team purpose they can be proud of and that inspires them. Involve them in helping work out how they can achieve their goals together. Giving people a say *engages* them — it increases their commitment, while sharing an overall purpose and goal whips up excitement. (To find out how to craft a potent team purpose, refer to Chapter 5.)

Team members also need to know their own individual roles in achieving the team purpose. Knowing how they contribute creates pride in what they do and builds team performance — when team members know how important their own contributions are, they don't want to let the team down.

To keep team members striving for their own and their team's purpose and aims, go around team members at your next team meeting and find out their priorities between now and your next regular team meeting. List these priorities on a whiteboard or flip chart and summarise them into team priorities; then post or distribute both lists. At the next meeting, track your team's and team members' progress and set new priorities.

Teams have role players

Everyone wants to be known for something in their team. One team member may become the expert in the technology the team uses; another may be known and respected for an ability to make people laugh and enjoy themselves; someone else is the one who generates enthusiasm and another may be the one to consistently come up with off-the-wall but useful ideas.

And then there are the roles leaders would rather people didn't play — the whinger, the know-all, the authority-resister, the cynic, the critic and so on. Squash these behaviours quickly and give these team members a more useful role to play. You may be sorry if you don't move quickly. (For more on how to change disruptive behaviours, see Chapters 18 and 19.)

Your team probably has an unofficial leader, too, someone the others respect or admire. This is the follower team members go to for advice or assistance, who speaks up on the team's behalf, and who influences their behaviour (for good or ill) in a variety of ways. The unofficial leader can be a great help to you, or a great hindrance. Know who this person is and get this person on side. (For more information on unofficial leaders, refer to Chapter 4.)

Teams have habits

Pay attention to the behaviours and activities your team members welcome and those they resist. For instance, team members have unspoken agreements — or *norms* — about how to dress, how to talk to and about their leader and each other, how important being on time is, how important turning in work on time is, their pace of work and their approach to work.

Teams also have traditions. For instance, team members have traditional ways to celebrate birthdays and other special events and have accepted procedures for giving and receiving gifts. The longer that team members are together, the more established and recognisable these rituals become. (For more information on norms, refer to Chapters 4 and 8.)

These team customs either help your team members and the team itself to succeed or they hold back success. Take the time to examine your team's traditions and when you see anything holding back your team, meet with your followers, discuss the problem openly and agree on better ways of working together.

Don't let your team's norms develop willy-nilly. As the leader, you're in a good position to initiate beneficial habits and customs and see that they continue.

Teams are 'us'

Teams need a sense of 'us' with which members can identify and feel proud. This sense of us is the glue that holds your followers together and makes each team different from every other team.

A team's *culture* combines with its norms to act as an invisible force that shapes team members' behaviour — how they relate to each other, to you and to outsiders, how they get jobs done, and so on. A positive, results-oriented and respectful team culture and norms are your team's backbone, providing strong support for its activities and achievements. (For more information on culture, refer to Chapters 4 and 8.)

Although team members have a lot of influence on the characteristics and personality of the team (that's why finding the right followers is so important), you build the culture you want and you demonstrate, by word and deed, the behaviours and attitudes you want team members to uphold.

Here are some ways to build a strong team culture:

- ✔ Build pride in the organisation and in your team.
- ✔ Encourage an enjoyable, pleasant atmosphere.
- ✔ Encourage the team and team members to be alert to problems and potential problems and raise problems early.
- ✔ Help the team come of age as quickly as possible.
- ✔ Make clear what you value and what the team's chief purpose is (refer to Chapter 5 for more on team purpose).
- ✔ Reward and respect behaviours that help achieve team goals and help the team members work well together.
- ✔ Set a good example for team members to follow.
- ✔ Speak — in private and straight away — to any followers who behave in ways that are preventing goals being achieved or who are holding the team back from working well together.

Meet with team members regularly to share news, solve problems and so on. Keep a flip chart or similar resource in areas where team members congregate on which team members can jot down any questions they want answered or any items they want discussed at the next team meeting.

Building Your Team's Muscles

Here's a quick review: You are making the most of each team member's skills, knowledge, experience, work preferences and style. You're building and supporting a sturdy team culture with strong and positive norms. Your team purpose, goals and measures of success are clear and worth working toward and team members understand their part in achieving goals and they understand their team-mates' roles in achieving those goals.

For the final sculpting of your team's strengthened muscles, you can generate plenty of the right types of communication within your team and between you and your team members. Take time out to do some heavy weightlifting with the team once in a while to formally build its muscles, and then nourish that muscle tone with daily team maintenance.

Strengthening communication

A large chunk of a team's culture and vigour comes from the way its members communicate with each other. In Table 15-1, I summarise communication categories to make some off limits and suggest ways to replace them.

Listen carefully to what your team members say. When you hear any comments that belong in the left-hand column, pause and ask your followers to switch to the suggested substitute in the right-hand column. This way, you can quickly build powerful communications habits.

Table 15-1	Communication Methods to Avoid
Not fair	**Try instead**
Blaming, shaming and scolding people and making them feel bad	Be a coach not critic; find solutions, not faults
Disagreeing	Before you disagree, summarise your understanding of your team-mate's views and say something like 'And here's how I see it ...' or outline your reasoning and finish up with something like 'And that's why I look at it differently'.
Dredging up the past (previous mistakes someone has made)	Skip the ancient history and concentrate on the future and what you want to achieve

(continued)

Table 15-1 *(continued)*

Not fair	Try instead
Interrupting (even when you're sure you know what someone is about to say)	Give people a chance to finish what they want to say, asking questions until you fully understand their points of view
Personal attacks, for example, name calling	Stick to correcting behaviour — what team-mates say and do that causes problems
Playing psychologist	Stick to the facts and stay away from personalities and psychoanalysing
Railroading, browbeating	Slow down and give your team-mates a genuine chance to say what they think
Sarcasm	Say what you mean, clearly and considerately
Telling people what to do, giving orders	Offer suggestions; say 'please' and 'could you ...'
Threatening	Tactfully persuade your team members that your point of view is worth considering

(See also Chapters 7 and 20 for more information on how to deal with disagreements.)

Leading a team workout

Leaders sculpt strong team muscles through special meetings known as *team building* meetings, designed to direct followers' attention to the job at hand (the team task) as well as the way they work together (the team process). (See the section 'Understanding What Goes On Inside a Team' earlier in this chapter for a description of task and process inside a team.) These team workouts are generally held off site over two or three days and most leaders bring in an external facilitator who specialises in team building to conduct the sessions, which frees up the leader to be a participant.

This time out for the team helps team members concentrate on what they are trying to achieve together and individually and examine the ways they work together. Team members and their leader establish clear team and individual goals and priorities, discuss problems and obstacles and find ways to remove them or deal with them more effectively and agree on ways to move the team forward by working together more effectively. The team members return to their normal routines with renewed vigour, a stronger culture, improved internal communications and a stronger commitment to their joint and individual goals.

Nourishing your team

Living organisms, machines and teams all need *maintenance* — regular upkeep. Every day, in large and small ways, leaders look after the health and fitness of their team members and the team itself to keep the team working smoothly.

Every time your team meets is an opportunity to

- Clarify its purpose
- Celebrate its achievements
- Check for any problems or obstacles preventing the team from performing at its peak
- Find methods to improve how the team members are working together or are working on team tasks
- Reinforce relationships
- Review the team's main goals and measures of success
- Strengthen team spirit

To maintain a strong team with well-honed muscles, look after these three areas:

- The task that everyone is there to complete
- The team as a whole
- The team's individual members

If you ignore any one of these three areas, the other two suffer.

Look after your team's task

No team can remain robust for long when it isn't succeeding in reaching its goals. Here are some ways to keep team energy and efforts directed towards the task:

- Advise the team of its progress and celebrate its successes.
- Develop clear plans and establish priorities.
- Ensure team members know how the team contributes to the organisation as a whole.
- Make sure each team member knows what they're responsible for achieving.

Look after your team

Strong teams have a clear sense of who 'we' — the team — are, what 'we' — the team — stands for and how 'we' — the team — operates. That shared understanding makes team members proud to be part of their team and proud of the team's results. Here are some ideas for looking after your team:

- Coordinate team efforts.
- Consult or involve the team members in making decisions and identifying and solving problems.
- Encourage ideas and suggestions.
- Have occasional, purely fun 'team time'.
- Help team members resolve conflicts.
- Help underperforming team members improve.
- Keep unruly team members in check.
- Provide the team with the resources it needs.

Look after your individual team members

Skilled team members make strong teams. However, every leader has experienced the one-bad-apple-spoils-the-barrel disease. Here are some ways to build the brawn of individual followers:

- Acknowledge and appreciate each follower's contributions.
- Allocate duties according to each follower's strengths and skill areas.
- Get to know followers as individuals.
- Make each follower's goals and measures of success clear, ambitious and achievable.
- See that team members have the time, information, equipment and other resources they need to achieve their goals.
- Train followers in the skills they need to contribute to the team's task and process.

Fortifying your team's physique with feedback

A client of mine once commented that followers have a right to hear from their leader how they're going and how they can do better. That put an entirely different slant on feedback for me — feedback isn't something to shy away from because it's awkward or embarrassing but something leaders owe their followers. In fact, feedback is a key leadership responsibility. It prevents followers from glumly concluding: 'When my leader doesn't say anything, I suppose I must be doing all right'.

A friend of mine calls feedback 'the wheel that moves the team machine'. This is true — no team functions well without feedback. No matter how old the team members are or how long they're in the team, followers need feedback. Your team as a whole needs feedback too.

Imagine if cricket fans waited until a batsman got a century or the team won the match before cheering. Working hard and making progress can be very demoralising when you don't hear any support.

The same is true of your team and its individual members. Don't wait until people have done a fantastic job or until the end of a project to say thanks — acknowledge effort and steps forward and celebrate small achievements that move the team towards its purpose.

Feedback keeps your team energetic and enthusiastic and builds the skills and knowledge of your individual followers and the team as a whole. In fact, feedback is your most powerful muscle builder. Setting the pace by giving the team and its members plenty of the right types of feedback promotes a learning culture where team members offer feedback to each other, too. But only when you use the right type of feedback.

Use the right type of feedback

Three types of feedback exist — positive, negative and none at all. No feedback at all is dangerous — in fact, feedback is so important to people that they do just about anything to get feedback. Even negative feedback is preferable to no feedback at all because at least negative feedback shows you're being noticed. So here's a double negative to mull over: Never give no feedback.

Never give negative feedback that's general, either. Generalised negative feedback, whether about the person, their personality or their behaviour, merely condemns and disapproves. Generalised negative feedback is hurtful and demoralising and doesn't offer any useful information. The only result of negative general feedback is the ill will and bad feelings it creates.

Specific negative feedback, on the other hand, points out exactly what you don't like or what needs to be done better. When you also explain or suggest what to do instead, this feedback becomes *constructive feedback,* which is very effective for building performance. (To find out more about this type of feedback, see the section 'Be a coach, not a critic' later in this chapter.)

The sandwich technique

You may have heard of the *sandwich technique* — sandwiching a negative piece of feedback between two positive pieces of feedback. This feedback system can work provided you don't use it so often that you train followers to wait for bad news every time they hear some good news from you.

Table 15-2 shows examples of positive and negative feedback and the results of offering no feedback.

Table 15-2	Different Types of Feedback	
Type of Feedback	*General*	*Specific*
Positive	Raises followers' morale	Ensures followers repeat the behaviour specified; builds performance
Negative	Demoralising; kills performance	Builds performance, especially if the feedback is constructive and explains what to do instead
No feedback	Demoralising; kills performance	Demoralising; kills performance

When you're giving feedback, be a mirror, not a judge. Help followers see themselves objectively by pointing out visible behaviour — what you can see or hear, not personality characteristics — and the effect of your followers' actions and what they can do differently.

Positive, general feedback is okay as a feel-good mechanism — even a few encouraging words are powerful. Supplement positive, general feedback with plentiful positive, specific feedback and watch the behaviours you mention multiply.

To make your positive feedback even more powerful, include these elements:

- Flag what you're about to comment on.
- Give an example of what you're commenting on.
- Explain why you appreciate what you're commenting on.

Here's an example of how you can fill in these categories:

- ✔ **Flag your feedback:** 'I liked your use of open questions with that customer.'
- ✔ **Give an example:** 'I thought it was very beneficial when you asked about the customer's goals for the business.'
- ✔ **Explain the benefits:** 'Your questions provided a lot of useful information that you can use to work with the customer to help build the business.'

A successful leader uses every opportunity to let followers know that their work is being noticed. You can offer feedback to your followers at any opportunity:

- ✔ At team meetings
- ✔ By marking major milestones with team celebrations — party hats and pizza, a fancy dress day, a team outing, balloons and so on — to keep your team members' spirits pumped and their energy directed at their goals
- ✔ By posting progress and thank-you notes on noticeboards
- ✔ During individual meetings with followers
- ✔ In emails
- ✔ When you pass followers in the hall or have a few minutes in the lift with a follower

Strong teams bounce along on lots of positive and constructive feedback that builds members' spirits and skills. Be specific whenever you give feedback — build a habit of never saying what you appreciate without saying why you appreciate it, or what you don't appreciate without saying why you don't appreciate it. (See Chapter 19 for more information on giving feedback.) Be generous with positive feedback and constructive feedback to build the behaviours and performances you and the team need.

Be a coach, not a critic

One of every leader's most important duties is passing on their hard-earned knowledge and wisdom, in part to develop the next generation of leaders and in part to build a high-performing team that hits its targets.

Offering constructive feedback and improvement suggestions turns you into a first-rate coach, helping followers find their strengths and refine their skills. You can ask questions to help your followers figure out situations or, when your feedback is more corrective than that, you can invite your followers to adjust what they're currently doing — that's much easier than asking them to change what they're doing. Think 'subtle shift' not 'complete overhaul' when you're coaching team members.

Think about how best to word your feedback before you give it. Put yourself in your followers' shoes and hear your feedback through their ears. Soften your feedback by saying 'I' more than 'you' — 'you' is pushy and invites resistance while 'I' is clear and reinforces your leadership.

You can choose from a buffet of ways to coach your followers and pass on your knowledge. The following suggestions begin with coaching simple tasks (show your followers) and move towards complex tasks where you encourage followers to have a go under your guidance. For tasks of moderate complexity, choose a coaching method from the middle of the following list.

- ✔ Show your followers patiently, step by step, what to do.
- ✔ Offer some rules to guide your followers.
- ✔ Tell a story about a similar situation so your followers can draw conclusions to guide them on how you want them to treat their situations.
- ✔ Ask questions of the 'What would happen if ...' type to help followers figure out the best course of action. (This is known as *Socratic questioning*.)
- ✔ Encourage followers to have a go at thinking through a problem or a course of action or completing a task (for example, preparing and giving a presentation) under your close supervision and then review the task with them to help analyse what can be improved for next time.

When you're coaching, stick to clear, measurable, non-arguable, objective behaviours — stick to what your followers say or do, or don't say or do. Here are four different ways to open your coaching session:

- ✔ **Guide your followers through a review.** Ask these questions:
  - Can you review the steps you took on this task for me?
  - What steps worked well?
  - What steps can be improved?
  - Knowing what you now know, what can you do next time to achieve an even better outcome?
- ✔ **Offer a suggestion.** Say something like 'I'd like to suggest an alternative method that may make the task easier for you'.

- ✔ **Set a goal.** Ask your followers

    - Where are you now (in this skill) out of 10?

    - Where do you want to be?

    - Do you want to talk about how to develop to where you want to be?

- ✔ **Use the Describe–Explain–Suggest formula.** This formula works this way:

    - Describe what you see happening.

    - Explain why what is happening matters.

    - Suggest what to do instead.

Don't overwhelm followers or lessen the impact of your coaching by discussing more than one issue in a session. If a follower needs coaching in more than one area, set up a different meeting for each topic.

Developing a learning culture

You can help your team members improve their work in many ways:

- ✔ Arrange for the team members to participate in formal training programs.
- ✔ Coach team members.
- ✔ Delegate duties that expand team members' skills.
- ✔ Encourage team members to develop their skills through reading, study or other self-development activities.
- ✔ Encourage team members to broaden each other's skills and knowledge.
- ✔ Offer secondments and special assignments to increase interest and enhance skills.

Followers gain an incredible amount of knowledge and information as they go about their normal activities. They gain from their own experiences and they gain from each other's experiences when you build what's known as a *learning culture* into your team.

A team really flexes its muscles when its members share their knowledge and experience among themselves. Reward team members when they support, help, advise and train each other, as this will encourage them to continue sharing their know-how around.

Chapter 16

Leading Special Teams

· ·

· ·

As the world shrinks and competition becomes ever-more fierce, organisations are responding with new ways to achieve results. Enabled by astounding advances in technology, new types of teams are springing up everywhere as a result of mergers, takeovers, globalisation and changing work patterns, such as part time, contract and home-based work. The new types of teams place special demands on leaders and their followers, demands that are over and above the more traditional challenges presented to teams and their leaders.

The types of teams — and the combinations of people and work practices within the teams — can be mind-boggling when you're used to more traditional teams where the leader and followers share the same workspace and see each other every day. Yet the special teams I describe in this chapter are the wave of the future, so don't be surprised when soon you find yourself leading one of these teams — if you're not already leading one of these new teams.

Leading in a virtual, hyper-competitive world demands flexibility, adaptability and special skills because special teams need to be led in different ways. Each special team has unique leadership challenges and demands and each requires skills in addition to those you need to lead traditional teams. For example: How do you lead followers who another leader also leads and who you seldom see or maybe never even meet in person?

In this chapter, I explain what the latest research and best practices have to say about leading special teams. You find out about supplementary skills that help you lead virtual, temporary, merged and mixed teams. I describe how to use technology to support these teams, how to build and keep the all-important communication channels open and how to get your special team off to a great start. I also look at how to wrap up your special team when and if the time comes. Finally, you discover the finer points of leading virtual meetings, particularly teleconferences and videoconferences.

Recognising the Challenges of Special Teams

In practice, the various types of special teams I describe in this chapter often overlap. You may find yourself leading, for example, a semi-virtual, mixed, temporary, matrix team. While temporary teams are established to achieve a specific goal and then disband, any of the other special teams can also be temporary — or permanent. They can all be virtual or actual, or a combination of virtual and actual. Special teams can also be mixed teams and/or matrix teams.

To simplify matters, I explain each category separately. First, I describe the four main types of special teams:

- **Merged teams:** These often are formed after an organisation takeover, merger or a major internal restructuring. Followers from once-competing marketing departments may combine into one new team as the result of a merger, for example. Or an organisation that's restructuring may contract out its day-to-day human resources functions and move one or two remaining HR professionals under the wing of the finance department and to a leader who is unfamiliar with their specialised skills. The result is that you face a group of followers who once competed but now must cooperate or a group of followers with entirely different specialisations and internal customers.

- **Mixed teams:** Spurred on by a shortage of labour, dual-income families with high mortgage repayments, the needs of organisations to reduce labour costs and the demand for flexible working conditions, teams are sometimes mixed to create new ways of working. Teams composed of a variety of members are appearing everywhere. You're likely to find yourself leading followers with different backgrounds and from different generations (see Chapter 17 on how to lead followers from different cultures, backgrounds and age groups). You're likely to see some followers regularly and others far less so.

Your mixed team can include full-time, part-time and casual followers, volunteer followers, followers who work from home some or all of the time and followers who work in other locations and even in other teams. Your mixed team can also include temporary followers and contractors, people you lead in name only and who may be highly skilled or specialised or unskilled.

✔ **Temporary teams:** These are often formed to complete a special project, solve a specific problem or create an innovative solution and then they disband. Although these teams are usually led by a full-time leader on a special, temporary assignment, team members are often part time and continue to report to their other leader for the rest of their work — teams where members report to more than one leader are called *matrix teams*.

When the project is specialised and complex, people from all over the world and even from other organisations are likely to be part of the team, so many temporary teams are also virtual teams.

✔ **Virtual teams:** Ten years ago, who would have thought that team members who have never met and who aren't even in the same hemisphere could achieve impressive results together? Today, team members across the globe do just that. Thanks to technology, team members can be in two places and even in two teams at once, work in familiar surroundings and cut down on expensive and time-consuming travel.

Virtual teams are made up of followers in different time zones, different countries and even different organisations who seldom or never meet face to face. Many are separated not only by time and distance but also by cultural, social and language differences (see Chapter 17 for information on how to lead cross-cultural teams). Sometimes these teams are set up for the long term and sometimes they exist just for a special project. Most members of virtual teams have expertise in different areas and may also be members of other teams and therefore have more than one leader.

Leading special teams

Cliques, mistrust, diversity, lack of proximity of team members, the 'newness' of special teams — all these factors are heightened in special teams and all these factors can drive any team apart. Paradoxically, these factors can be the potential downfall of special teams and also can be their potential strength. And here's the rub: The way you lead your special team largely determines which way your team is to be.

The more complex your team's goals, the more likely it is that your special team is made up of diverse members with different skill sets and specialisations; teams like this are known as *cross-functional teams*. As a result, team members speak and think in different 'languages' — the languages of their own functional specialisations. When your team is global, team members may literally speak and think in different languages and follow different cultural customs, too. This makes the potential for misunderstandings, miscommunication and conflict high.

Temporary teams, virtual teams and merged teams are almost always 'new' and the membership of mixed teams often comes and goes. Building a culture and guiding followers in long-standing teams is difficult enough; the job is much harder when the members may not know one another and harder still when the team is temporary or merged. Building (and keeping) a sense of team and commitment of team members to each other takes even more effort.

Building special teams

One way to quickly forge followers into a team is to set them a big challenge. This fulfils the deep need people have to be part of something worthwhile. Bring a bit of emotion in to really engage the new team and bind its members together. Then invite team members to share their ideas for rising to the challenge and making the challenge worthwhile for them as well as for the organisation. (For more on this subject, see the section 'Sustaining trust' later in this chapter.)

Agreeing early on to a clear and inviting team purpose, to clear goals and measures of success and to clear ground rules for working together points your team toward success. Get to know your followers and help them to get to know each other. A quick way to do this is to assign short projects to team members who don't know each other so they can work on the projects together.

As quickly as you can, create a team culture and norms and establish some team traditions. You need to make norms more explicit in special teams than you do in traditional teams (refer to Chapters 8 and 15 for more information on norms).

Special challenges of virtual teams

Leading virtually is not the same as leading face to face. Distance makes the job harder when you're building relationships and makes sweeping aside problems, difficulties and misunderstandings easier, clearing the way for disasters. However, these problems are not inevitable.

Building trust and creating open communications is essential. Find out about your followers, and help them find out about each other — as people, not just team-mates. Spend up to 50 per cent of your virtual team's early communications time discovering information about each other — families, hobbies, social activities and so on. This time spent together leads to a culture that acknowledges and discusses difficulties, slip-ups and misunderstandings. (See the section 'Leading by Supporting' later in this chapter.)

When you can't meet face to face often, create a team scrapbook every year, building it as the year progresses. Include a photo and brief paragraph about each team member, personal bits and pieces of news and team accomplishments. You can even include family and holiday snaps and put in something about a few key, interesting or quirky customers and suppliers and their feedback. The more team members know about each other, the more tolerant they can be toward each other's foibles and even errors.

Special challenges of temporary teams

When you unite a disparate team of individuals to achieve a single goal, it is critical that you create a common purpose, carefully plan its achievement and develop a series of milestones and success measures is critical (refer to Chapter 5 for more on this subject). Assigning particular responsibilities to team members is high on your list of priorities, too. When your temporary team is virtual or partially virtual, or when your team members are from around the organisation, take special care to develop relationships and open communication as soon as possible.

Split loyalties of team members are a concern in temporary teams, particularly when team members are assigned to the team part time and retain membership of, and duties in, their normal team. All of the other challenges special teams present to their leaders also apply to temporary teams. Here are some additional tips.

- ✔ Keep team members' other leaders informed about your team's progress and the progress of the people they loaned to your team. This lessens the temptation to keep pulling the individual off the temporary team and on to other work.
- ✔ Make sure that team members and their other leaders know how much the organisation and the team member stand to gain from their followers' participation.
- ✔ Negotiate in advance the amount of time team members can devote to your temporary team.

Special challenges of merged teams

Members of merged teams almost certainly speak different languages in terms of their culture, values and norms. Even when team members come together as a result of an internal reorganisation, they feel uncomfortable and bring their former team's subcultures, philosophies and ways of working with them.

The territorialities and suspicions that usually abound in merged teams result in a leader needing three top priorities. These priorities are

- ✔ To align team members to the organisation's values, vision, mission and goals, particularly in the case of teams merged as a result of a takeover or merger

- ✔ To make clear what you stand for (and what you won't stand for), since you're probably unknown to (and possibly distrusted by) a large portion of the team

- ✔ To unite your followers' very different cultures, values and norms into shared goals and a team purpose so each team follower is facing the same direction (see Chapter 5 to find out more about how to keep your followers facing in the same direction)

Be aware that many of the team members may bring a sense of grief over the loss of their former team and former team-mates who haven't been brought into the new team. Many may resent the new team (and its leader) that formed as a result of a takeover or merger, and most are likely to feel fearful for the future. You have lots of baggage to recognise and deal with when you lead a merged team.

Special challenges of mixed teams

Different types of followers in mixed teams have different expectations of you, their teams and the organisation and they demand different leadership from you in terms of the style of leadership you use and how often and even how you communicate with them. Whatever their expectations, however, all team members want to be — and feel like — active and effective members of the team and the organisation. Use your team purpose and the organisation's values, vision and mission to build a sense of identity and unity.

As with any team, establish clear measures of success and monitoring procedures but — unless you have a good reason not to do this — leave the methods up to each follower. Make sure your team members understand the workflow and who does what so they know which of their tasks can hold up others when not done well or on time. See that all members of the team know how to find the information they need, paying particular attention to the needs of casual and temporary followers and contractors.

Create opportunities for get togethers, both informal and work related, to give team members a chance to build relationships within the team and help forge a team identity and culture. Pay particular attention to give part-time team members a chance to build relationships across the organisation with people they rely on and who rely on them.

Involve all team members in meetings, whether they're virtual or actual meetings. If you hold an in-person meeting and one or two members can't attend, ask them to phone in and participate.

Special challenges of off-site followers

Telecommuters — off-site followers — present the same challenges as followers in other virtual teams and then some because these followers are mixed with on-site followers. The natural human tendency to let 'out of sight' become 'out of mind' is stronger for leaders in mixed teams because you see your on-site followers more than your off-site followers. When you're used to leading people who you can see, using a variety of other ways to build your relationship with your off-site followers and keeping up your contact with them is high on your list of priorities. Keep reminders in your diary if your need to have reminders.

Not feeling part of the team or included in the team drains motivation and, ultimately, followers' willingness to produce results. The extra care you take to communicate with 'invisible followers' — by telephone, email, instant messaging — on both task and personal matters, pays off. Keep them involved and up to date with the gossip (when you don't, the grapevine takes over and you lose control of the information network). Check in on your out-of-sight followers at least once a week just to pass on any news, see how they're going with their work and, generally, find out whether you can provide any information or other assistance. Resist any urge to get straight down to business. Begin your conversations with a bit of small talk, even with task-oriented followers.

Being comfortable with managing off-site followers by results (not time spent working) and leaving the way they work up to them is important. Set them a goal, agree timelines and other constraints and let them achieve the goal in their own way.

Train on-site followers in how to work with their off-site team-mates. They may hesitate to contact them at home for example, even though they're probably working and not sitting with their feet up watching re-runs of *Neighbours*. Every few months, meet with all your followers and discuss successes, goals for the next period, and any difficulties team members are experiencing. Provide an informal lunch so you can all enjoy a bit of down time together to maintain your important relationships. In between, keep your on-site followers up to date on the contributions and activities of their off-site team-mates.

Dialling into actual meetings

One of the worst forms of torture is dialling into an actual meeting and not being able to hear the other participants clearly. Remind those physically present of the virtual presence of other meeting members and ensure actual participants speak clearly into the microphone. Check frequently that your virtual colleague can hear everyone.

Special challenges of part-time and casual followers

Part-time and casual followers often have a lot of 'baggage' to overcome. In the past, they may have been seen as less committed (usually not the case — dedication and professionalism have nothing to do with hours spent on the job) and less able to produce. The evidence is just the opposite — half-time and casual followers are often able to produce two-thirds or three-quarters of the results of full-time followers because of the extra attention they bring to their tasks. Instead of falling for those old myths, realise that these followers offer your team skills, experience and knowledge that you probably don't otherwise have access to in these times of *follower deficit* — yes, that means a shortage of followers.

As you do with off-site followers, become used to managing part-time and casual followers by results and take special care to include them in social and task-related team events (including meetings). Communicate frequently with part-time and casual followers to keep them up to date and feeling part of the team.

Special challenges of temporary followers and contractors

Contractors and temporary followers can, like their part-time colleagues, suffer from the perception that they aren't committed to the team and its results. That perception is generally a furphy too. The loyalties of contractors and temporary followers generally lie with the specialised tasks these people do, so you can rely on their professionalism to do these tasks well. Think of temporary followers and contractors more as service providers, professionals, specialists and individuals rather than as followers.

Just because temporary followers and contractors may not be with you permanently and you don't lead them directly, don't ignore them. Be explicit about goals, work norms and other expectations and establish a relationship with them, however short it may be. You and your team benefit and your organisation as a whole benefits from the goodwill this generates.

Since temporary followers and contractors are likely to have wide experience with other organisations, have a coffee with them and pick their brains when their time with you is up: What did they enjoy about working with you and your team? What changes do they see may help the work flow or procedures? How do they describe your team? And, when temporary followers and contractors bring skills to your team that you need and are in short supply, suss out their availability and willingness to come back and work with your team in the future.

Gaining the Technology Advantage

Technology has advanced more in the past 30 years than it has in the past 2000, helping us to live and work faster, smarter and easier. You can manage just about everything a team needs to do electronically by creating a *platform* — an infrastructure that lets your far-flung team or temporary project team work together and share data seamlessly.

Shared *collaboration technology* — online workspaces, real-time application sharing, shared calendars and tasks lists — enable temporary project teams and virtual teams to work together quickly, creatively and flexibly. Your team can supplement its collaboration technology with other technology, such as instant messaging and SMS.

Every member of your far-flung team must use the same version of software. When you don't get that right, your team and its work become frustratingly slow and unnecessarily costly.

 Instant messaging (IM) enables team members to see when their colleagues, and you, are available and it is a great way for team-mates to share 'Eureka!' and 'Oh, No!' moments. Put everyone on your team on the same IM program to avoid creating IM cliques, and see that security is covered. Discuss and agree on some protocols to prevent IM constantly interrupting whatever team members are working on.

When you and your team members are not fully familiar with the advanced technologies you're likely to use, arrange training. Struggling through and figuring out technology as you go wastes precious time and energy.

 Many teams have found that email is a poor way to collaborate. Part of the reason for this is that one-on-one exchanges can cause others to feel left out, reducing trust and damaging the team's effectiveness (yet copying everyone on emails is overkill). Email also has poor documentation and storage features, making it hard to find information quickly.

Creating an online team room

A virtual work space that captures the team's ongoing work, which members visit at least daily, is essential for virtual teams and many temporary teams. Every document of substance generated by the team, decisions and the rationales behind them, commitments, schedules, a continually updated progress report — everything important to the team is always current, neatly categorised and accessible to all team members twenty-four hours a day, seven days a week through shared virtual work spaces.

Virtual team rooms increase understanding and trust within the team by giving team members a place to meet, discuss, solve problems, share ideas, monitor progress, keep themselves and each other up to date and build a sense of team. Virtual team rooms also build a valuable knowledge base, promoting continuous learning and improvement.

As the team leader, you manage the virtual team room, updating it and moderating online discussion threads. Build your team site by assigning a different, clearly labelled section to each aspect of the team's work, for instance:

- ✔ **Action plans:** These plans detail the steps the team is to take and which team members tick off as they complete each step.

- ✔ **Bulletin board:** This is where team members can post any problems and issues where other team members may be able to offer assistance.

- ✔ **Contact page:** This page contains each team member's contact information and professional information (experience, areas of expertise and so on) and personal profiles (hobbies, interests and so on).

- ✔ **Home page:** The opening or home page can show team members' photographs set out in a circle, like a clock face. This stresses equality and enables team members to identify themselves until they get to know each other — 'This is Kris at 3 o'clock'. Your home page can display other important information such as your team purpose and mission statement.

- ✔ **Key activities summary:** The summary documents what members have learned and the best practices relating to the activity.

- ✔ **Leader's blog:** This space allows leaders to share their thoughts, post team news and so on.

- ✔ **Meeting centre:** Here you find the information for teleconferences — notices of when teleconferences are being held, attendees, agendas, minutes, actions arising and so on.

✔ **Team goals and timelines:** These show everyone what's completed so far and what's yet to be completed.

✔ **Team responsibility chart:** Each team member has one of these charts.

✔ **Virtual discussion threads:** These are subjects for team discussion that are listed by the topic.

✔ **Working documents:** Organising these documents into clearly numbered versions (so team members don't mistakenly work on the wrong one) is important.

Making the most of threaded discussions

Team members can hold virtual conversations for problem solving, sharing information, generating ideas and options, developing activities and so on, through threaded discussions sections in their online team room, which leaders generally manage (although sometimes a team member volunteers to facilitate a thread in their area of specialisation or key responsibility). Organise online conversations by topic to make the conversations easy for followers to follow each thread.

Agree on protocols early. For example, agree on how quickly you need to respond to a question or thread when you have information (typically within a week). At the end of the time period, generally enough comments exist to warrant summarising what's been said, highlighting areas of agreement and disagreement (summarise topics that generate a lot of discussion more often). The thread initiator is usually responsible for the summary.

Before virtual meetings, ask team members to post their work progress electronically and check each other's reports to see their team-mates' progress. When a topic of a threaded discussion is coming up on an agenda, post links on both the thread and the agenda to encourage discussion before the meeting; and use the meeting time to discuss problems and disagreements, which are more effectively handled through conversation than in writing. (For more information on leading virtual meetings, see the section 'Leading Virtual Meetings' later in this chapter.)

Getting Your Special Team Up and Flying

Your mission, should you choose to accept it, is to forge a collection of strangers with little in common into a mutually supportive, successful team working together to achieve the team's purpose and goals.

Establishing trust is easier when 20 to 40 per cent of the team members already know each other. When team members aren't trained in the fine art of team working, get them some training as a priority. The more skilled the team members are in the following areas, the better your team can function:

- ✔ Appreciating others
- ✔ Building effective relationships and networking
- ✔ Clear communication
- ✔ Coaching
- ✔ Holding difficult conversations
- ✔ Resolving conflicts creatively

Make sure each team member is briefed on your organisation's strategy and values, too.

Although the members of special teams are often coming together for the first time, special teams are expected to begin producing results quickly, so pay special care and attention to getting your team started properly and up to speed quickly. Laying the groundwork for building trusting and cooperative relationships within your special team is your first critical task. Establishing a clear team purpose and clear team and individual goals is your next critical task. Your first few meetings are critical to achieving these outcomes.

Holding a launch meeting

A launch meeting that generates some excitement about the team and its goals gets a team off to a great start. You have three goals at a launch meeting:

- ✔ To formally welcome the members to the team and briefly explain your vision for the team, its goals and the timelines for achieving them
- ✔ To help team members begin getting to know each other professionally as well as on a more personal level, which makes subsequent meetings much easier and begins establishing the trust that your special team needs to succeed
- ✔ To set up ways of working together that can last for the lifetime of the team

Four types of team trust

Research has defined four types of trust that can be applied to leadership:

✔ **Deterrence-based trust:** This causes team members to do their work because they fear punishment if they don't do it.

✔ **Knowledge-based trust:** This develops when team members know each other well enough to predict each other's behaviours with confidence.

✔ **Contractual-based trust:** This type of trust occurs when team members know they can rely on each other to honour their commitments.

✔ **Identification-based trust:** Built on empathy and shared values, this type of trust arises when members identify with the team and with each other.

While traditional teams tend to move through these four types of trust sequentially, the type of trust established in special teams at the start usually sticks.

Start building trust

Trust develops in virtual teams differently than in teams where team members physically work together. Trust is established (or not established) more quickly when the team first forms. The first few electronic messages and the first team meeting are decisive in establishing which kind of trust becomes the norm for the team. Plan your messages and meetings ultra-carefully because when you fail to establish trust, low morale and poor performance can haunt your special team and affect your outcomes.

Building trust when you work with people in the flesh is easiest. When your team is fully or partially virtual, try to hold the launch meeting with a face-to-face meeting and create as many face-to-face opportunities as your budget can manage. These meetings bolster working relationships and help team members become familiar with each other's communication styles, nuances and foibles. That's not to say that teams that only meet virtually can't succeed — they can, but only when they are led well.

The less team members know each other, the more important it is to help them build relationships quickly. Helping team members find areas of commonality to build bonds based on mutual respect, trust and understanding is important too. At your launch meeting, ask team members to introduce themselves to each other, describing their

✔ Experiences gained from similar teams with which they worked

✔ Particular knowledge, experience, skills, and abilities they bring to the team

✔ Personal background information as well as outside interests and hobbies

✔ Working style

These introductions and sharing of descriptions serve these important functions. They

✔ Begin the process of trust-building between team members

✔ Build confidence that the right people are on board and able to contribute meaningfully to the team

✔ Convey information about what each team member can contribute

✔ Generate rapport and respect among the team members

✔ Foster cooperation by providing a sense of a shared history that substitutes for the actual shared history of long-standing teams

✔ Help the team identify and make best use of individual strengths and experience to help the team succeed

Warn team members you intend to go through this exercise of introduction and descriptions so that they can consider what to say beforehand and won't be caught unawares; you want genuine and beneficial answers. Include yourself in the introductory process too and, when everyone has introduced themselves, highlight each individual's expertise for the rest of the team.

Don't spend so much time on the getting-to-know-you part of a meeting that members form the impression the team is more about fun than results. As leader, you have a fine line to walk. Make the task at hand the main point of your first few meetings and establish each team member's roles and responsibilities. Then, once the task is humming along, switch your attention to strengthening relationships.

Please don't take offence

A friend of mine has led many a temporary virtual project team and always includes this information about herself during introductions: 'I'm not a touch typist so my emails are short and to the point. Don't take offence from this — I'm not being rude!' Her virtual followers then understand why she isn't very 'chatty' in her emails.

Establish a clear task

A team can't start producing until its individual members are reaching for common goals. After the opening introductions, turn the attention of your meeting to your team goals. Review what the team is expected to accomplish and the success measures and key milestones that are going to show that you have accomplished your goal.

Then get down to the nitty gritty: Clarify your expectations regarding work methods, operating guidelines and parameters and how you want the team members to work together. Make your expectations about performance and behaviours ultra-clear.

Brief the team about the extent to which you plan to involve them in decisions that affect the final outcome of the project, its overall timeline and the work of other team members. Ask that any team members with a decision or issue that affects the whole team bring the matter to you with options and recommendations; and explain that you expect team members to make decisions if they have the skills, knowledge and experience to make them.

At the close of the launch meeting, ask team members to begin thinking about their own key result areas and measures of success. Meet with each of them individually, virtually or actually, to establish a clear role, responsibilities, objectives and outputs — their *deliverables* — along with agreed check points and follow-up procedures.

At your next team meeting, ask each team member to outline their key responsibility areas (KRAs) and measures of success to the others so that everyone in the team understands each other's roles and goal responsibilities. Then plan the team's work against its goals and establish timelines and the resources the team needs to achieve its goals. Graph the timelines and milestones so your team members can more easily chart their progress.

Now the time is right for your *risk analysis* — consider what can go wrong so that you can avoid slip-ups before they happen. Planning the team's work together like this ensures all team members understand what's needed and feel ownership and accountability for achieving their goals.

Once you're clear about the resources your team needs, set about obtaining them. When you fail to get your team the resources it needs, enthusiasm quickly fizzles and efforts fade away.

Keeping up to date with regular reports

A helpful type of report is a weekly, oral, half-hour update known as the *Two-Pager*, covering

✔ What the team planned to do this week

✔ What the team did

✔ Where the team members are now

✔ Where the team members are on special risks and issues

✔ What the team members are going to do next week

This type of report keeps your team members current and their energies directed at the next phase of their work. You can discuss these points with your team members individually, or with your entire team, depending on what your team is working on.

Saying goodbye

If and when your special team disbands, capture lessons learned for the next special team you lead. Conduct a team brainstorming session to collect ideas about what worked and what went wrong. Look for what to do differently to prevent similar glitches from occurring and what to keep doing to ensure similar successes in future teams.

Highlight and celebrate the achievements of the team as a whole and of individual team members with a celebratory conference call or an actual get together. Do something special — present everyone with a cake, a bottle of bubbly or, in global teams, different mementos in different locations, depending on their cultures.

Offer feedback to team members individually to help them in the next special team they join. Finally, write a report assessing how the team performed, regarding budget, managing risks, deadlines, team work and so on. Acknowledge the team's efforts and individual team member's contributions.

Leading by Supporting

Although most special teams depend on technology, special teams depend even more on the human touch. You don't necessarily need to be an expert on whatever your special team is doing to keep your team humming along productively, but you do need to be an expert in building relationships. In fact, as the leader of a special team, relationship management is one of your key result areas. (Refer to Chapter 4 for more information on developing your key result areas and Chapter 9 for information on working well with everyone.)

It's not an exaggeration to say that without communication, trust and clear goals, special teams can't function. Although this rule applies to traditional teams, too, building and maintaining communication and trust and respecting the usual protocols that go along with trust are vital in special teams.

Communicating intensively

Developing communication channels that ensure a free, fast and easy flow of information in all directions and keeping them lubricated takes extra work in special teams. Clear guidelines — which make airing difficulties and dissension safe — and staying in frequent contact are mandatory.

Leaders and team members must be clear and thoughtful communicators, too. You set the example, you and your team agree the 'rules', but you still want to bring good communicators on board.

Establish open lines of communication

Agree on clear communication guidelines early in the life of your special team. Include arrangements for written, electronic and face-to-face (if relevant) communication for different aspects of the team's work, such as when to copy in everyone on the team and when not to bother and how quickly to respond to queries. Develop a set of code subject titles and an importance flagging system to indicate the nature, importance and urgency of messages you send each other to help everyone decide whether to read them now or file them to read later. These guidelines also help overcome differences in communication styles between the team members.

If team members are widely scattered and/or diverse in terms of backgrounds, languages, culture and/or specialisations, adopt a common language for the team. If necessary, compile a glossary of technical terms and figures of speech that may not be familiar to everyone.

Team members need to speak up about any reservations, doubts or misgivings they may have throughout the life of the team. Tabling setbacks and looming problems without delay is also important. Right from the start, make dissension safe and raise differences of opinion early.

Maintain open lines of communication

The further away your followers are and the less often you see them in person, the more you need to communicate. You're the critical conduit between your special team and the organisation. Become the primary source of information about the team's progress and the organisation as a whole to defuse the rumour mill. Listen as well as talk, so that you can find out your followers' concerns and deal with them.

Delivering small chunks of information frequently rather than in one occasional big hit not only keeps the team informed and up to date but also establishes a sense of connectedness. An online team room that is always open also helps spread information (refer to the section 'Creating an online team room' earlier in this chapter).

Welcome different views as ways to explore ideas and options and use these views to generate a full discussion and reach a common view that includes everyone's points. Tacit agreement isn't good enough — find out specifically whether everyone agrees by asking 'What do you think about this?'

Use threaded discussions, electronic bulletin boards and your leader's blog to communicate with your team members between meetings. Speak to team members individually between team meetings using a variety of channels (email, telephone, SMS, instant messaging, online chats, web conferencing and so on.) You can phone team members regularly to check in and catch up, too. You may need to phone team members daily when the team is at a critical juncture and only weekly when the team is sailing along smoothly. Successful leaders avoid *leadership by crisis* — only talking to their team members when a problem arises.

Successful leaders also respond quickly to emails and return phone messages promptly. The more remote your team members are, the more you need to be available, so they don't think they're working alone, with no support. Inform your followers that your door is always open — metaphorically — even though team members working in different places can't actually see that open door.

You can stay in touch with the team's progress by monitoring and participating in the virtual team room and by tracking the team's and individual team member's performances against success measures. Help the team see its progress, too, by regularly plotting the team's progress showing its actual, against its planned, achievements.

Part of your job as a leader is to keep your followers and the team concentrating on the task. Providing plenty of positive, enthusiastic and helpful feedback is a great way to achieve this aim, but don't depend just on email and the virtual team room — give your support and feedback personally — and often.

Provide constructive or corrective feedback without criticism when it's needed. Use phrases such as 'This isn't working — let me explain why' and 'That didn't meet our needs. What can I do to help?'

Sustaining trust

Team members initially have a tendency towards excessive politeness because they don't know each other well and trust hasn't built up to assure them that disagreeing and airing problems is safe. However, trust grows quickly as relationships between team members build, as team members communicate frequently and openly discuss dissension and difficulties. Trust grows still further as team members see they can rely on each other to deliver quality deliverables on time.

To earn and keep the trust you need from your team members, base your actions and decisions on values and principles, not expediency. Keep your agreements and, if you must break an agreement, explain why and promptly renegotiate a new agreement.

Leading by results

Monitoring results is different in special teams, where the priority for leaders and followers shifts from seeing and being seen to outcomes. Your followers' results are really all you have because you can't see whether many of them — those working in other places — are beavering away at their tasks. (Becoming used to working in different places can be difficult for some leaders and followers.)

If you haven't already, shift your mindset from observing followers as they work to measuring their outcomes. Develop a clear way to recognise achievements so that followers know how to measure their successes. Agree how often and in what format you expect to receive progress reports.

Special teams often operate in a state of flux, so be flexible and stay adaptable. When changing circumstances affect your team's goals, deadlines or budgets, obtain written agreements from the people who matter.

Leading Virtual Meetings

Thanks to teleconferences, videoconferences, multimedia conferences and your desktop computer, you can meet with your team in real time, speeding up your ability to make decisions, solve problems and achieve results. Yes, technology can be the special team leader's friend — yet technology also simultaneously creates new leadership challenges.

Beware the following pitfalls that can affect the quality of virtual meetings:

- ✔ Communication is more difficult because the body language that helps people interpret and understand meaning is zero in teleconferences and limited in online, video and multimedia conferences.

- ✔ Lack of, or limited, visual elements in virtual meetings also make it easier for participants' attention to wander.

- ✔ Speakers can feel as though they are speaking into a void at virtual meetings.

- ✔ Speakers don't actually know who is paying attention unless the meeting is an online videoconference.

- ✔ Virtual meetings can lack the level of psychological satisfaction that an actual meeting provides unless the meetings are very well led.

Clarifying the general principles

Leading and participating in virtual meetings is similar to actual meetings with a few added complications. (Refer to Chapter 13 for general points on leading meetings.) Luckily, you can overcome many of those complications by establishing crystal-clear guidelines from the outset. (When new team members join, take the time to brief them on the guidelines privately before their first virtual team meeting.)

Develop procedures for gaining the floor, asking, acknowledging and dealing with questions and develop some ground rules for general meeting etiquette, such as:

- ✔ Be extremely courteous and tactful because you don't have the advantage of body language to help people interpret your comments.

- ✔ Don't hold side conversations; when you must speak to someone in the room, use the mute button.

- ✔ Don't shift and move about in your chair or tap pencils, shuffle feet and so on because the microphone picks up these sounds as distracting background noise.

- ✔ Never interrupt a speaker.

- ✔ Speak clearly and avoid slang, jargon and other expressions that may not be familiar to everyone.

- ✔ When you fail to hear a comment, say so; others probably didn't hear the comment either.

Accents can be tricky so be sure to speak clearly and to listen sharply when meeting virtually with people whose first language is not English. Help non-native English speakers feel comfortable so that they don't deprive the group of their experience. You can welcome these speakers by opening meetings with a quick *go-around* asking everyone to share a work-related win since your last virtual meeting or to share an anecdote about a recent event in their lives, either work related or personal. These stories warm up the participants, give non-native English speakers a chance to tune in their English 'ears' and 'thoughts', and bring them into the swing of speaking English. This exercise also reminds the native English speakers not to use slang and not to speak too quickly and helps switch on everyone's cultural sensitivities. As a final benefit, the sharing builds relationships as team members learn more and more about each other with each meeting.

Here are some tips to make the virtual meetings you lead fabulously fruitful:

- ✔ Begin with something unexpected or some news so that meetings are special and no-one wants to miss them. Then move on to a topic that gets people talking, giving each member a minute or two to comment.

- ✔ Coach any particularly quiet team members between meetings to help them speak up; ask for their opinions, thoughts, experiences, ideas and so on during the meeting and, if they remain non participators, consider replacing them.

- ✔ Include a list of participants and their locations, contact details and job roles with the agenda and any other papers you send out before the meeting until the team members get to know each other. (This isn't necessary when you use an online meeting centre.)

- ✔ Show the start and finish times on the meeting's agenda in the local times of the participants so that participants are aware of the time of day in other meeting locations.

- ✔ Take short breaks when the meeting runs longer than an hour.

- ✔ Try to balance the number of participants from each location whenever you can.

- ✔ Weigh up the mood of the meeting occasionally by going around the participants in the different sites and asking how they're going or whether they have any questions or comments they'd like to add.

When some team members work at the same location, ask them to participate from their desks on different phones or computers rather than clustered around a speaker phone or conference room video camera. This encourages equal attention to the meeting from everyone because when you have some team members face to face and others virtual, the virtual people fade as the face-to-face participants start talking to each other. The remote participants are left wondering what's going on because they can't follow.

Leading worthwhile teleconferences

Because you can't see everyone in a teleconference, forgetting who is present is easy. Until you get to know each other's voices, ask team members, particularly those new to teleconferences, to draw a map to keep fully tuned in, writing the names of people on the call on a piece of paper and keeping the piece of paper in front of them. It often helps to draw the map as if the participants were sitting around an actual conference table.

Using instant messaging to hold side conversations during teleconferences can be very helpful (silence your key strokes or use the mute button, though). Instant messaging can be a bit like passing notes at school, only better — you can send messages such as, 'The answer to the question you were just asked is ...'.

Here are some other tried-and-tested ways to ensure your teleconference is a success:

✔ Ask participants to inform the meeting when they need to leave the room so other participants don't address comments to them and receive no response.

✔ Ask people to say their names when they speak and the names of those to whom their questions or comments are addressed.

✔ Before you begin the meeting proper, announce all the participants by name and ask them to say a few words of introduction (when they don't know each other well) or just say hello so people can orient themselves to the voices of the other participants.

✔ Have participants slow down their speech or repeat what they say when some people indicate they didn't understand.

✔ Keep your attention from wandering by taking clear notes of who is saying what.

✔ Know who is to call the others in case the connection breaks. When you regularly hold teleconferences, make this a standard procedure.

✔ Sit up straight and wear a pleasant expression — the other participants can sense your body language from your voice even though they may not be able to see you.

Leading productive videoconferences

Video and multimedia conferences, conducted in a conference room with special equipment or using inexpensive *Voice over Internet Protocols* (VoIP) from desktop computers, are rapidly becoming the way of the future. Follow these pointers when you're leading and participating in these types of conferences:

- Ask participants to put large name cards in front of them when they don't know each other or until they get to know each other.
- Bear in mind that a time delay can exist between the spoken word and when others hear it.
- Don't lean into the camera and toward listeners because this position can make you look aggressive; sit up straight, with your face straight to the camera (not at an angle) and your head aligned over your hips.
- Know who's operating the camera (when you're holding a videoconference) and know what's to happen if the connection breaks.
- Maintain eye contact with the camera (and therefore the other participants) and use the monitor to see the other participants.
- Mind your body language — other participants may be able to see you even when you're not speaking.
- Try to select wide-angle shots rather than close-ups. Stay two to three metres back from the camera.
- Use slower and smaller gestures than you normally do to avoid creating distractions.
- Wear plain, solid colours except white, which can be glaring; red, which can bleed; and black, which can make you disappear or look like a corpse. Also avoid small designs, patterns, plaids or stripes, which the camera distorts and which can be disconcerting to others. When your video has a monitor that enables you to preview your image, do so.

 Take minutes during multimedia conferences so people can see them on their screens and can comment and correct any errors or omissions as the meeting progresses. This also means you can post accurate minutes in your virtual team room as soon as the meeting ends.

Multimedia conferences

Also known as *data conferencing*, multimedia conferences are videoconferences that allow collaborative computing. The technology has an additional window that displays the data file so that participants can simultaneously exchange and manipulate Windows-based data to exchange, work on or view a computer application during the videoconference. Participants can, for example, collaboratively edit a document or spreadsheet, view a presentation or update computer-aided design drawings.

Chapter 17

Leading Across Cultures and Across the Globe

*O*ne fact is for sure — as a leader in the 21st century, you're likely to lead a wide-ranging group of followers. For example, in Australia, followers may be drawn from 160 ethnic groups speaking many languages and may belong to three distinct generations. A similar mix applies to New Zealand. These people have different religious and educational backgrounds, different values and abilities, and different literacy and numeracy skills. Because of different marital, carer and parental statuses, they have different personal-life commitments affecting how much and how often they can or are willing to be a follower. The one-size-fits-all approach to leading doesn't work Down Under.

The variety of differences in backgrounds and attitudes means that miscommunication and misunderstandings, wrong assumptions, problems, irritations and conflicts can mushroom and fester. Smart leaders know they can't afford the luxury of accepting only followers like themselves — and anyway, they wouldn't find enough followers that were the same as them.

Leading a smorgasbord of followers can be a nightmare or can be fun and rewarding. The result depends on how you, as a leader, view the situation. You can try to force your followers into little pigeonholes of similar behaviours and ways of working, or you can reap the benefits of drawing on their differences.

This chapter gives you the tools you need to make the most of diverse followers. I describe how to lead young people just entering the workforce and older people getting ready to retire and how to lead the knowledge workers that are the engine of the New Zealand and Australian economies. Finally, I turn to leading followers from different cultures.

Leading in a Diverse World

No doubt your followers are a mixed bunch. (When you're leading a diverse group of followers who live in another country or countries, and you're leading them remotely, refer to Chapter 16 for advice on how to deal with followers who work separately from you.) However different your followers are from you and from each other, each needs to feel secure and respected. Followers can't follow when they're busy figuring out how to fit in, looking over their shoulders, trying to protect themselves physically or psychologically or tuning out unpleasant comments or remarks. No matter who they are, what they do, where they're from or how different they are, people can't produce their best when they feel uneasy and unappreciated. Followers need and have a right to know that they as individuals and their contributions and potential contributions are understood and valued.

Diversity is the best way to inject creativity and innovation into your team. A variety of followers gives your team the ability to tap into a range of perspectives and knowledge and experience bases, and generate new ways of working, solving problems and meeting customer needs. That's why, given the right leadership, diverse teams out-perform *homogeneous* teams (for more about leading teams of people with similar backgrounds, refer to Chapter 15).

To benefit from diversity, you and your team members need to *value* differences, not merely tolerate them. Developing a reputation as a leader and developing a team that welcomes diversity helps you to attract the types of followers you need.

Because communication is such an important part of everything you do as a leader, begin by paying attention to the subtleties of communication inside your diverse team. You can smooth relationships by communicating in ways your followers understand and in ways that are similar to the ways they communicate. Watch for the nuances of body language, gaze and intonation and adjust yours to be more in tune and therefore less jarring.

Notice what makes different followers comfortable and uncomfortable. For example, vague instructions may make some followers uncomfortable, so give them precise instructions; some followers may speak more quietly than others, so drop your own volume a bit when you speak to them.

Notice how followers from different cultures deal with issues, such as authority and differences of opinion, and take their approaches into account during team and individual meetings.

Here are some other ways to gain the diversity advantage:

- ✔ **Be accommodating.** Followers with commitments outside work — for example, carers of elderly parents or young children — appreciate flexibility, such as flexitime and telecommuting, part-time working and job sharing (for more on these types of working, refer to Chapter 16).
- ✔ **Be flexible in your thinking.** Consider individual requests on their merit, consider unusual solutions and accept different styles of working.
- ✔ **Have a multi-faith calendar.** Encourage followers to mark and celebrate events together and learn from each other's cultures.
- ✔ **Look for similarities.** Don't concentrate on differences between your followers — similarities are the base on which to build your team culture.

Leading the Generations

If you're leading more than a handful of followers, you're probably also leading three distinct generations. Although not every individual in each generation is the same, people in the same generation have more in common with each other than they do with people in other generations.

Differing abilities

Followers have different intellectual and physical abilities, nervous and emotional conditions and injuries and illness that can restrict activities and speech. The range of abilities isn't surprising when you consider that 15 per cent of the population has a disability. In fact, you yourself have an 18 per cent chance of becoming disabled at some time during your working life (a disability is considered to be a physical or mental impairment or restriction in activities or participation due to health conditions.)

Followers with disabilities can contribute significantly to your team. Studies show that these followers have above-average productivity and retention rates and below-average absenteeism. They have a genuine desire to appreciate the value and benefits, both social and economic, which flow from participating in the workforce.

Generally, leaders can expect that most followers who grew up in the same era, in the same circumstances with the same social and global events shaping their thinking share similar values, beliefs, ways of working and motivations. You can also conclude that followers of the same generation share similar expectations about what they want from you, their leader, from their organisation, and from their lives.

Leading Baby Boomers

Born between 1946 and 1964, the *Baby Boomers* are your older followers whose life experiences often enable them to grasp the wider tasks as well as the details. Life and work experience help Baby Boomers think through problems, decisions and difficult situations calmly. Brought up to consider the needs of others, Boomers are reliable and adaptable followers. Baby Boomers are also willing to adjust in order to fit into the team and the organisation (whereas younger followers often expect a team and an organisation to adjust to suit them).

Because inductive reasoning and spatial orientation skills peak in a person's 50s and verbal abilities and verbal memory peak in a person's 60s, the life experience of Baby Boomers, combined with their brain power, enables Boomers to apply their skills more effectively than many younger followers can. All of this makes Baby Boomers potentially valuable mentors to younger members of your team.

Although they tend to resist change, Baby Boomers follow directions more readily than younger followers (who, with their fresh eyes and prove-it-to-me attitude, examine instructions and procedures to see whether they're the most effective or efficient way to do a job — and often uncover better approaches as a result).

Boomers are beginning to retire, making those older workers still with your team valuable assets because younger workers aren't replacing the retirees in enough numbers. Fortunately, your followers in their late 40s and older are less likely to move on than younger followers. Boomers thinking about retiring can be enticed to stay by offering flexibility (for example, part-time work, working remotely some or all of the time, a career break to assess whether they want to retire, phased retirement that gradually reduces the number of days they work or working one month a quarter). Offer Boomers interesting and challenging assignments and duties that recognise and make the most of their experience, skills and abilities and continue training them to show you're interested in updating their skills and consider they have a relevant future in the organisation.

Leading Generation X

Born between 1965 and 1979 to overworked parents, *Generation X* followers are the first generation to grow up with both parents working or to grow up in single-parent families as children of divorce. Also called the *Peter Pan generation*, Xers don't see themselves as adults until their late 20s and so many are only starting their own families in their early to mid 30s.

Xers aren't as intimidated by authority as Boomers and are more comfortable with female leaders than the older Boomers. And, unlike the change-resistant Boomers, Xers have a go at adapting to change. Resourceful, individualistic and self-reliant, Xers are more comfortable with technology than Boomers, too. They're not big readers, though, so when you need to train them, give them information in small, easily digestible chunks and use lots of graphics to convey key points.

Xers are casual in their dress and communication style and slightly cynical, having seen their parents work hard for little thanks; they don't want the same for themselves. Instead, Xers want to enjoy their jobs but know that enjoying their lives is important, too. Your Gen X followers who put in long hours only do so for limited periods and they expect adequate compensation for their sacrifices.

Less motivated by money and more by personal satisfaction, Generation Xers see themselves as free agents and want to grow and learn to increase their marketability. They don't expect lifelong employment with one organisation, but, before leaving a job, they try to change work situations when they're not happy — so listen carefully to your Gen X followers' suggestions and complaints.

Generation X followers want you to provide learning opportunities through job rotation and varied assignments and are drawn to leaders who provide lots of feedback and a fast, stimulating pace. Give them goals and explain the constraints but don't tell them how to do their jobs. Don't micro-manage your Generation X followers and remember to ask for their opinions. Recognise their contributions in informal ways, such as with free days off.

Leading Generation Y

The first generation raised on the Internet, computers and interactive technology, *Generation Yers*, born between 1980 and 1995, are already in the workforce. Intelligent, self-confident and motivated, these offspring of the most age-diverse group of parents ever and the most coddled and confident generation ever, are also the most formally educated generation ever.

Having been entertained and kept busy by their dual-career or single parent parents since they were toddlers, your youngest followers are likely to be stimulus junkies who don't know how to be still. They spend their money on travel, clothes and entertainment, go into debt and don't invest. Spoiled, hedonistic, materialistic and self-absorbed, your socially conservative youngest followers grew up in good times and think they're entitled to wealth and success just for showing up. In fact, leaders often complain that the Yers want the money and the perks but on their own terms. Unlike the Boomers, Yers are not concerned with their leader's or organisation's needs but expect you to bend the rules to suit them and meet all their requests.

No-one appears to have explained to the millions of Aussie and Kiwi Yers — also known as *Millennials* — about short-term sacrifice for long-term gain. Their parents just gave them what they wanted because they were too busy to explain why they couldn't have it or didn't need whatever it was they demanded. As a result, Yers in general tend to be short term in their thinking and, consequently, impatient with strategy and planning. So when you communicate rules, policies and strategies, make sure that they're practical and necessary and, when the rules, policies and strategies are important, explain them and the rationale behind them clearly.

Before these young followers agree to join your team, expect them to have a look at the values of your organisation and team — Yers have enough self-confidence to want to know whether they'll *enjoy* the jobs, not whether they can *do* the jobs. They want to work for socially responsible organisations in non-hierarchical, egalitarian set-ups. They highly value work–life balance and job interest and see jobs as a series of stepping stones across organisations that can progress their careers. Yers don't want to commit to an organisation long term. They're not into vertical career paths as much as they're into training and opportunities. They want to try their hand at a variety of assignments and challenging tasks that give them a real sense of purpose and achievement.

Gen Y followers see adults, including their leaders, as people who help them solve their problems. They want a coach, not a boss. Yet, because of their inexperience, Yers need your supervision, structure and attention. Mentor, guide and support them, give them lots of positive feedback and recognition, show appreciation for a job well done and take the time to give them lots of informal reviews and chats. Help them learn to deal with difficult people and authority figures, who can intimidate them, and be sensitive to conflict between Your Gen X and Gen Y followers.

Expect your young followers to question everything you and they do. They don't question to challenge your authority but because they're curious; they want to understand how what they're doing fits into the larger project and how what they do makes a contribution to the team or organisation or world.

Your Gen Y followers want to be connected to their jobs and they expect state-of-the-art equipment, lots of variety and interaction and workplace flexibility, continuous learning and freedom to try new methods. When you don't provide these opportunities, Yers are likely to be off faster than you can blink. Similarly, when they feel you're ignoring them, they pick up their Blackberries and move on — they won't try to change what they don't like or even complain — just leave.

Millennials are easily bored so keep them moving and learning, feeling tested and feeling a sense of belonging. This stimulation can retain their interest and keep them on your team for more than two or three years. Give them responsibility as a mark of your trust and faith in their abilities.

Generation Y followers are generally fast learners who love change (not just trying to adapt to change or resist it) and they're usually enterprising, creative and good at innovating and finding ways to improve things. They're also good team players and value belonging to a mixed, diverse, sociable, fun, happy team. Build a team culture that says: 'This is work, not play' to keep Yers productive, not just having fun.

Your youngest followers tend to think they know everything, so manage their egos while you see that they get enough of the right training to contribute meaningfully to your team. Involve them when you're training them, don't just talk at them. Since they're probably pragmatists who don't muck around, don't bother trying to show them something that isn't relevant to what they're doing or has no practical application or value.

Many leaders are reluctant to tell Gen Y followers that their performances aren't up to standard — they're afraid the Yers may spit their dummies and leave. But compromising your performance expectations is a mistake. Approach performance managing or correcting a Gen Y follower as an exercise in coaching and helping them to gain new skills.

Leading Knowledge Workers

Nearly 40 per cent of workers today are knowledge workers. As a leader, you're a knowledge worker yourself. (Most knowledge workers can work from anywhere — far north Queensland, China, India or the Antarctic. When your knowledge followers are remote, refer to Chapter 16.)

Described as the horses that pull the plough of economic progress, workers who think for a living — *knowledge workers* — are essential to modern economies, such as those of Australia and New Zealand. But how do you know if your knowledge followers are pulling their full weight? Their work is intangible and often invisible and they use their experience and expertise to make judgement calls, to improvise and to team up with other specialists inside and outside your team. They often work off site and even when you can see them, knowing whether they're sitting thinking or just sitting is difficult to judge.

Knowledge workers demand high levels of autonomy and thrive when working with others in their fields. You may know as much about their tasks as they do and work alongside them as well as lead them. Or you may not know much about the tasks they do and primarily be a supportive leader who understands their world without being fully part of it. If that's the case, you can still acquire the resources they need and translate what they do and sing their praises to the rest of the organisation.

Either way, the best way to lead knowledge followers is to lead from underneath, supporting them and helping them (refer to Chapter 2 for more on leading from underneath). Think of yourself not so much as their leader but as their coach, developing, mentoring and training them. Give them quiet spaces where they can think without distractions and the freedom to get on with their jobs without worrying about organisational red tape. Give them the communication tools they need (for example, instant messaging) and other technologies to help them network effectively so they can find and share valuable information. And give them the equipment, funds and other resources they need.

Put what your knowledge followers do into the context of the entire organisation because your knowledge followers want to feel they're contributing to a larger whole and that their work and the work of their organisation is meaningful.

Assign projects they find personally interesting and challenging. Give them access to information and opportunities to demonstrate their skills through delegation and involvement to prevent the problems that come when knowledge followers are bored or not challenged. Agree on meaningful measures of success so you can assess your knowledge followers on results.

Leading Followers from Other Cultures

In Australian organisations, one in four followers was born overseas and many of them come from non–English-speaking countries. They come from various social, cultural and economic backgrounds and diverse circumstances, from privileged to poverty-stricken and war-ravaged countries. Some have experienced horrors that born-and-bred Australians and New Zealanders can't even begin to imagine.

New Zealand followers are a similarly mixed group — 33 per cent are of non-Pākehā (non-European) background and include Māori, Asian, Pacific Islander, Middle Eastern and African followers.

A mixed bag of followers holds the potential for all sorts of situations, from the fun of learning about different cultures and customs to the challenges of learning to understand people with belief systems very different from one's own.

Sometimes, people are so immersed in their own cultures that they don't even notice their culture — it's just the way life 'is'. They consider themselves normal, and *others* different, with their different ways of looking at the world and different ways of expressing themselves. To people whose understanding of other cultures is limited, those *others* can be scarily tidy or horrifyingly disorganised, bafflingly quiet and secretive or garishly loud and pushy.

When people consider their own culture to be the 'norm', they usually see other cultures and people from other cultures in general terms — as *stereotypes* — and in a critical light. People who think in terms of stereotypes assume they know why someone says or does something or what people's intentions are, based on their own culture. This perception leads to misunderstandings based on lack of knowledge, which in turn lead to conflict. Clearly, stereotyping is not an ingredient of high-performing teams.

Leaders often learn from their followers and this is never more true than when you're leading followers from other cultures. You're enriched by the gift of another set of lenses through which to view the world.

Responses to different cultures

Culture is so ingrained that it appears to be common sense and universal. That's why cultural differences can be so puzzling and even frightening. Here's a range of responses you may see in your followers when they're joined by a team member from another culture. These responses begin with the negative and move toward the positive:

✔ Xenophobia: Are fearful

✔ Ethnocentrism: Feel superior

✔ Forced assimilation: Become like us

✔ Segregation: Remain separate

✔ Acceptance: Get together, accommodate and build relationships

✔ Celebration: Value other cultures for their differences and the fun, excitement and new ways of thinking they bring

Leading a team of followers with different cultural backgrounds makes an enjoyable, stimulating and often innovative and creative team environment once you get all the followers facing the same direction and pulling together. Building understanding by addressing and discussing cultural differences and different ways of working prevents your followers from dismissing or even distrusting each other and helps them appreciate and value each other's differences and the different contributions everyone can make.

Understand your own culture first

If you understand your own culture, you're more able to see your culture and other cultures as they are — just different ways of thinking and behaving, based on different ways of looking at the world, yourself and the people around you. The more you understand your own culture and how strongly your culture influences your beliefs and shapes your behaviour and interactions, the more you can understand and successfully lead and work with people from other cultures. Here are some cultural questions and tips to help you become aware of cultural differences:

✔ Do you give a short, firm handshake or a lengthy, limp handshake? If you're a polite African, you probably give a limp handshake that can last several minutes, but if you're from a European culture, you probably go for strong handshakes that last only a few seconds.

✔ Do you shake your head from shoulder to shoulder or nod your head to indicate agreement? What you do depends whether or not you're from India.

✔ Do you think crossing your ankle over your knee with the sole of your foot or shoe pointing towards another person is okay? You wouldn't do that if you were from the Middle East or some parts of Asia.

✔ Do you think slurping your food is okay? Or speaking on your mobile phone during meetings is okay if you stand up and go to the back of the room? You probably do if you're Asian and you probably don't if you're from Down Under.

✔ How do you beckon someone? With your palm facing down and moving your fingers in a scratching motion towards you? Or with your palm up and fingers moving towards you? You guessed it — the answer depends on where you grew up.

✔ Would you pass something to someone using your left hand? You wouldn't if you were Muslim or from Thailand.

✔ When you have a runny nose, do you prefer to sniff or to blow your nose? How you handle this depends on where you're from: if you're Asian, you probably consider sniffing more hygienic and acceptable; if you're an Aussie or Kiwi, you probably blow.

✔ If an older fellow leader were assigned an unpleasant job by your mutual leader, would you try to do the job for him because he's older, or would you let him get on with it because your leader assigned the job to him rather than to you? Your approach depends on whether you're from a Pacific island or a Māori or an Anglo-Aussie or Pākehā.

Cultural differences are more than just personality traits. Although differences within cultures exist, greater differences exist between cultures and these differences persist over generation. Whether you're leading followers from other cultures, working with other leaders from other cultures or working with suppliers or customers from other cultures, awareness of and sensitivity to the culture they come from greatly strengthens your hand.

The following sections analyse important cultural differences, followed by some tips for leading followers with English as a second language. Think of each of the these cultural differences as scales, with some cultures falling to one end of scale, other cultures towards the other end and still other cultures lying more in the middle.

Go out of your way to build trust and help your followers value their cultural differences. Include all your followers in all team activities, formal and informal. Get to know each follower as an individual and look for similarities and common interests to help build bridges between yourself, your followers and their team-mates.

Leading followers who deal with uncertainty differently

Various leadership tendencies are applied to different cultures that find their sources in social, religious or other behaviours common to certain countries or groups of countries. For example, generally speaking, Latin American, Middle Eastern, Japanese, Russian and Southern European cultures are high in *uncertainty avoidance*, which means they tend to prefer certainty, order and agreement.

Generally, people from these areas believe there is a single best way to solve a problem or achieve a goal and they expect their leader to know that solution or how to achieve that goal. They look to their leader to reduce uncertainty by providing correct answers and expertise, precise objectives, a clear structure to fit into. They also appreciate rules to tell them how to behave and what to do in different situations. Lead these followers from the front (refer to Chapter 2 for more on leading from the front).

Some cultures — such as those from Australia, New Zealand, Northern Europe, North America and much of Africa and Asia (particularly China and Singapore) — are low in uncertainty avoidance, which means they tolerate uncertainty and ambiguity and are open to many ways to solve a problem and many ways to achieve a goal.

People from these cultures value innovation and experimentation, are comfortable with figuring out solutions for themselves, with taking risks, with change, with broad goals and with flexible ways of working. These people are also comfortable agreeing to disagree because they believe that looking at a situation in lots of different ways is okay.

For followers who are low in uncertainty avoidance, it's a good idea to lead from the back or the centre and underneath (again, refer to Chapter 2 for details on leading from different angles).

Leading loners and cooperators

People from *collectivist* cultures emphasise the group and its needs, wants and achievements whereas people from *individualistic* cultures place importance on the individual and prize an individual's needs, wants and achievements.

Japanese people have a saying: 'The stake that sticks out gets hammered down.' Japanese culture — like most Asian, Indian, Pacific Islander, Māori and Arab cultures — has traditionally been group-oriented or *collectivist*. Russia and many African and Latin-American nations have also had strong group-oriented cultures. 'One for all and all for one' sums up the desire to be part of a group, whether family, tribe or community.

Making a mistake or doing something silly costs people from group-oriented cultures more than mere embarrassment — the results can be personally devastating for them. Errors can cause people from these cultures to 'lose face', resulting in shame and humiliation because they believe their mistakes reflect badly on their entire team, family or community.

Followers from collectivist cultures emphasise modesty; generally, they dislike making presentations and speaking up at meetings, particularly with a dissenting opinion or to point out a flaw in the team's thinking or approach. These people also place a high value on cooperation and prefer to avoid competition; in fact, they may expect rewards for cooperation more than for getting results. They're loath to openly disagree with others, much preferring expressions such as *maybe* or *differently* to *no*. Even a *yes* can mean *maybe* or *no way*.

Your cooperative followers probably prefer to work and reach decisions in small groups, helping each other and learning from each other. They see the results they achieve from the perspective of the quality of their joint efforts. Make the most of this by asking these followers to mentor and coach their team-mates and lead them from the front or the centre and from underneath.

To make it easier for your cooperative followers to speak up at meetings, you may need to directly ask them for their opinions: 'Tell me, where could this plan go wrong?' If they still hesitate, try collecting their opinions and ideas before the meeting and presenting them as bullet points to the rest of the team. Explain that you did some pre-meeting exploration with a few people and here are some points already gathered to get the team started. This takes more time from you as the leader but this may sometimes be the only way to get some of your cooperator followers to open up.

In most Northern European and English-speaking cultures (including Australia and New Zealand) the emphasis is on *me* — the approach is individualist. *Each for himself* describes this approach. These cultures emphasise individuals and their results over relationships. They value action, frank and direct communication and winning, and they expect to be rewarded for results and performance. They relate to people as individuals and judge people based on their achievements, not as members of families, tribes or communities.

Individualists are comfortable working on their own with minimum direction. They speak up when they have something to say and often get a buzz from hotly debating the pros and cons of various approaches. Lead them from the centre or the back and from underneath, supporting them as they get on with it.

Group-oriented *we* cultures prefer stable longer-term relationships and are reluctant to do business with strangers. In contrast, people from individualist *me* cultures are quite open to doing business with strangers and don't spend much time building relationships or establishing trust (often to their detriment, even in individualist cultural settings). Make the most of your cooperative followers' skills at building relationships with other parts of your organisation and your suppliers and customers.

To those who were brought up to cooperate in group cultures, individualists can seem offensively blunt, rude, arrogant and uncaring whereas people from individualist cultures can perceive people from collectivist cultures as inscrutable, secretive and unforthcoming with information.

Engender trust and prevent nasty surprises by building a team culture that values open communication and exploration of issues, problems, solutions and ideas while respecting for each member's cultural background.

Leading followers who accept authority and followers who respect authority

Vast differences exist in the ways cultures view and deal with hierarchical relationships and authority. Some Chinese and Arabic people are trained to treat some employees as inferior, whereas most New Zealanders and Australians are trained to treat followers as equals who deserve respect (though it may not always happen that way).

Pacific Islanders and Māori have a pecking order among themselves based on respect for age. Thus when the leader assigns an unpleasant task to an older Islander or Māori, a younger Islander or Māori generally does the task instead because in their culture, the elders deserve the better assignments. The degree of respect for authority is called *power distance*.

Cultures that endorse distinctions and respect authority are more formal and hierarchical. Such cultures include most Asian countries, India, countries in the Middle East and Brazil, Mexico and Russia. People from those cultures relate to *ascribed status* — that is, they relate to people based on factors such as gender, race, age or caste.

Like cooperative cultures, authority respecters value procedures, rules and conformity. They emphasise the importance of rank and status, creating a big gulf between them and their leader. They seldom develop personal ties with their leader and they expect to take the blame for their leader when something goes wrong. They show respect for their superiors through their formal behaviour and use of titles and surnames, such as Mr and Mrs (or even Madame) rather than using first names.

Since your authority-respecter followers expect you to have all the answers and the wisdom of experience, they don't mind you telling them what to do without inviting their input and opinions. You can be quite directive and lead these followers from the front. You can make the pecking order among your followers clear with people who are comfortable with hierarchies, too. For example, you may nominate a deputy to lead in your absence when you go on holidays because these followers can be uncomfortable in a leadership vacuum. You may also, for example, nominate a technology guru, an equipment guru and a procedures guru when a lot of your followers appreciate and respect hierarchy. Make your role as the leader and your expertise clear, highlight deadlines and provide clear goals and structure. If authority-respecters come to you with problems, they expect you to tell them the answers.

At the other end of the scale are the followers you need to lead from the centre or the back — those from the egalitarian, informal cultures of Australia and New Zealand and the countries of North America and Northern Europe. They value people, whatever their station in life, for *achieved status* — and respect people for what they achieve. These followers behave and dress in diverse ways and can be insensitive to those who prefer cultural uniformity.

Your informal followers expect you to cop the blame when something goes wrong — to pass the buck to them would be cowardly and weak. They also expect cordial, matey relationships with you and are comfortable getting to know you personally and socialising with you. And none of this Mr, Mrs or Madame stuff.

Agree on (don't set) deadlines with these followers, avoid telling them what to do without asking for their input and don't pull rank. Try to avoid an obvious chain of command, too. Lead from the back and underneath — be a resource and a coach. When they come to you with a problem, help them figure out the solution; don't take over and fix the problem for them. Egalitarian followers are generally self directed, so assign them tasks that they can get on with completing themselves.

Leading direct and indirect followers

Some cultures have lots of shared knowledge and understood ways of speaking and behaving and are often very homogeneous, too. As a result, people from these cultures don't need to be explicit when they communicate. Many people from Asian countries and the subcontinent communicate this way, paying attention to non-verbal sources of information to understand meanings. People from these cultures expect people to keep up with what's going and place the responsibility on the listener to understand their meanings. (This is known as *high-context communication.*)

In contrast, people from North America, New Zealand, Australia and Northern Europe are in the habit of clearly spelling out what they mean — they need to because their cultures are more diverse. The emphasis is on words and straight talk, not on non-verbal cues. This is known as *high-content communication.*

Communication and relationships can easily break down when some people assume more shared understanding than really exists. A team culture of open communication where people ask for more information or explanation when they're not clear about what someone is saying is the answer. (For more on this subject, refer to Chapters 15 and 16.)

Leading followers who use time and space differently

People from Singapore, Northern Europe, North America, Australia and New Zealand see time as a limited resource to be divided up, meted out and managed in order to achieve results. Not surprisingly, these people tend to do one thing at a time, work in an orderly fashion and dislike interruptions. People from these cultures are optimistic about the future and believe they can shape the future through planning, acting and taking control. They stick to their plans once they're made, too. Since these cultures also respect private property and value privacy, those followers — known as *monochromatic* followers — prize their space and their property and are in heaven when you give them a private office.

People from Latin-American, Middle Eastern, Asian and Indian cultures, on the other hand, produce people who tend to see time as abundant, a gift to be used freely and without constraint, taking the emphasis off punctuality, promptness and planning. Since plans and time are more flexible, allotting time to various activities can be pointless. These followers are *polychromatic* — comfortable doing several tasks at once, fielding interruptions as they go and starting meetings only when everyone is there — that's why they expect your door always to be open.

Followers from Latin-American, Middle Eastern Asian and Indian cultures look more to the past and value traditional ways of doing tasks, so expect them to be more conservative and slower to change. They give priority to family and relationships, not privacy and schedules; in fact, many of these cultures don't have a word for privacy, which explains why these followers are happy to share work space and belongings, chatting as they go about their business.

When it comes to personal space, followers from Latin-American and Middle Eastern cultures part ways with their Asian team-mates. Latin-Americans, Middle Easterners and Southern Europeans are generally comfortable with quite direct and intense eye contact; they gesture more and are more expressive facially. At the other end of that scale are your Asian followers and somewhere in between are your Northern Europeans and people from English-speaking countries.

Your Asian followers may also speak more softly and be more comfortable with silence than followers of European and North American descent. Your time-controlling followers probably stand, literally, at arm's length, with little physical contact, whereas your laid-back followers tend to get a bit more up close and personal (making the time-controllers quite uncomfortable at times). Observe the way your followers from different cultures use their personal space and do the same when you're with them.

Leading followers who don't (yet) understand Aussie and Kiwi English

When you lead followers who are learning English or who speak a different style of English from Australian and New Zealand English, a little patience, understanding and careful listening and speaking goes a long way. Here's how to help these followers perform well:

✔ Arrange, when you can, for others who speak the follower's first language to support them. However, when that's someone from your team, avoid letting a clique form.

✔ Avoid using slang. People who are new to Australia or New Zealand cannot be expected to understand the complex slang the people of these two countries use. In fact, Kiwis and Aussies can sometimes have trouble understanding each other!

✔ Avoid complicated and lengthy sentences and explanations; stick to essential information at first.

✔ Be aware the follower may hesitate to ask questions, so keep the communication lines open.

✔ Don't add unnecessary words or distract your follower with small talk while giving instructions or training.

✔ Don't speak more loudly than usual — that's insulting.

✔ Explain and reinforce the basic vocabulary of your work team frequently.

✔ Explain tasks step by step, in the correct order, using as many diagrams and illustrations as you can.

✔ Pause every few sentences to allow your followers time to process what you said and look for understanding in their facial expressions.

✔ Speak slowly and clearly, in complete sentences (pidgin English is insulting and harms the followers' chances to improve their language skills).

✔ Show and tell: Use examples, hand movements, models and graphs to make your points clear.

✔ Watch quietly as your followers complete tasks to check that you're communicating clearly.

Part V
When the Going Gets Tough

Glenn Lumsden

'I've got some good news and some bad news.
The good news is that we're about to have one of those
character-building conversations that will, in time,
be the making of you . . .'

In this part . . .

Two thousand (or so) years ago, Publius Syrus remarked that anyone can hold the helm when the sea is calm — when the going gets tough is when captains show their mettle. The same is true of leaders. Leadership that's plain sailing is lovely but, sadly, conditions are seldom calm. This part explains what to do when followers don't follow or don't perform and how to navigate through deep waters. You find out how to survive the tough leadership challenges that are sent to try almost every leader. This is the stuff that makes or breaks a leader.

Chapter 18

When Followers Don't Follow

Sadly, not all followers are perfect. They can occasionally let you down in surprising and disappointing ways. And to be fair, when they do let you down, you may find that it's because you've let them down in some way.

I begin this chapter by explaining how to stay in control when you think you may be in danger of losing your cool. Then I guide you through a bit of navel gazing to determine your own role in situations where followers are not following. After that, you find out how to deal with followers who refuse to follow an instruction and how to deal with followers who reject you or the team and go their own way. Finally, I describe a range of tools for sorting out team squabbles.

Keeping Your Cool

First things first: Whatever the problem, stay in control. Losing your temper or making threats always makes matters worse. You're the leader; set the example.

Don't let other people, your followers, events or situations call the shots — stay in control of what you think, say and do. You're diving into your primitive *limbic brain* when you feel yourself losing control, which generates the fight-or-flight response — just what you *don't* need.

Controlling your frustration can be tough when your followers are in their limbic brain and responding emotionally. Your brain is programmed to respond to other people's emotions in kind — this is known as *interpersonal limbic regulation*.

To rise up from your limbic brain and think clearly, take three deep breaths. This delivers oxygen to your *thinking brain*, the seat of your creative and logical thinking, judgement, foresight and self-control. This area of your brain controls your ability to pay attention and make decisions — just what you *do* need. (See Chapter 19 for more information on your limbic and thinking brains.)

Asking Yourself a Few Hard Questions

The Chinese have a saying: 'Wisdom is the comb that nature gives you after you're bald.'

So that your hard-earned 'comb of wisdom' doesn't come too late for you, take some time for introspection — basic navel gazing. To avoid blaming everyone but yourself for a problem, think about the role you may have played in the creation of the problem. Here are some areas to consider. Ask yourself

- Are you giving and earning respect?
- Are you helping your followers to feel like winners and explaining how important they are to your team and the organisation?
- Are you setting a good example?
- Are you using your power and authority correctly?
- Do you honour your commitments and build team trust?
- Do you include the task, team and individual needs in your considerations?
- Do you look and sound like a leader?
- Do you seek your followers' input into matters that affect them?
- Have you been fair dinkum and honest, and developed a reputation as fair and reliable?
- Have you built a strong team?
- Have you developed a clear team purpose with your followers?

✔ Have you explained your vision and values clearly enough and shown your followers how they benefit too?

✔ Have you gained your followers' cooperation and commitment, not just their compliance?

Leaders who think they're perfect, that problems are caused by their followers and have nothing to do with them, are almost certainly kidding themselves. That line of thinking leads to leadership with arrogance, blindness to one's own shortcomings and failure to mature, grow and develop as a person and as a leader. (Refer to Chapter 3 for more on mastering your qualities as a leader.) Sorry to be harsh about this subject, but that's the way it is. Leadership is all about building skills and making discoveries about yourself. Unfortunately, that often means you make mistakes and later reflect on what went wrong so you can learn from them — which is fine, as long as you *are* learning from them.

Dealing with Followers Who Refuse Instructions

So you're giving an instruction to a follower and the follower simply refuses to do what you ask. Before saying or doing anything else, count to ten and think through your request. Ask yourself these questions:

✔ Are you assigning a task the follower isn't yet capable of doing and training is the missing ingredient? If that is the case, check whether the follower is open to training or ask someone who is trained to do the job instead.

✔ Are you explaining the importance of the assignment or the reason for giving the job to this particular follower? If not, brief your follower on the details.

✔ Are you giving the directions in an inappropriate style? If you are, then the time has come for you to nibble a little humble pie and reword the request.

✔ Is your instruction reasonable? You may need to modify your request and explain the background to it.

If you're still stumped, switch to detective mode. Discuss the refusal with your follower to find out what lies behind it. Do this in private, so your discussion doesn't become an interesting sideshow for the rest of your followers. Use your best listening skills to dampen any emotion and find out why your follower is refusing the request. (Refer to the E.A.R.S. formula in

Chapters 7 and 19.) Here are some possible reasons why your follower may be refusing your request:

- Your instructions aren't clear.
- Your follower is so flat out on other duties that no time is left for more.
- Your follower is tired of being ordered around and told what to do.
- Your follower thinks your request is unsafe.
- You're asking your follower to take on a task to which he or she is unsuited.

Finding out what's going on often leads to a compromise or a course of action that you and your follower are both able to live with.

Whatever you do, don't threaten the follower with 'Do it or else!' or any similar controlling order. Threats are actually a sign of leadership weakness. Unless you're absolutely certain you can — and will — carry out a threat, you only end up looking silly and losing credibility in the eyes of your followers and anyone else who hears about your threat. (Try comparing how you assigned the work with the various ways of assigning duties explained in Chapter 12.)

Engage, energise and prize

When you want your followers to follow you, involve them in meaningful activity, enthuse them and show you appreciate them.

Help your followers see the bright and shining beacon you're leading them towards and get them involved in charting the course towards your and their goals. Giving people a say increases commitment and sharing the overall aims of a project whips up excitement. That's known as *engaging* people.

Now you want to *energise* your followers. First of all, don't go around issuing orders. Ask, don't tell, and remember your pleases and thank-yous. Try to match followers to tasks (see Chapters 3, 12 and 15 for more on matching people and tasks). When your followers enjoy their assignments, they're willing to invest their energy in their work. Equally important, see your followers have the tools and equipment, training, information, time and other resources they need to do a good job When that isn't the case, people feel like they're just beating their head against a brick wall and that's a sure way to sap the energy you're after.

Finally, *prize* your followers' efforts by showing your appreciation for their contributions. Make it clear you value what they're doing because they're helping the team move closer and closer towards the beacon. When your followers don't think their contributions are worthwhile and welcome, why would they bother making contributions?

Dealing with Followers Who Reject Your Team's Culture and Values

Sometimes, you and your team are heading in one direction except for one or two followers who are charging off in a different direction, or who are refusing to accompany you on a new course. I once worked with a large government organisation on a major job redesign project aimed at enriching and enlarging jobs and empowering staff. Once the staff understood the goals and that they were to be a part of redesigning their futures, most were, not surprisingly, very receptive to bringing their jobs into the 20th century (as it was then). But as I went around working with the various teams to help them regroup and reassign duties and smooth out the work flow, I occasionally came across someone who flat-out refused to take on any additional duties, even though any necessary training was part of the process. 'This is what I was hired to do, this is what I will continue to do — you can't force me to change my job' was the attitude. (Yes, this is a true story.)

Some offices were large enough for me to place these recalcitrant followers into work teams of their own so they were able to carry on as before. Sometimes that wasn't possible and we couldn't; at those times we had to use the north-bound bus approach, which I discuss in the following sections.

Explaining your expectations

Followers don't know what you expect of them unless you tell them. Before bringing new followers on board, check first that their work habits help them fit into your team (for more on this subject, refer to Chapter 15). When new followers join your team, explain your organisation's values and expectations, your performance expectations and your expectations regarding work habits clearly, so no grey areas or misunderstandings exist. When you're the newly appointed leader of an existing team, make your expectations regarding work habits clear in that situation too. When your team or organisation is changing direction, communicate the whys and wherefores of the change fully and often, explaining precisely what you need from your followers.

Only when all your expectations are clear and in the open can you legitimately act when a follower is not meeting them. When your expectations aren't clear, the first step is to make them clear. Sit down and discuss what you expect from your follower and talk about which expectations and values your follower is meeting well and where you need to see your follower making some adjustments. While you're at it, find out whether your follower has any expectations of you that you're not meeting. Fair's fair, right?

Taking the north-bound bus

Some people change when they see the light, others when they feel the heat. Use the *north-bound bus* approach when the time is right to apply a bit of heat. In essence, you say: 'Here is the direction the team is heading (north). If you want to join the rest of the team members, you're very welcome. If you don't want to join the rest of the team members, be aware that the team is still heading in that direction (north), so you need to find another bus to take you where you want to go (south, east or west). The choice is entirely yours and if you decide to join the team, I will do everything I can to help ease your journey.'

The north-bound bus approach applies to accepting change as well as to fitting in with the way your team operates. Say, for example, your team's culture is open and cooperative, with team members sharing information freely to speed and ease the flow of work and helping each other out whenever someone needs a hand. As well, the team's norms are to keep work spaces tidy and put team equipment away after use. Everyone in the team works happily along those lines except for one follower who is untidy, doesn't put equipment away and doesn't offer to help other people when they need it. Clearly, you have a problem (refer to Chapters 8 and 15 for more information on team culture and norms). When a follower still fails to conform to these expectations after you expressly point them out, you may decide this is a 'firing offence' because the behaviour of the follower is damaging your team's ability to function at its best.

Using the north-bound bus approach, you can say something like, 'You know, I've explained, three times this month already, what I expect from everyone on this team in terms of helping others out and working tidily. To me, this is very important. Everyone on this team needs to meet my requirements in terms of tidiness and helpfulness and if you can do that, you're very welcome on my team. If you can't meet my standards, I believe that you may be happier on another team. It's completely up to you and I will support you as best I can in whatever decision you reach. I will meet you on Friday to discuss your decision.'

When you discuss the subject of followers leaving your team, you're entering into the realms of performance management. When your followers appear unwilling to make a decision about conforming to the team or leaving, find out your organisation's policy on dismissal and follow that policy to the letter. Ask your human resources specialist and your own leader to walk you through how the policy applies to your situation. You may think it's easier to allow your follower to remain on your bus but, in the long term, the morale and performance of your whole team suffers.

Dealing with a Team Barney

Working with people is like being part of a family — you're together with people with whom you may not normally have anything in common. That alone is bound to produce tension. When you consider the diversity in the modern workforce in New Zealand and Australia, people from different age groups, abilities, cultures, backgrounds and so on, misunderstandings are bound to arise.

Differences can make people uncomfortable. On the other hand, differences can also make life interesting — after all, life can be very boring when everyone in a team thinks the same way.

The first move you make to prevent differences in backgrounds, differences of opinion and differences in priorities from creating tension and strife is to build a culture of openness that values differences. Differences provide a variety of understandings, solutions and viewpoints and can bring creativity and fun to a team.

The second move is to realise that disagreements are only destructive in two situations:

- When misunderstandings are covered up, they fester and are likely to eventually erupt into a major blow-up that reduces team morale and productivity.
- When the disagreement results in winners and losers, this leads to entrenched opinions, hard feelings and often the desire among team members to get even.

If you ever see icy stares between team members or sense ill will, bad vibes or discord, step in. Differences can quickly develop into short, sharp exchanges. Tension builds and starts to prevent the entire team, as well as the bickering followers concerned, from performing well and eventually normal team functioning becomes difficult.

Here are some danger signs. Don't wait until the following occur.

- Bad feelings become such a big issue that some of your followers are forced to raise the problem with you (by that time, the problem is well advanced and is difficult to solve).
- Differences between team members escalate and then erupt into a major blue (when your whole team may suddenly become involved and take sides, making the run-in really hard to solve.

Hurters and helpers in squabbles

This table shows some subtle, but powerful moves you can make to help you help your followers reach agreement on disputes. I've contrasted these helping situations with situations that can hurt your chances of finding agreement between followers in disputes.

Bringing Together Followers Who Are in Conflict

Helpers	Hurters
Sit your followers next to each other to show they're (literally) on the same side	Sit your followers opposite each other to show they're opponents
Keep the attention on what your followers agree on and on outcomes both sides want	Turn your attention to the subjects on which your followers are disagreeing and the different outcomes each side wants
Insist your followers say what they want clearly	Keep talking about what your followers don't want
Stick to one issue at a time	Permit your followers to argue about everything on their minds and to dredge up 'ancient-history' complaints
Insist your followers use neutral words and a neutral tone of voice	Permit your followers to use emotive words and words that put down the disagreeing followers
Insist your followers seek solutions, not faults	Allow your followers to continually remind the other side what they are doing wrong or what they are mistaken about
Ask or make suggestions (but only when you must do so)	Tell your followers what you think

Call your quarrelling followers together and explain that you plan to help them find a way to turn their arguments into an agreement about how they intend to work well together in the future. Ask followers to explain their points of view neutrally, objectively and non judgementally and help them to articulate their views when necessary by asking questions to draw out and explore their positions. Ask your followers to explain their understanding of the other side's point of view before commenting or making a new point.

Don't allow your followers to dredge up the past, but keep the conversation firmly directed to the future (for more on this subject, refer to Chapter 15).

Keep the conversation moving along with lines such as these:

- ✔ I understand that. Is there anything else I need to know?
- ✔ What else can you tell me?

Here are some questions to ask when discussions become deadlocked:

- ✔ I don't want to leave the discussion like this. Do you have any ideas?
- ✔ What do you agree on?
- ✔ What do you want to happen next?

When the core issues are identified and both points of view are in the open and understood, look for the common ground between them. This may mean helping your followers to change the ways in which they view an issue — this is called *reframing*. For example, show them how to stand back to look at the situation from a different angle or to see a point of view in a different light.

Then ask your followers to say how they think their differences can be resolved or what they want to happen next. For example, what do they want the other side to do from now on? Help them to explore their options when they seem to get stuck. Ask them if they have any other ideas. Don't let them say what they *don't* want — have them state what they *do* want in positive language. This turns the disagreement into a goal they can move towards together.

Turn complaints into goals

When two team members or team factions declare war, ask each to complete these sentences in this order:

- ✔ My problem, complaint, concern or issue is ...
- ✔ My real concern about that is ...
- ✔ What I'd really like is ...
- ✔ Therefore my goal is ...

The answers your followers provide give you an insight into your team members' true needs and fears and give your discussions a constructive starting point. (For more information on handling complaints, refer to Chapter 7.)

Meeting with conflicting followers together is better than speaking to each side individually and relaying one follower's position to the other. When you present one side's views to the other side, you can sound as though you're taking sides, and you end up with both sides of followers alienated against you as well as each other.

See yourself as a referee or a peacemaker in this *mediation* process, remaining neutral and helping your bickering followers find a way to work together. When push comes to shove, state that the quarrelling cannot continue, suggest you meet again in a day or two's time and try again. Explain that if that doesn't work, you're going to *arbitrate* — impose a solution which they may or may not like but that they must accept. When you need to do that, go for a compromise so no side is a winner or loser.

When grievances become official — that is, when they are reported to human resources officers or to higher management — always follow your organisation's grievance procedure to the letter.

What's the problem?

Knowing the cause of a conflict can be the first step to resolving the conflict, so guide your followers to identify and acknowledge the source of a problem. You can divide possible sources into these categories:

- **Facts:** When your followers are arguing about facts, suspend the discussion until you can find out exactly what the pertinent facts are.

- **Goals:** Everyone wants a different outcome. Help your followers work through what each side of the conflict wants so they each end up with a solution that satisfies them. Help your followers find some common goals by, for example, looking at the overall project or how they want to work together.

- **Personalities:** Followers' mannerisms, traits, habits, quirks, their general personality styles or approaches may annoy other followers. You can't change people's personalities so usually you're best to overlook these differences or learn to live with them.

- **Values:** Disagreements based on differences in values are usually quite difficult to resolve. Probably the best move is help your followers recognise that everyone is different and no-one can change another person's values — values are too deep-seated to change and have no rights and wrongs (refer to Chapter 3 for more information on values). Help your followers to respectfully agree to disagree.

- **Unclear expectations:** Help your followers clear up the confusion by outlining their expectations of each other.

Chapter 19

When Followers Don't Perform

*O*ne of your primary responsibilities as a leader is to ensure your followers are all performing at the expected standard. That sometimes means you need to help a particular follower who is performing below standard. This process is best approached with a one-to-one session between you and the follower. When you give followers your individual attention, you have a better chance of succeeding in turning around their performances.

You may occasionally need to remove a follower from your team or from a project when that follower isn't able to give you the level of performance you need. Difficult as that may be, removing an underperformer is in everyone's interests. Floundering followers are never happy followers and the negative effects of underperformance quickly spread across the rest of the team. Your reputation and your team's reputation can suffer as a result.

Failure to deal with underperforming followers costs you the respect of the rest of your followers and your credibility in the organisation. Morale suffers when followers need to carry other followers. Longer-term problems set in as performance continues to erode and the underperformance becomes more and more difficult to address. The longer you leave poor work habits or negative attitudes to fester, the more difficult turning them around becomes and the more drastic your options become.

In this chapter, I show you how to recognise when what appears to be a performance problem isn't really a performance problem at all; how to tease out the facts of performance problems; and how to successfully work with your followers to improve their performances. You find out how to address performance problems with small weapons early on and how to progress all the way to a major attack on the problem when necessary.

Thinking Through Your Followers' Performances

For some reason, many leaders jump into performance discussions thinking they know why a follower's performance isn't up to scratch and then start shovelling on the advice. Do these phrases sound familiar to you: 'Look, just try harder'; 'Do it this way'; 'This could cost you your job'; or 'I'll have to ask someone else to do that if you can't get it right!' This is definitely not the way to go.

Seeing yourself in others

A few years ago, a man I'll call Joe attended a two-part management training program I ran. One of the topics examined during the first week was turning around below-par performances from his followers. Joe told about one of his followers who always went for smoko at exactly 10.30, even when the rest of the team members were busy. This really annoyed Joe: 'It's so *selfish*!' he said. 'Every day, even when the team's flat-chat, he takes his smoko and he eats a pie and plays Sudoku. This has to stop. I don't mind when the others aren't busy. But when the team members are busy, he's *selfish* to take that break when he's meant to be helping his team-mates.'

Others at the training program began asking Joe questions: What other breaks did this man take? (He took lunch when the team wasn't busy and skipped lunch or ate later when the team was busy, which was great teamwork.) What about his time-keeping? (Excellent — in fact, he was always first in and had the coffee brewed ready for the others.) What about his performance generally? (Excellent — top performer — but he's just so *selfish* about those smokos!)

Can you spot what the other people at the training program saw that Joe couldn't see?

A couple of months later, the participants on the training program were together again for the second part of the course. One of the first questions was to Joe to find out how he'd succeeded in counselling his 'selfish' follower.

'It's funny,' Joe said, 'I invited him to sit and have a chat with me and I had my opening comments all ready, the ones I practised here at the training session. But when I opened my mouth to begin, I suddenly realised that *I* was the one being selfish! Here was one of my best performers and I was getting cranky about the one and only break of the day he takes? What was I thinking?'

When Joe was seeing his follower's performance as selfish, he was actually looking in a 'mirror' and seeing himself as selfish. That's hard to admit. People can make the mistake of *projecting* characteristics that they don't like in themselves onto other people.

You may be wondering why no-one pointed that out to Joe during the first week of the training program. The answer is that sometimes people need to find out the reality of situations for themselves. Mirror projections are one of these situations. And I guarantee you this fact: Leaders gain a lot of knowledge when they look at themselves objectively in the 'mirror'.

So-called performance shortfalls may be shortfalls that are worth addressing. Here is where you need to concentrate all your efforts on solutions that are going to bring you the best results.

Getting your intentions clear

You can't make people perform their work to a higher standard by making them feel bad or by making them feel like losers. That approach doesn't work for you, your followers or the organisation.

When you want to help a follower perform better, make these your two overall goals:

- ✔ Enable your follower to accept and correct the performance shortfall.

- ✔ Maintain or enhance your follower's feelings of self-worth (for more information on self-worth, refer to Chapter 3).

Bearing in mind these intentions, think through your follower's performance, in this order:

- ✔ Consider what your follower is doing well in terms of *results* and *behaviour* (what your follower is saying or doing).

- ✔ Isolate any substandard performance — what your follower is saying or doing that's below expectations or what targets your follower is not meeting.

- ✔ List the facts and document the *performance gap* accurately. This gap is the difference between the performance you expect and your follower's current performance. A factual performance gap makes for an honest and constructive discussion.

People do what is easiest or most rewarding. When a follower isn't performing up to your standards, the reason may be that poor performance takes less effort or is somehow more rewarding than meeting the performance standards you set. Figure out how you can find a way to make improved performance easier or more satisfying than poor performance.

Specifying the performance gap

Performance problems come in two types — *behaviour gaps* and *results gaps*.

Behaviour gaps

Behaviour gaps occur when a follower says or does something that you consider incorrect or inappropriate. For example:

- Having to be reminded two or three times a day to do routine tasks
- Interrupting people at meetings
- Keeping customers waiting for more than one minute without acknowledging them
- Not putting equipment away after using it
- Speaking abruptly and curtly to team-mates or customers
- Taking a break instead of helping busy team-mates

What you see depends mainly on what you're thinking

Leaders are not the only people who see what they expect to see. Here's a story that illustrates that a negative attitude can produce negative experiences, while positive produces positive.

On a recent visit to Japan, I met a scientist who was engaged in cutting-edge genetic research. 'How do you like living here?' I asked.

He replied in no uncertain terms. 'Not much. The weather is cold in winter and hot and humid in summer, getting to know the local people is difficult and I don't care for the food.'

Surprising, I thought. Struggling to make conversation, I asked where he'd worked before coming to Japan.

'I ran a lab in New York', he said.

And did he enjoy living in New York?

'No, not really. The people were loud and rude and living in New York was very expensive and crowded.'

'Oh, well, you must miss your own country a lot,' I suggested, knowing he came from Eastern Europe.

'No, not really. It's quite poor and the living standards aren't very good. It's good to be away.'

One more try: 'Where do you plan to go when you're finished your work here in Japan,' I asked.

'Oh, I'm thinking about running a lab in Sydney. The people there are doing some very interesting work and the lab has wonderful facilities. I've never been to Australia before, so I'd like to go there.'

This scientist's leader may not be able to change his outlook on life in general. But the scientist's positive expectation of Sydney can be harnessed to produce a positive outcome.

Results gaps

Results gaps occur when a follower fails to meet a target. For example:

- ✔ Missing the 90 per cent on-specification target by 5 to 15 per cent for three weeks in a row
- ✔ Missing a sales target by 10 to 15 per cent for the past 8 weeks
- ✔ Not answering the telephone within three rings and not identifying the department
- ✔ Selling up only 5 per cent of sales rather than the targeted 15 per cent
- ✔ Turning in the last three reports one to three days late

Pinning down performance shortfalls

In my performance management workshops, I often ask the leaders attending to list the performance shortfalls of the followers they lead. These leaders are generally quite vague on this subject at the start, stating shortfalls such as poor time-keeping, inattention to detail and so on. Next, I ask the leaders to remove any value judgements or labels (lazy, irresponsible, bad attitude and so on) and ask questions about the performance gap to make the gaps more specific. The more specifically leaders state a performance gap, the more obvious how to deal with the gap becomes.

For example, a leader with a poor time-keeper may say that a follower is 10 to 30 minutes late in the mornings two to three days a week and 10 to 15 minutes late back from lunch breaks 8 out of 10 days. That doesn't sound good. However, after further questions, the leader reveals that this follower often works late and takes work home and provides work that is thorough, well presented and always on time. This begs the question: Is this really a performance problem worth addressing? When no particular reason for stringent timekeeping exists and the follower works in his or her own

time and turns in good work, you may well not have a performance gap and you probably don't need to take any action.

A leader with a detail avoider may explain that the detail avoider turns in reports that are poorly presented because the reports lack white space to make reading easier, they don't have enough headings to help readers find information and they're inaccurate due to transposed figures and putting the wrong tables or graphs under a heading. The leader may then explain that the detail-avoiding follower is rushing and not proofreading reports because he or she spends too much time socialising. The leader is concerned because these reports are important — they ultimately go to important people outside the organisation. Upon further questioning, this leader may explain that this particular follower has never done a good job with these reports and is poor at detailed work in general. This information indicates that this leader may be assigning this duty to the wrong follower and perhaps even that the follower is not suited to jobs that contain a lot of duties requiring attention to detail.

Concentrate on results and the contributions followers are making to the team or department and ignore traits that are not related to performance. For example, when you're a neat freak, guard against seeing your followers with untidy desks as disorganised, ineffective slobs. When you're a fast-paced go-getter, guard against seeing slower, more thoughtful followers as unmotivated dolts.

Once you define the performance gap clearly, you often find that a performance problem doesn't exist at all and that your course of action becomes obvious. (Refer to Chapters 10 and 12 for information on setting clear goals or measures of success.)

Knowing precisely what a performance gap entails enables you to explain the shortfall clearly and objectively to your underperforming follower in your one-on-one discussion. Get the facts by logically thinking through the gap using these headings, in this order:

- ✔ **What the performance shortfall is:** Make your description of the performance shortfall factual, specific, free of assumptions, hearsay and value judgements and as measurable as you can.

- ✔ **When the performance shortfall takes place:** Collect times and dates to support your description.

- ✔ **Where the performance shortfall takes place:** Clearly and accurately describe the location of where the performance shortfall occurs, if appropriate.

- ✔ **Who the performance shortfall affects:** Collect names of any other people involved.

- ✔ **How long the performance has been unsatisfactory:** This may be a sudden or a long-standing problem.

- ✔ **How to substantiate the performance shortfall:** Have evidence or specific information to support your description of the problem (hearsay is never substantial evidence).

Depending on the performance gap, the change you need your follower to make to correct the gap can be a large or small change. Small changes are objective, measurable and non arguable. Big changes are difficult to measure and subjective. Bad attitudes fit into this latter category. Table 19-1 demonstrates how the *change continuum* — from easy-to-make small changes to difficult-to-make major changes — works.

Table 19-1	The Change Continuum
Easy	*Difficult*
Objective	Subjective
Measurable	Not measurable
Clear target not met	Questionably enforceable target not met
Enforceable standard of behaviour not met	Attitude
Poor attendance record	Behaviour toward team-mates
Failure to follow a specific safety procedure	Untidy attire

Checking the five keys that unlock performance

When you decide you have a performance problem and you consider the problem worth addressing in a one-on-one meeting with your followers, think through the five keys that unlock performance to make sure the responsibility for change lies with the underperforming follower and not elsewhere. (Refer to Chapter 10 for more information on the five keys that unlock performance.) Approach the five keys by

- ✔ **Being sure followers know what to do:** When an underperformance is a results gap, check that your follower knows what standards you expect and understands the importance of the task concerned. When the problem is a behaviour gap, find out whether your follower is fully aware of the behaviour you expect and why that behaviour is important.

- ✔ **Confirming followers know how to do a job:** Has your follower been properly trained and had enough time to build experience and confidence? Has your follower met the standard in the past? If so, think about what may have changed.

- ✔ **Ensuring followers want to do a job:** Is the task one that you believe the follower has the aptitude or attributes to do? Or have you mis-assigned the task to a follower who has no interest or aptitude in it or to a follower who is tired and bored with this task?

✔ **Giving followers a chance to do a job:** Is your follower bogged down by cumbersome systems or procedures, faulty or inadequate tools or equipment, too much to do, lack of information or difficult team-mates? Or is a personal problem or happy event outside work sapping your follower's energies and ability to perform?

✔ **Knowing how you can lead followers to peak performance:** How sure are you that you're leading properly? For example, when you don't set a good example, treat each of your followers respectfully and fairly and build a team where the members help each other, your followers are unlikely to want to perform well for you. Or perhaps you're sending signals that you don't expect your follower to succeed. (Refer to Chapter 3 if you need to find out more about how to be a leader for whom followers are willing to perform well.)

Now that you know the details of the performance problem, you can invite your follower for a one-on-one discussion. Generally, beginning gently is best — 'Come in for a chat about this target you seem to be having trouble reaching'. You can become increasingly directive — firm — in specifying precisely what needs to happen in terms of performance. Essentially, your message becomes: 'This is the target you must meet or the standard of behaviour you must display if you want to keep your job.'

Holding Performance Discussions

Ignoring your follower's faults often can be easier than taking your follower to task. Sometimes, ignoring faults is the smart move to make. You can't change a follower's personality or working style any more than you can change a follower's height or eye colour.

But when a follower's bad habits or poor results are harming your team or your team's results, you have a responsibility to address the problem — quickly and without nagging or pushing and in a way that's fair, just and reasonable. The tougher the message you need to get through, the less people want to hear your message and the more carefully you need to think about how to best get across the changes that you want to occur. Begin with a quiet chat.

Too often, performance discussions occur after a series of incidents that end up with the leader losing patience and taking action that is punitive and motivated by fear, hurt or anger. These discussions generally leave in their wake resentment, guilt, anxiety, fear, stress and frustration and contribute to a decline in morale and an even worse performance by the follower concerned. The longer you wait, the more difficult a performance discussion becomes.

Poor excuses for waiting

Leaders who use any of these reasons to delay or avoid a performance discussion are very probably engaging in wishful thinking or self-deception:

✔ If I wait, the situation may resolve itself.

✔ I don't want to disrupt our relationship or seem harsh.

✔ I'll just hint and make sarcastic remarks until the offending follower figures out what I want.

✔ I'll wait until I feel the time is right.

✔ I'm afraid the offending follower may leave if I say anything and then I'll have problems finding and training a replacement.

✔ I'm not perfect either, so who am I to judge?

✔ No-one wants to hear (or give) bad news — better to say nothing.

✔ This has been going on for so long, it's too late to fix it now.

Here are some methods that are guaranteed to begin a performance discussion poorly:

✔ **Apologies:** 'It's not really such a big deal and I hate to sound picky, but you've been arriving back late from breaks for the past few days.' Facing up to your responsibility to turn poor performance around is not a subject for apology.

✔ **Backhanded 'compliments':** 'That's not bad, but I really expected better.' Followers are left feeling deflated and irritated.

✔ **Hearsay:** 'It has come to my attention that . . .', 'I've heard . . .', 'I've had a report . . .' Followers have difficulty concentrating on your feedback when they're wondering who the dobber is.

✔ **Humble requests:** 'I'd really appreciate it if you'd put in a bit more effort.' You may as well save your breath because few followers respond to weak requests.

✔ **Threats:** 'You'd better change your attitude if you want to stay on my team!' Followers are more likely to respond by digging their heels in and crossing their arms.

✔ **Vagueness:** 'You'll just have to work harder in future.' Followers can't correct a problem when they don't know what the problem is.

None of these approaches can help your follower face up to the difficulties that underperformance is causing and none can help your follower choose between unsatisfactory performance (and ultimately loss of position) or improved work performance. And make no mistake: The choice of whether or not to change lies solely with your follower.

How not to nag

Nagging never works — be it at home or in the workplace. The following table has some nagging lines to lose and some positive lines to choose.

Followers respond well to the differences in these lines. For example, a successful leader avoids saying: 'You should have worked on that instead of doing that,' and instead says 'You could have worked on that instead of doing the other'. The word should creates guilt about something that may have happened in the past and that cannot now be changed. The word could doesn't condemn. Instead, could shows followers they have a choice and helps them to make better choices in the future.

To Nag or Not to Nag ...

Lose These Lines	Use These Lines
You don't seem to be able ...	I see you're having trouble ...
You're not doing X properly	I'd like to run through how I want you to do X
You didn't ...	You may find it easier if you ...
You always ...	Next time ...
You never ...	From now on ...
You don't understand	I can run through that again
Mistake	Valuable lesson
Bad (judges a person's character)	Not wise (refers to the natural consequences of a person's actions)
I've told you before not to ...	How about trying it this way ...
That was great, but ...	That was great, and ...
You shouldn't ...	It's faster to ...
Should	I could ...

Performance discussions are made up of three steps:

1. **Giving good information:** You set the scene and describe the performance shortfall.

2. **Gathering good information:** You help your follower out of the limbic brain and into the thinking brain and listen to how your follower sees the situation (for more on the limbic and thinking brains, see the section 'Drain any emotions' later in this chapter).

3. **Moving toward a solution:** You and your follower put your heads together and figure out the cause of a performance gap and work out how to close it.

Giving helpful information

At a communication workshop in Sydney, a participant once offered this homily: 'It's important to say what you mean, but don't be mean.'

That clever line applies to performance discussions too. You can't hold a useful discussion when you get your follower offside at the outset. While making clear that you need your follower to improve an aspect of their performance, you also make clear that you're not criticising your follower on a personal basis by

✔ Keeping on the discussion about behaviours or skills

✔ Keeping your discussion about the future

✔ Turning a performance gap into a performance goal by saying what you do want, not what you don't want

The way you begin a performance discussion is important, so plan your first few sentences and your description of the performance gap. Follow the *KISS* principle: Keep It (your opening statement) Short and Simple. Keep it clear, objective and non arguable, and unpolluted with blame, innuendo, generalisation or exaggeration. Avoid getting into personalities and subjective observations and stick to the facts.

When you're uncertain about how to begin a performance discussion, think of another leader you know who appears to do well in this area. What do you think that leader says and does? Use that information to get your discussion started.

Saluting the stars

Corrective feedback and performance counselling have their place in turning around or weeding out underperformers. Just remember that followers need positive feedback too so they know what they're good at doing and can further develop their skills. You don't want your followers to waste time shoring up areas where they're naturally weak either — that prevents them from spending their time doing what they do best and improving their skills.

And remember your top performers — they may not need as much feedback from you as the poor performers, but they still appreciate knowing that they're working well and achieving their goals. Thank your stars for particularly outstanding efforts and be sure to spend time coaching them to the next level.

Think about where to hold the discussion (for example, in your office or in a neutral conference room) and when the best time is to have your discussion. Make any arrangements you need to make so that your discussion won't be overheard or interrupted.

Set the scene

Begin the discussion with a *framing statement* that says, in essence, this is what I want to discuss. In your one-on-one discussion with your follower, frame your words in a way that enables your follower to engage in an honest and open discussion, not in a way that gets your follower's back up. Here are some lines to use:

- ✔ 'I don't want to discuss your overall performance, which is excellent, but I do want to talk about the incident with Jay yesterday.'
- ✔ 'I want to discuss how you're travelling on this project and see how you and I can increase your effectiveness.'
- ✔ 'Your sales have fallen steadily over the past four weeks and this week, you are 15 per cent under budget. I'd like to explore what's standing in your way and figure out how to improve your sales.'
- ✔ 'You and I have spoken twice over the past three weeks about missed deadlines and yesterday's deadline was also missed. I want to find out what's holding you up so we can fix the problem and have you meeting your deadlines again.'

Present positive and constructive information

Give your follower these three pieces of information:

- **What the current situation is:** Clearly state the results gap or the behaviour gap.

- **Why the performance gap matters:** Explain how your follower's current performance is affecting your team's service, output, yourself, the team or team-mates, customers, efficiency — that is, explain why the current performance is a problem.

- **What your goal is:** Say what you need to happen. Describe the change you need to see (the target to meet or the behaviour to adopt) and the time frame in which the follower needs to make those changes.

Next, stress that your primary concern is satisfactory performance. You now have two choices depending on whether the performance gap is complex or straightforward.

When a performance gap has several causes or when several solutions are available, begin exploring the possibilities. For example, you may say:

- Can you suggest what may be holding you up?

- Do you have any thoughts on how to get your performance back on track?

- You and I need to decide what to do to bring you up to speed so what are your thoughts?

- You and I need to work out what's preventing you hitting your target and fix the problem, so what do you think is holding you back?

When you've asked your questions, wait five seconds to let each question sink in. (Remember, your follower may be struggling because the limbic brain may be responding to your questions.)

When a performance gap is clear-cut, you probably don't need to go into a major fact-finding expedition — you're safe suggesting the course of action you expect your follower to take. But this works only for very straightforward gaps.

Gathering helpful information

Now the time has come for your follower to take the floor. Listen carefully and show you're listening by making eye contact with your follower and by other body language that shows you're listening. (For more on body language, refer to Chapter 7.)

Your follower has three possible responses to the helpful information you're offering:

- ✔ **'Okay — sorry, I'll fix that problem':** Double check that your follower knows how to rectify the performance gap. (Notice and acknowledge the performance improvement that follows to ensure the improvement continues.)

- ✔ **'Well, I'm stumped':** When the follower indicates doubt about how to improve a performance, you may be looking at a complex performance problem that you need to explore in depth together to discover the best course of action. Analyse the problem using the five keys as a guide (refer to Chapter 10 and refer to the section 'Checking the five keys that unlock performance' earlier in this chapter). After you isolate the cause or main cause of the performance gap, concentrate on what needs to happen for the follower to close the gap.

- ✔ **'I'm not doing anything wrong':** When a follower denies a performance problem exists or throws in red herrings to divert you from the problem, keep presenting your evidence of the performance shortfall calmly and objectively. Don't be side-tracked by excuses or diversions.

R. A. M. home minor changes

Asking people to change is not as simple as it may seem to be. Here's a little memory jogger — a R.A.M. — to remind you how to ram home what you want changed without ramming the point down your follower's throat.

- ✔ **R is for Realistic:** Make sure what you ask is sensible and practical. Is your follower interested in doing what you're asking? What's in it for your follower?

- ✔ **A is for Achievable:** Make sure your follower has the time to do what you're asking, that your follower knows how to do it and has the necessary resources in terms of tools, equipment and so on.

- ✔ **M is for Measurable:** Making your request measurable ensures that what you're asking is clear so your follower knows precisely what you're expecting. Unless your follower is a mind reader, when you don't make what you want clear, the chances that your follower can provide what you want are slim. Explain clearly *what* you want, *why* you want it, *when* you want it and *how* or *how well* you want the job done (when that information isn't immediately obvious).

Your opening statements

Here are two examples that show the information you need to provide your follower with at the beginning of your performance discussion. The first example relates to a complex performance gap that may have several causes and several possible solutions and therefore includes a question that encourages the follower to explore possibilities and diagnose the problem. The second example relates to a more straightforward performance gap and so the leader states what is to happen as the goal.

Here's the first example:

- **Frame the discussion:** 'Bruce, I'd like to discuss your monthly sales report. Do you have some time now?'

- **Describe the current situation:** 'Your accuracy is fine, as with all of your other work. But your last three reports have been one to three days late and I'd like to discuss any problems you may be having with the report's timing.'

- **Explain why the performance gap matters:** 'I need your report on my desk on the first Wednesday of each month so that I can compile the analysis for all the regions and get the results to the sales manager by Thursday. When I don't receive your report, the entire process is delayed.'

- **State your goal:** 'You and I need to find out what's delaying you and fix the delay so that you can complete your report on time.'

- **Explore options:** 'What seems to be holding you up in preparing the report?'

- **Wait five seconds:** Now let your message to Bruce sink in and give him time to think.

In this next example, the problem is straightforward in that the solution is obvious, eliminating the need to explore options; the leader can offer an improvement suggestion as the goal.

- **Frame the discussion:** 'Sheila, I'd like to discuss this morning's meeting.'

- **Describe the current situation:** 'You cracked several jokes and made a lot of side comments, which held up the meeting.'

- **Explain why the performance gap matters:** 'I couldn't get through the agenda on time, and that annoyed me because I don't like my meetings to run over time.'

- **State your goal:** 'Sheila, from now on, please keep your comments relevant to the topic under discussion and save the jokes until after the meeting. Can I count on your cooperation?'

- **Wait five seconds:** Now allow time for your message to Sheila to sink in and for her to respond.

Drain any emotions

No matter how tactful you are, followers can feel under threat when you point out a performance shortfall and go into defensive mode. When that happens, a primitive part of the follower's brain, called the *limbic brain*, kicks in, preventing clear thinking and information processing.

Setting the scene carefully with your first few words can help prevent your follower from diving headlong into, but only slightly slipping into, the limbic brain. When you then switch to listening mode, the follower feels understood and valued and, as a result, can climb out of the limbic brain and into the more sophisticated *thinking brain*. Once the thinking brain is in action, you and your follower can get on with figuring out how to turn your follower's performance around. (Refer to Chapter 18 for more information on your limbic and thinking brains.)

Briefly recap what your follower says, particularly when defensiveness, resistance or emotions creep in. Summarise in your own words or repeat a couple of key words or a key phrase from what your follower has said and then pause to listen some more. This draws out your follower's thoughts and feelings, helps drain any defensiveness or other emotions and increases your ability to see the situation from your follower's point of view. (For more on how to listen, refer to Chapter 7.)

The high-wire man

I once attended a wonderful *Cirque du Soleil* performance and marvelled at the team work, the professionalism and the outstanding feats of performance I witnessed. As it happened, the show I attended was the premiere in Adelaide. Early in the first half, a man on a high wire danced and leaped around. Then he jumped into the air and attempted a somersault with a twist. He fell. He climbed back up the ladder, danced and leaped and attempted that somersault again. He fell for the second time. Back up he climbed and continued on with his act. The falls were plainly not part of his act and, although he recovered well from them and carried on like a true professional, he unmistakably had messed up.

As luck would have it, I was conducting a workshop on how to build staff performance for a client a few days later. I related the falls to the leaders attending and asked them how they would handle the inevitable discussion were they the leader of the high-wire performer. The leaders immediately switched into investigation mode to find the real issue so they could help fix the problem that caused the man to keep falling. They wanted to know whether he had done the somersault with twist successfully in practice sessions and in the dress rehearsal and they wondered whether he'd had enough training and practice or had perhaps been pushed too far too soon. They were clear that asking questions of the man and listening to his replies was the best approach. One leader suggested the possibility that the man may have received some bad news before going on stage that had affected his concentration.

The leaders wondered how the man was feeling about having fallen twice during his act and whether his leader needed to undertake some damage control to boost the man's self-confidence. They agreed that asking him what he needed to avoid the falls in the next performance was wise and asking him whether he needed any extra help, coaching or other support was helpful too. And they said they would explore whether continuing his act without the somersault and twist was a possible solution, at least until he was ready to resume that part of his act.

Now that's the spirit of a true-blue leadership performance discussion.

Stay on track

Let your follower speak without interruption. In other words, give your follower the opportunity to state a point of view and listen objectively to that point of view. This process is known as _due process_ and is an indispensable part of every performance discussion.

However, keeping control of the conversation is very important. Don't become involved in long, rambling explanations or, when a follower becomes aggressive or defensive, don't become defensive or aggressive in return. Keep recapping your follower's comments using objective words in a neutral tone of voice.

Don't argue; don't justify; don't defend yourself. When you know that a follower is wrong, put that aside for the moment. Keep listening and recapping what your follower is saying until you think you've drawn out all the information.

Don't follow red herrings or be deflected by other devices used to distract you from a performance shortfall. For example, when followers compare their situation with those of others — 'Well, Jane does that too and you don't come down on her like a tonne of bricks!' you could respond with answers such as these:

- ✔ 'Jane's situation is different. You and I are not discussing Jane's time-keeping, we're discussing your time-keeping.'
- ✔ 'That may be, but we're not discussing Jane right now. What we're discussing is ...'

Keep repeating your information about the current situation and your goal, which is to close the performance gap.

Similarly, when followers deny a performance shortfall and you're really sure that a problem gap exists, keep repeating your evidence and the fact that you expect the performance shortfall to be rectified.

When followers come up with excuses and more excuses — and you're sure they're just excuses rather than explanations — keep asking how the performance standard you need can be reached. When you're not sure whether you're being offered an excuse or a genuine explanation, ask the question: If you and I removed that excuse or reason, can the target then be met? When the answer is yes, you may have a valid reason for the performance shortfall and you need to fix it; when the answer is no, you may be facing an excuse, so keep looking for a genuine reason.

Searching for a solution

Once your follower accepts that a performance shortfall exists, you can get down to the real business of looking for the cause of the performance gap and figuring out how to close that gap. Your follower can probably suggest some reasons for the gap; when that is not the case, work through the five keys to analyse what is preventing the follower from meeting expectations. (Refer to the section 'Checking the five keys that unlock performance' earlier in this chapter.)

When you're exploring possible causes for a performance shortfall, make sure your follower knows you're on the same side. Sit next to your follower or at right angles to send a clear message that you're literally on the same side.

Encourage your follower to take the lead in finding and isolating the cause of the performance gap because your follower is more likely to identify causes and find solutions than you are. In these situations, the more you keep the energy coming from your follower, the more you keep the performance problem where it belongs — with your follower. Performance shortfalls belong to your followers and you're there merely to help your followers close their performance gaps.

Once you believe you have the cause of a performance gap, begin searching for a solution. Again, keep the energy with your follower by placing the responsibility for closing the gap with the follower. When you want to suggest solutions, do so, making clear that your solutions are suggestions only and that your follower must make the final decision. Make clear that you're willing to assist in any reasonable way and remember that you may need to fix any problems not under your follower's control which are causing or contributing to the substandard performance.

When you and your follower agree on the cause of a performance gap and how to close that gap, summarise the specific actions you and your follower plan to take and agree on a monitoring procedure. Always end the discussion on a positive note.

Following up

You guessed it — speaking to a follower about a performance shortfall isn't the end of the matter. After your performance improvement discussion, monitor your follower's performances so that you can either offer positive feedback or initiate a further discussion.

Followers remember criticism, but they respond best to praise. Criticism leads to defensiveness and resistance while praise leads to confidence and the desire to perform better.

Recognise improvements

Don't necessarily expect an overnight virtuoso performance, especially when the performance shortfall is large — your follower may need to build new skills or habits. Recognise every sign of improvement, even small ones.

Deal with failure to improve quickly. When the quiet-chat approach fails, the time has come to escalate your intervention. Hold another discussion, stressing that the performance gap must be closed. When you need to escalate further, continue stressing that the performance gap must be closed and set a reasonable date by which your follower needs to close the performance gap. Continue to offer any reasonable help you can.

When followers lose their edge

Sometimes followers who once did sterling work go off the boil. The reasons may be because they've done particular tasks for so long that they're now bored and the tasks are no longer challenging or even remotely interesting to them. Sometimes the reasons are that followers feel they're working hard with no or fewer results than they expect — inadequate tools and equipment or silly systems and procedures may be stopping them reaching the expected standards. Occasionally, followers experience events in their private lives that affect their work (for more on this subject, refer to Chapter 10).

When these situations exist, you can hold a discussion with your follower along these lines:

✔ **Acknowledge the change in performance:** 'Russell, you used to be one of my top performers. Lately, though, you seem to be having some problems.' (Be sure to provide Russell with an informative example to support your comment.)

✔ **Find any problems:** 'I'm wondering whether anything is the matter.' (Try to find information to explain why Russell's performance has changed.)

✔ **Look for solutions:** 'Russell, I really need you back to your best again. What can you and I do to get you back up there?' (Assure Russell that you're looking for solutions, rather than criticising his work performance.)

These discussion points follow the three stages of a performance discussion with your follower, described in the sections 'Giving helpful information', 'Gathering helpful information' and 'Searching for a solution' earlier in this chapter.

The ultimate sanction

When your gradual escalations don't work, the time may have come for the ultimate step — to leave the organisation. Make clear to your follower the need to choose one of two possible actions — to close the performance gap or to move on. The decision entirely belongs to your follower. Explain that you're willing to act as a resource and to help your follower. However, ultimately, your follower is responsible for his or her performance.

Before taking this step, be absolutely certain that nothing, other than your follower's own efforts, is preventing satisfactory performance. When that's the case, the time has come for the change–time–consequence message before further harm is done to your team or your team's results.

The change–time–consequence message works like this: If this *change* is not made by this *time*, the *consequence* is that . . .

Consequences may be loss of job, demotion, removal from the project or reassignment to other duties. The consequence must *not* be a punishment or threat designed to force your follower to resign. For example, a transfer to the Back o' Bourke or reducing your follower's working hours and therefore wages — neither of these consequences can change your follower's performance, so they are pointless.

Review your follower's measures of success and decide who is to collect what information about the performance, from where or from whom, and when. Then set a date to meet — either the date specified in your change–time–consequence message or at a halfway point that seems reasonable.

The rest is up to your follower. The decision to turn a performance around is the follower's decision and no-one else's decision. You can sleep knowing that you have done all you can (refer to Chapter 18 for more on leading your followers in the right direction).

Most organisations follow the 'three chances' practice. Warn your follower — three times — that when a particular change in performance or behaviour does not occur by a certain date, you have no choice but to ask the follower to leave.

Preserve your follower's dignity and self-respect by separating the person from the problem. Find ways for your follower to save face, even when you must part company. When a follower doesn't turn out to be right for your team, that doesn't mean that follower is a loser. Think of the follower and that particular job as a bad fit and realise that your follower can be a valuable asset to another organisation.

Chapter 20

When You Find Yourself in Deep Water

A strait is a passage or channel, and dire straits are a leader's rites of passage. Dire straits test your leadership dexterity and give you a chance to prove your mettle.

Entering a challenging channel signals the time to draw fully on the leadership muscles you strengthened, honed and toned (in Chapter 3) to see you through the dangerous waters and safely to the opposite bank. Once there, you can breathe a sigh of relief, thank your lucky stars and reflect on the experiences you gained.

Successful leaders aim to avoid dire straits and this chapter starts with some tried and true advice on how to do just that. Then you find out the first steps to take when the tide turns and you're forced to get yourself and your followers out of trouble.

In this chapter, I walk you through how to recover from poor decisions and other mistakes, how to deliver bad news and how to deal with crises. Finally, I consider what are perhaps the most painful dire straits of all — how to take bad news that's aimed at you.

> ✔ Explode and use language that would make pirates faint
>
> ✔ Swallow hard and bottle up your frustration

Natural though these options may be, they do nothing to change the situation. Channel your emotions into productive actions instead.

But forget a quick fix — quick solutions are seldom productive. The following sections offer ideas for charting your initial course when first confronted with a grim situation.

Keeping calm

In chimpanzee troupes, the leader sits at the centre, and every 30 seconds all the other chimps check him out. When he's feeling nervous or worried, they feel nervous and worried too. When he's feeling calm, collected and confident, that's how they feel. Human followers also take their cues from their leaders. In an emergency situation, human followers need you, their leader, to keep calm.

This is the time when your body and brain can let you down. The time when you need to think clearly is the time when your brain is most likely to freeze. To prevent your brain and thinking processes freezing, take three deep breaths. Inhaling oxygen calms your nerves and the oxygen moves to your thinking brain, helping you think clearly and rationally and keep your emotions in check (for more on this process, refer to Chapters 4, 18 and 19).

Listen to your subconscious

If you aren't too stressed, preoccupied or confused, your subconscious brain, which is active whether you're awake or asleep, can transmit ideas and insights to your conscious brain. Here are some ideas to help your brain do its job:

✔ Build your brainpower by building variety into your life.

✔ Create a structure and overview of your responsibilities with key result areas and measures of success (for more on how to do this, refer to Chapters 4 and 5).

✔ See problems and goals clearly.

✔ Set time aside for relaxing and vegging out.

✔ Write down ideas as soon as they occur to you.

Next, you can assess the situation logically:

- ✔ Gather the information and facts that you can.
- ✔ Check for information or facts that you may have missed. They may be staring you in the face but you're just not seeing them.
- ✔ Decide what other information and facts you need.
- ✔ Look at the situation from different angles, not just the way the situation first presents to you.
- ✔ Question your assumptions.
- ✔ When other people are involved, check that you're all working with the same information and towards the same results.
- ✔ Steady your nerves with the knowledge that the worst-case scenario that you may imagine rarely occurs.

Now is the time to draw on your networks, inside and outside the organisation. When appropriate, discuss the situation with people you know you can rely on for their discretion as well as for sound advice and useful perspectives, based on their experience and common sense.

Use the facts you gather to dispel any rumours, particularly within your team. When your followers are aware of or sense you're in a fix, give them as much information as you can without breaking confidences or leaking confidential information.

Managing your stress

Few situations are as stressful for a leader as thinking you're painted into a corner. This is when you're glad you took the time to figure out your own signs of stress and how to manage them. Managing stress as you navigate dire straits can help you think clearly in the short term and can keep you healthier in the long term.

Give the media a miss

If your dire straits are organisation wide and attract media attention, no matter how tempted you may be, how nice and honest looking the reporters seem or how innocent their questions or your comments may seem, never speak to the media. The only exception to this rule is when your organisation formally requests that you liaise with the media, when you're fully briefed on the situation and when you're trained in media relations.

Here are some stress busters for tight spots:

- ✔ **Do a brain dump.** Depending on how far you travelled through the dire strait, you can write down everything you know about the situation, what you want to happen, your options for dealing with the situation, your criteria for selecting a solution, a list of To Dos (people to speak to, information to find and so on). This takes your mind off the negatives and moves your attention on to constructive action, giving you a sense of control, which lifts your confidence. In case you feel overwhelmed by all you're writing — relax. You don't need to do every task at once. You can work your way through what needs to be done one step at a time.

- ✔ **Do something constructive with your pent-up energy.** When you don't have time to go to the gym, take a short walk or trot up and down a flight of stairs.

- ✔ **Do something enjoyable.** Take your mind off your woes on your day off and do something you really enjoy — play golf, take a bush walk with your family or go for a swim.

- ✔ **Listen to your self-talk.** The messages you're sending yourself about the situation can help you get out of it. Handling difficult situations well on the inside helps you handle them well on the outside. Recognise that the situation is probably not as dire as you believe and, even when it is very serious, worrying about a situation doesn't fix it. Trust yourself to deal with the situation as best you can.

- ✔ **Talk your difficulties through with someone.** Talking helps release some of the pressure you may be feeling. The someone you choose to talk to doesn't need to have solutions, just open ears.

Recovering from Poor Decisions and Other Mistakes

All leaders want to be perfect leaders but that's just not possible — everyone makes mistakes once in a while. Just see to it that your mistakes aren't through carelessness, through rushing because you aren't on top of your duties, through not checking facts or information or through any other easily avoidable causes.

Don't get angry with yourself (or anyone else) when you make a mistake or make a poor decision. Don't make your error bigger than it is — one mistake doesn't make you a poor leader or mean that your team is useless. And one mistake probably won't ruin your life for all eternity. Put errors in perspective but realise that when you do make a mistake or implement a poor decision, your credibility is almost certainly on the line. In that case, follow these four steps:

1. **Own up:** Don't pretend a mistake hasn't happened. Don't make excuses. Don't blame anyone else. Don't pass the buck. Don't try to put a positive spin on your mistake. Those actions sink your credibility even further. Own up and accept responsibility.

2. **Communicate:** Notify anyone who needs to know, who is affected or who is likely to hear about your mistake. Also, inform these people of how you plan to fix the situation or, failing that, ask for their input into how best to resolve the situation when you think they can assist you.

3. **Fix the mistake:** You have two choices — go back to square one and start over or salvage the situation by adjusting what you did to fix the problem your mistake has caused. If the situation is a total failure and can't be fixed, cut your losses and try another solution.

4. **Gain experience from your mistake:** Don't let the mistake make you averse to taking risks in the future. Treat your mistake as an instructive experience. Figure out what went wrong so you avoid that mistake in the future.

Brain tricks

Your brain can play havoc with your ability to deal effectively with difficult situations. Be especially careful to avoid the following brain tricks when you're in deep water:

✔ **Anchoring:** This locks you onto your first set of assumptions about a situation. You can counter the anchoring effect by making an effort to think laterally and to look for other ways to view a situation and find ways out of it.

✔ **Selective vision:** Selective vision causes people to see what they want to see or what they expect to see. You can counter selective vision by getting more information and seeking evidence and points of view that contradict your assumptions and beliefs.

✔ **Sticking with the status quo:** Desperate situations call for serious measures, so be prepared to cut your losses and step away from the status quo — the way something has always been done or the way something always is. Be prepared to try different solutions.

(For more information on brain tricks, or *heuristics*, refer to Chapter 11.)

The trick that can help you the most when you're in a predicament is the brain's ability to work while you're asleep. When you need help finding a solution to a sticky situation, set your brain to work as you fall asleep by thinking over the facts and other information you have and what, ideally, you want to happen. Then instruct your subconscious to work on that information while you sleep. Generally, your sleeping brain can supply you with solutions within three nights of 'sleeping on it'.

Taking action

When you find yourself in dire straits, you need to take action, but not just any action. Try these checks before you decide how to act:

✔ Check that you aren't burning any bridges.

✔ Check that you're keeping a few options open.

✔ Check your motives to see that you aren't acting out of fear or pride.

When your team makes a mistake, be sure to provide cover for your team members while they fix the mistake. Coach your followers through the problem and assist them to solve the problem and recover from their mistake. As you work through your options, guard against the blame game and against groupthink. When the mistake is behind you, congratulate yourselves on your recovery and be sure to find the value in what went wrong so you can prevent similar mistakes in the future.

Delivering Bad News

Delivering bad news is never easy and never pleasant, in part because you often feel badly for the recipients and in part because of the negative reactions you anticipate. Recipients of bad news can feel a range of emotions — shock, anger, blame, disbelief, disappointment or bewilderment. Even when you're not the cause of the sorry situation, prepare to receive the brunt of those emotions. (When you have any concerns at all for your own safety, make sure you're between the door and the recipient for a quick getaway in the highly unlikely case of a violent reaction.)

You need to be strong to deliver bad news, but don't let that make your delivery harsh, cold or calculating. Here are three steps to saying with compassion and grace what you'd probably rather not have to say.

1. **Think through the bad news first.** Mentally rehearse how to deliver the news. Anticipate questions. Avoid giving bad news on a Friday. Arrange to see your follower in private, organise seating and leave time to talk; delivering bad news quickly and leaving — 'hit and run' — is cowardly.

2. **Deliver the bad news calmly.** Don't dance around the subject or stretch out the news. Get straight to the point. Flag the bad news ('I'm sorry, but I have bad news'). Then give it — tactfully, respectfully and

politely. Aim to be clear and direct without being blunt. Use neutral or objective language but don't hedge, don't use euphemisms or try to put a positive spin on bad news. Your followers can see through spin and may resent the fact that you thought they were that stupid. Be as honest as you can; maybe the whole truth is not appropriate but what you do say must be true. Think about what the follower needs to hear.

3. **Listen to the responses.** When your follower expresses emotion or seems to be emotional, give them time. Show empathy and explain their responses as a natural reaction. Deal with emotions rather than ignoring them or telling your follower to calm down or control himself. ('I've upset you. This must be awful for you.') Use your E.A.R.S. to let the followers express their feelings and to show empathy. (For more on E.A.R.S., refer to Chapters 7 and 19.) Allow silences and even tears. Be prepared to match your follower's pace — don't rush the discussion to end your own discomfort.

When you have to deliver bad news and your follower blames you or argues with you, don't be drawn into defending your decision or the message because that makes you sound unsure and weakens your position. Similarly, don't be drawn into an argument — rise above it. People make out-of-character comments and say words in the heat of the moment that they later regret. Try these strategies:

✔ **Summarise the news.** When your follower has responded, review the situation. Because of the emotions involved, people receiving bad news often don't retain everything that's been discussed, so go over the most important points.

✔ **Plan the next steps.** Talk about what steps your follower may be able to take. Help your follower to develop a strategy when appropriate. When you can, offer other help, for example, offering counselling provided by of the organisation.

Smart mistakes and foolish mistakes

Failure is part of success. Mistakes are part of growing and becoming better at what you do. Mistakes come in two varieties — smart mistakes and foolish mistakes. When you're smart about a mistake, you find out valuable information — smart mistakes have potential.

Foolish mistakes, on the other hand, are those where you fail to find out valuable information and, as a result, you keep repeating the same mistake, even though the mistake doesn't help you add value, improve a situation or get the results you're after.

When people are out to get you

Sometimes, other people in an organisation can set you up as a target. You may be in the way of their ambitions, they may need to put others down in order to build themselves up, or they may simply enjoy watching you squirm. Keep calm, assess the situation objectively and counter their efforts.

Rule number one is: Don't take attacks, snide comments, or obstructive actions personally (that's also rule numbers two, three, four and five). Even when the attacks are personal, not rising to the bait gives you power, takes away your opponents' satisfaction and helps defuse potential conflict.

Don't ever think about getting even — and when you're tempted to get even, refer to the details of the mirror test in Chapter 3.

Not taking the matter personally and not stooping to settling the score doesn't mean that you allow people to belittle you or to take advantage of you. You still deserve to be treated with respect. Aim to draw respect from your other colleagues, your own leader — possibly your attackers — through your personal demeanour rather than giving in to hand-to-hand combat.

When the bad news is out of the blue, follow the three steps I gave you — think through the message, deliver the message and then listen. In other bad news situations, you can reverse steps 2 and 3. For example:

✔ When the bad news takes the form of a poor performance review, you can ask questions and listen first to your follower's thoughts — 'How do you think you went this last period?' Your follower may pre-empt the bad news for you; when the opposite occurs — when the follower genuinely seems to have no inkling of what you're about to say, at least forewarned is forearmed.

✔ When you're about to confirm a rumoured closure or takeover, find out your followers' expectations or how much they know or suspect. That helps you fill in the blanks and provide the right amount and type of information.

Sit at right angles when you're delivering bad news to a follower. When you're delivering bad news to a group of followers, sit facing the group at the same level. This is not a time to be towering above your followers.

Dealing with a Crisis

An accident in your department, a natural disaster such as a fire or flood, a disruption to services that puts a halt to operations, the loss of a key follower due to illness or resignation or, less serious, defective equipment or delayed or inaccurate information — these situations are examples of the unforeseen difficulties leaders contend with every day.

Take some comfort in the knowledge that the crisis doesn't mean the world is coming to an end or that a situation is so bad you and your team can never recover. Stay calm, rally the troops when appropriate, and assess the situation to decide what you need to do — right now — to minimise the fallout and get on the road to recovery. For example, when a project is in danger of missing its deadline, maybe you can bring in someone to help with the workload or eliminate some of the non-essential tasks in order to get the project back on track.

When you're the piggie in the middle

Leaders are sometimes caught between the conflicting expectations of their followers and their own leaders. When you're in a similar dilemma and must announce a decision or a new policy that you expect to be unpopular with your followers, here's what to do:

✔ Find out your leader's reasoning, what lies behind what you're being asked to do, and what other alternatives were explored so that you can communicate the rationale to your followers.

✔ Don't describe your leader's idea as dumb or useless or say you think your leader has lost the plot. This makes you sound weak and powerless and can cost you the respect and confidence of your followers. You don't have to pretend to like your leader's instruction or the new policy or decision, but you do have to support your leader as you expect your followers to support you.

✔ Present the information neutrally, without making it sound either better or worse than it is.

✔ Explain how your followers are affected and avoid giving false hope by being as realistic as you can be.

✔ Remind followers who are difficult that you don't have the authority to alter the situation or remind them that the board of directors made the decision. (This is different from saying 'I'm just following orders'.)

✔ Acknowledge and hear out your follower's feelings and concerns but don't allow their protests or complaints to become prolonged.

✔ Explain what you or the organisation need or expect from your followers now.

✔ Listen to any suggestions for a different approach your followers offer and discuss these suggestions with your leader when you feel they have merit.

Avoiding Dire Straits

Some dire straits appear out of nowhere, but most don't just appear like that. Many surface gradually through poor planning, failure to recognise and act on looming problems and failure to heed warnings from your subconscious or from other people.

Here are my top ten no-brainers for staying out of trouble:

- ✔ Anticipate problems, try to prevent them and have sound contingency plans just in case.

- ✔ Do right by everyone and benefit from the boomerang principle as they do right by you.

- ✔ Don't get bogged down in detail and other non-leadership activities you can delegate to others.

- ✔ Don't make promises you can't or don't intend to keep.

- ✔ Find ways to say 'Yes', help people save face and avoid winning at someone else's expense.

- ✔ Keep good records. How often do you refer back to simple things like telephone conversations, asking yourself, 'Now, when did I say I'd get back to her with an answer?' or 'What did I agree to send him?'. Good records, in the form of confirmatory memos and emails, also protect your back.

- ✔ Keep *kaizenning*, or looking for ways to do a task better, easier, faster or cheaper (for more on *kaizen*, refer to Chapter 5).

- ✔ Manage your time well and concentrate on your priorities so you aren't forced to do a job a second time because you didn't have the time to do the job right the first time.

- ✔ Plan properly and always check your plans with your doom-and-gloom specs to spot weak areas and where your best-laid plans may go wrong.

- ✔ Stay on top by monitoring results and looking for trends.

Putting First Things First

As a leader, expect situations that sometimes frustrate you, confound you and even make you angry. Your first inclination may be to

- ✔ Bury your head in the sand and hope the problems go away
- ✔ Complain to anyone who cares to listen

When you disagree with a request or decision

Your leader may occasionally ask you to take an action with which you disagree or to announce a decision you consider a mistake. When that happens, follow this advice in this order:

✔ Double check that you understand the request correctly.

✔ Ask a few questions (in a non-challenging way) to find out more about what may lie behind the request or decision.

✔ Look for areas where you agree and highlight them.

✔ Explain your reservations about the other areas.

✔ Offer an alternative or ask if you may suggest an alternative or two in the next few days.

When the decision remains unchanged — and you can't argue that it's unethical or contrary to the organisation's values and vision — then accept the decision. Your leader probably has access to information that you don't have.

Don't go over your leader's head to his or her leader unless you're prepared to face the consequences — a ruptured relationship with your leader.

With your initial action — or *interim action* — in place to bring the situation under control, at least temporarily, you can then draw breath and analyse the situation with the following questions:

✔ What actually happened?

✔ How many people — and who — are affected and how are they affected?

✔ What else — after your interim action — can you do to rectify the situation or reduce its seriousness?

When other people are involved, tell them what's going on and what your recovery plan is. When the crisis is your fault, a sincere apology is generally a smart move.

Do what needs to be done and when you have time to catch your breath, figure out what caused the crisis in the first place, not so that you can lay blame but so that you can avoid similar crises in the future.

Receiving Bad News

Over your years of leadership, you're bound to be on the receiving end of bad news occasionally. Perhaps the news is about redundancy, perhaps your department is to be closed or your organisation taken over by another organisation with its own leaders. Whatever the bad news is, remember that giving you bad news is often difficult for the other person. You can help them by staying calm, not becoming defensive or argumentative and hearing them out. Breathe deeply as you're listening to ward off fear or anger and stay in your thinking brain, where you can listen properly and decide whether you need any further information at this point.

Sometimes your leader, or other leaders, or someone in your network that you respect — a mentor or even a follower or a delegation of your followers — may have some feedback for you that you may be wise to listen carefully to and take on board to improve your performance and increase your effectiveness. When that happens:

- **Listen.** Don't brush the feedback aside, deny its truth, defend or excuse yourself or blame others.

- **Check you understand clearly.** Recap the feedback in your own words and ask questions to clarify the message when you need clarification.

- **Concentrate on the future.** Listen to find out what you need to do to improve your performance. If you want to, ask the person offering you the feedback for suggestions — you don't have to accept the feedback if you don't want it.

- **Thank the person for their feedback.**

When the person delivering the message offers you criticism rather than feedback, here's what to do:

- **Put your shields up.** As you listen to the criticism, picture a protective shield surrounding you and filtering out any negative or hurtful emotions and allowing only the facts through. This filter helps you respond to the useful information and not get caught up in the emotions.

- **Mentally examine your critic's intentions.** This helps you decide how to deal with the information. Criticism may be aimed to help you or to hurt you, or perhaps the other person just needs to let off steam.

- **Be a detective.** Ask for clarification and examples when you're unsure about what your critic is saying. Make clear that you're not being defensive but genuinely seeking more information. For example: 'When you said the report was incomplete, what can I add to make it more complete?' Or 'When you said X, could you give me an example so I can be sure I understand what you're saying?'

- **Don't make excuses.** Replace the 'Yes, but . . .' with 'I agree and . . .'. When appropriate, accept responsibility.

- **Focus on the future.** Find out what you can do to improve your performance. This strategy helps your critic to become a coach.

- **Say, 'You're right'.** It's easier than saying 'I'm wrong'.

Part VI
The Part of Tens

Glenn Lumsden

'I've been studying the wisdom of great leaders and I've concluded that this looks like a job for ... Captain Ultra-Guy!'

In this part . . .

Here are two short chapters, packed with quick ideas about leadership and which you can read any time you have a few spare minutes. The facts in these chapters make a great way to psych yourself for a presentation or a meeting. Read these tips to adjust your attitude and re-energise yourself whenever you're not too excited about a job you're about to start. And use the Part of Tens to quickly brush up on your leadership skills when you need a refresher.

Chapter 21

Ten Characteristics of a True Leader

*I*n this chapter I want to make one point clear straight away — when I talk about a leader's characteristics, I don't want to imply that these are in-born traits and that, therefore, leaders are born, not made. Each of the ten characteristics I discuss in this penultimate chapter can be developed and perfected.

I list here the ten traits that true leaders have in common. The only questionable trait is that of leading a balanced life. Occasionally, you find leaders who work long hours to transform organisations at a cost to the rest of their lives. These people are the extreme exceptions, not the rule. And, unless you want to give up your valuable personal life, you probably don't want to emulate them.

To perfect leadership characteristics in yourself, get to know other true leaders. Watch how they behave and try out these behaviours yourself. Concentrate first on your self-mastery skills to strengthen the consistency of leadership that keeps your attention on developing and perfecting your other leadership qualities.

Mastering Yourself

Failure to understand yourself, value yourself and stay in control of yourself — in short, failing to master yourself — is the most common source of leadership failure. The package of values and beliefs about yourself, others and your world that makes you the person you are and guides your thoughts, actions and decisions is critical to your ability to lead well. This package guides you and drives you to do what you do, to interpret information in certain ways (and to miss some information entirely) and to tackle chores, duties and situations with gusto and pleasure or with indifference and lethargy. (Refer to Chapter 3 for more information on self-mastery.)

True leaders do what's necessary and sensible without needing to be urged to do so by someone else. True leaders are directed from the inside, not from the outside. Self-mastery gives true leaders control over their emotions and actions, not to repress them but to wisely choose when to act or not to act and when to act later at a more appropriate time. Self-respect leads to self-mastery and when you have both firmly under your belt, you have true power.

Staying Positive

Here's a saying relevant to staying positive: Some people bring joy *where*-ever they go and other people bring joy *when*-ever they go. The same can be said of leaders. One characteristic that is guaranteed to make people glad to see you is a positive, can-do approach (and one characteristic guaranteed to make people glad to see your back is a glum, negative, everything-is-a-pain approach). Research has shown that people with a positive approach are happier, healthier and live up to 20 per cent longer than gloomy people (for most of us, that's more than ten years).

A positive approach is energising and refreshing. A positive approach attracts people to you and your optimism rubs off on them.

A positive approach isn't just about cheeriness and smiles, though. Optimism is also about a can-do attitude. True leaders don't explain why they can't do a task or why a task is difficult to do. They emphasise what you can do and create solutions and possibilities. A positive approach is about finding your way over and around obstacles and figuring out how to add value and make a difference.

Optimism breeds confidence, faith in your abilities and the willingness to keep working toward a goal or at a job until you succeed. Optimism keeps you going even when you stumble.

Here are some ways to boost your positivism quotient:

- Congratulate yourself when you succeed at a task or achieve a goal.
- Don't blame yourself for failures and mistakes. Take responsibility for them, fix them and remember what not to do next time. Then move on.
- Don't let problems in one area of your life influence other areas of your life.
- Recognise that setbacks are usually temporary.

Staying Motivated

Asking your followers to walk with a spring in their steps is difficult when you don't have a spring in your own step. Whether undertaking a task they dislike, beginning a difficult conversation or even getting out of bed on a Monday morning after a fantastic but tiring weekend, true leaders know how to find the get up and go to ... well ... get up and go. Three qualities help leaders get going:

- Clear goals and the desire to reach them
- Commitment to put in an effort, even when the going is tough
- Self-confidence to take action

 Don't look to magic tonics or fairy godmothers to motivate you. Motivation comes from inside — you're the only person who can motivate yourself. Here's what to do when you have an attack of lethargy — look and act motivated (even if you know you're not feeling too motivated that day). Stand tall, hold your head high and smile to get your *endorphins* — the feel-good chemicals that swish around your body — to do their work for you. The mind–body link is so strong that the act of making yourself look and act motivated soon has you feeling motivated as well.

 Use *pull motivation*, not *push motivation*, to get you going. Pull motivation is when you act because you *want* to; pull motivation is like a magnet. Push motivation is based on fear or the desire to avoid an unpleasant task or situation; push motivation is never as strong as pull motivation.

Being Genuine

True leaders are genuine people. They identify and express their thoughts, feelings and needs openly, honestly, tactfully and considerately, seldom dramatically; true leaders don't turn up with hidden agendas. True leaders are willing to say 'I don't know' and to admit to mistakes so they can correct them.

True leaders have no *facade* — outer masks or false fronts that hide who they really are or pretend to be something they're not. To use that common leadership catchphrase, true leaders 'walk their talk' and others intuitively sense that what they see in the true leader is what they get. The primary motivation of true leaders isn't pleasing others but doing what is right in a particular situation.

This authenticity builds the true leader's reputations as reliable, straightforward leaders that followers want to follow. It also attracts people who appreciate true leaders for what they are (and are not). Even when people don't like what these leaders say, they respect their opinions and are prepared to support and help them.

The authenticity of true leaders is based on a strong understanding of themselves (for more on this topic, refer to Chapters 3 and 4). True leaders take a good look in 'the mirror' (refer to Chapter 19 for more on the mirror of projection) and understand their own quirks, motives and characteristics.

Being Dependable

No-one wants to sit on a chair with weak, wobbly legs. No-one wants a watch that doesn't tell the time, even when it's a beautiful timepiece. And no-one wants to work with people who aren't dependable. Dependability and reliability are essential features of a leader's reputation. These qualities show respect for others, as well as for yourself. Being dependable makes you trustworthy; people know they can count on you because you're not just hot air and empty promises.

True leaders follow up and follow through. True leaders do what they say they intend to do, when they say they intend to do it. When you say you're going to do a task or make a change, you may not be able to do so straight away. But you can do the following:

- ✔ Figure out what your next step to deliver on your promise is to be.
- ✔ Mark your next step in your diary or put it on your To Do list.

Dependability also means returning calls and responding to emails promptly (48 hours is my own outside limit). Dependability is about punctuality and doing what needs to be done without being asked to do it. But dependability isn't just about doing tasks. Dependability is also about being available when you're needed, stepping up, rising to challenges and helping others.

You can't finish what you start when you're over-committed, so a true leader's dependability is built on a foundation of good self-management and time management (for more on these skills, refer to Chapters 4 and 6).

Learning from Your Mistakes

How many mistakes do you reckon you make before you become proficient at tasks you're now good at completing? To succeed at any job, you need to make a lot of mistakes in the run-up stages. Everyone makes mistakes, even true leaders. The only choice you have is whether or not to turn your mistakes into smart mistakes and gain wisdom from them.

When you're smart, mistakes can become opportunities. Mistakes provide information about what's working and what isn't. (Refer to Chapters 4 and 20 for more on handling mistakes and gaining wisdom from them.)

Mistakes are not to be scoffed at. Here are some popular products that are the consequences of people's mistakes:

- ✔ Friction matches
- ✔ Potato chips
- ✔ Roulette
- ✔ Scotch tape
- ✔ Telescopes
- ✔ X-rays

Communicating Generously and Effectively

Leaders spend an incredible 75 to 90 per cent of their time communicating — speaking, writing, listening and reading. Paradoxically, poor communication is the cause of the majority of organisational ills and below-par team work. Leaders' days are so hectic that taking communication shortcuts can be tempting and sitting down for a quiet chat with a follower or another leader can seem like a luxury.

True leaders are generous communicators. True leaders keep others informed and are generous listeners, too, seeking out and taking on board the ideas and opinions of others. True leaders keep up a continuous flow of communication with their followers and their own leaders, sharing their thoughts and ideas. True leaders nurture helpful and supportive networks inside and outside an organisation.

Whether writing or speaking, successful leaders express themselves tactfully, articulately and clearly. They explain their reasons and priorities and help people understand their instructions and requests. (Refer to Chapter 7 for more information on how to communicate like a leader.) First-rate communications skills are the hallmark of true leaders.

Balancing Your Life

Leadership is a time-consuming vocation and the temptation to work, work, work is great. Striking a balance between leading and the rest of your life isn't easy. Sometimes one of your personal hats conflicts with a leadership hat (refer to Chapter 2 for more on the different types of hats leaders wear). For example, your parent hat may need you at a child's school concert when your negotiator hat requires you to be interstate, or your spokesperson hat calls on you to work late to meet a critical deadline, eating into the concert you want to attend. Or your partner hat may need you at home to celebrate an important anniversary or milestone when your connector hat takes you to an important conference where you're speaking on behalf of your organisation.

While true leaders are willing to work hard and put in the hours, they also realise that no law exists that says they must be available at all times, rain or shine, in sickness and in health. Think about working from home once in a while. Most leaders find they get more done without the endless interruptions, which lightens their workloads (and their stress loads) and increases the time they have available to wear their personal hats. For example, you can work from home while looking after a sick child or an elderly parent or while working on a report or special project.

Here are a few other ideas to help you round out your life and balance your personal demands with your leadership demands:

- ✔ Combine your personal and work To Do lists.

- ✔ Ensure that when you're leading, you're leading; when you're at home, you're at home.

- ✔ Don't drag work back and forth; only take work home when you actually intend to do it.

- ✔ Know which of your personal hats are the most important to you and set yourself clear goals for each one. Work as hard towards reaching your personal goals as you work towards reaching your leadership goals.

- ✔ Fill your team with winners, the most talented people you can find, to take some of the pressure off and help you have a life beyond work.

- ✔ Help your followers to achieve work–life balance for themselves. Skill shortages are biting ever more sharply and quality followers are becoming ever more scarce. When your followers can't find work–life balance, your best followers are likely to vote with their feet and move to organisations and leaders offering sensible and flexible hours and other life-friendly policies.

Being Prepared

Leaders don't just hop into situations — they think through the situations first. Whether communicating, solving a problem or reaching a decision, true leaders think about their actions and words from the perspectives of others and from their organisation's perspective, looking for down-the-line fall-out and up-the-line implications. True leaders consider longer-term ramifications, too. This helps them choose their words and actions wisely and anticipate and be ready for questions and possible reactions.

True leaders prepare for whatever they tackle. When making a speech, true leaders practise like mad. When they have a meeting to lead, true leaders think through their opening comments and how to introduce each topic on the agenda. When they're visiting clients, true leaders find out or remind themselves of basic information about the clients' organisations and the clients, and think about what clients may need and want, as well as what needs to be said and how best to say it.

Getting Straight to the Heart of the Matter

Compare these two descriptions of a country scene:

> The sun is shining high in the sky and the clouds have fled temporarily, although there is a threatening and darkening sky in the distance.

> It's a fine day but rain is forecast for later so I'll bring an umbrella.

Which one do you think gets to the heart of the matter? Pretty obvious, isn't it?

All the best leaders I've worked with have a knack for cutting straight through to the core of an issue. They simplify without making issues simplistic. They pare down complex concerns to their main elements in a clear and insightful way. They turn the convoluted and complex into the succinct and concise and don't get caught up in peripherals or bogged down by minor details.

Real leaders can see an overall project and read which steps in a process are the critical steps to get right. True leaders invariably choose the KISS approach — keep it short and simple — when solving problems.

Chapter 22

Ten Ways to Be a Successful Leader

*L*eadership is about action, not about having a fancy job title. People sometimes want to be a leader but are not willing to put in the hard work. To be a successful leader, you need to want to do what a leader does, a lot of which is difficult and challenging and most of which needs skills that are developed only with effort and practice.

I've worked with hundreds of leaders, many of them truly excellent. Here are the ten behaviours that the best leaders use and that I consider key ingredients of their successes.

Successful Leaders Use Time Wisely

Leaders work hard, but in bits and pieces. Recent research indicates that most leaders have less than five minutes between interruptions and need to get their work done in the intermissions between those interruptions. It's incredible they ever get any work done!

The only way successful leaders can achieve their goals is to know what their key result areas (KRAs) are and to concentrate on them. KRAs tell you what your high priority activities are. They tell you when to say yes and when to say no. They tell you where to concentrate your energies and efforts — between all the interruptions.

Match the way you use your time to your key priorities and attend to activities that add value to your job or to your project or the organisation. Otherwise, you end up working hard but achieving little.

Successful Leaders Give Feedback

Successful leaders help their followers reach their full potential. Successful leaders correctly identify and make the most of their followers' strengths and are coaches and mentors, spending a considerable portion of their time developing the next generation of leaders. This passing on of leadership skills is, perhaps, the most important legacy of a true leader.

Successful leaders also listen. They ask a lot of questions and listen to the answers. They listen with their eyes and hearts as well as their ears, so they understand what's said and what's being left unsaid. Their sensitivity to *vibes* — the feelings of their followers or the tone in the workplace — keeps successful leaders a step or two ahead of the others.

Successful leaders cultivate followers, peers and more senior leaders to give them ongoing advice and feedback. They ask questions to make sure they understand, thank the person offering the feedback, think about feedback and act on feedback when they feel doing so is in their and their followers' best interests.

Successful Leaders Stay True to Themselves

Successful leaders have their own leaderships styles based on the needs of their followers, their organisations and their own core values. Successful leaders aren't copies of their own leaders or leaders in the media and they don't imitate what they think the ideal leader is. (Ideal leaders don't exist — just the right leaders in the right situations at the right times.)

If you don't know what your core values are, refer to Chapter 3 to find out. Knowing your core values and honouring them are the way leaders stay true to themselves and lead in ways that are comfortable for them. When you know what you stand for, you won't fall for the most expedient course of action — you can lead with integrity.

Successful Leaders Deal Gracefully with Change

The rate of change in today's society doesn't appear to be slowing down — if anything, the rate of change may be speeding up. That means that organisations in which you're a leader, the people you lead and the requirements of leadership keep changing too.

The successful leaders I know stay on top of the game and are often one step ahead. They keep up to date and abreast of trends, which means they can often predict what's coming. They find out what their followers and other influential people in their organisations are thinking, too, which helps them adapt to different situations. They keep learning — about leadership, about the fields they lead in, about technology and about new ways of tackling tasks. They know what's happening in other organisations and what is considered best practice and figure out how to apply those methods in their own teams.

Standing still in leadership doesn't exist — when you're not progressing, you're going backward.

Successful Leaders Surround Themselves with Winners

Leaders thrive when surrounded by the best people. Leaders are not afraid of strong followers who can eventually take their places because true leaders know that strong followers support them in achieving their goals and free up their time to concentrate on leading.

Successful leaders invite high-calibre followers to join their teams. They train them well and support their efforts. They generate enthusiasm and work to grow their teams into high-performing masterpieces.

Successful Leaders Know that Leadership Isn't a Popularity Contest

Successful leaders are respected and admired. They're often liked, too, but not because they're soft. Quite the opposite.

By setting challenging goals and expecting the best from their followers, successful leaders bring out the best qualities in their followers. They support their followers and encourage them to achieve goals that the followers hadn't realised they were capable of achieving.

 Successful leaders genuinely care about their followers but they expect them to live up to their high standards. In families this expectation is called *tough love*. Successful leaders don't flinch from the hard messages they sometimes need to give to help followers perform better and they don't flinch from holding their followers accountable for deliverables and meeting their goals. They don't select the most expedient or easiest courses of action but the ones that achieve their desired outcomes. That's what earns true leaders admiration, respect and loyalty — not indulgence or leniency.

Successful Leaders Love What They Do

The more satisfaction you get from what you do, the better you're able to do the job. Add enjoyment to satisfaction and you really begin to fire. The buzz, the thrill, the charge — Yessssss! Not every day is full of thrills but enough days are to keep successful leaders pumped and loving the leadership role.

 You need to have a burning desire to lead well. But successful leaders go one step further — they get a huge kick from leading. Not from the power, the glory, the status or the title, but from nurturing their followers' performances and watching their followers and their teams blossom. True leaders love everything that strong leadership entails (okay, well, most of what leadership entails).

Successful leaders delight in developing and living visions and team purposes; in working with their followers to make meaningful contributions to their *internal customers* (people inside their organisations who depend on their work); and in looking after their *external customers* (the recipients of their work outside the organisation). True leaders get a warm glow when they stand back and observe their followers getting on with their jobs and achieving results.

The moral here is to stick with what you do best: Runners run. Singers sing. Leaders lead.

Successful Leaders Take Responsibility

Imagine you're at home after a hard day's leading. You have a glass of something cold in your hand and you're putting your feet up. Two children are in the kitchen and you hear a splat. 'What's happened?' you ask.

'Nothing!' (That's *denial*.)

'Don't tell me "nothing" — I heard something drop,' you say.

One of the children responds: 'She pushed me!' (That's *blame*.)

'I still want to know what happened,' you call.

'Well, the milk carton was wet and slipped from my hand.' (That's an *excuse*.)

Instead of denial, blame or excuses, you may prefer to hear, 'I dropped the milk carton and I'm just going to get the mop to clean it up.' (That's called *taking responsibility*.) I know — pigs might fly too — but your kids aren't leaders yet, although you can't start training them too early with tough love. (Refer to the section 'Successful Leaders Know that Leadership Isn't a Popularity Contest' earlier in this chapter).

My point is this: Successful leaders don't deny problems, blame others for them or make excuses for them. They accept responsibility and do what needs to be done — to fix problems, to achieve goals, to honour their commitments. They don't stand back and wait for their goals to be achieved through earnest wishing but no action. They don't wait for their skills to blossom unaided. They don't wait for others to develop good working relationships with them. They start the ball rolling and get the job done.

Successful Leaders Keep Searching for Better Ways to Work

Successful leaders expect the best and make situations, procedures and other ways of working better — all the time, over and over again. They pay attention to what's happening around them and are always looking for ways to improve work practices — to make jobs easier, faster or more economical. They're always looking for ways to streamline processes and add more value (refer to the information about the *kaizen* mindset in Chapter 5 if you want to find out more about searching for better ways to work).

The *kaizen* mindset keeps true leaders involved and prevents burnout because that mindset motivates true leaders to innovate and improve situations. No leader (and no team or individual follower, for that matter) can afford not to be in a permanent *kaizen* state of mind.

Successful Leaders Stay on Top of Stress

Pressure and stress are part of leadership. Successful leaders recognise their own signs of stress and manage them appropriately so they can act in ways consistent with their own and their organisations' values.

Identify the types of events that create pressure for you and work out how you behave under pressure. Giving in to stress sets a bad example for your followers because they watch you closely in difficult patches and what you do has a profound impact on them and on the culture of your team. Think about the signals your behaviour sends to your followers and whether those signals are sufficiently helpful.

Before you respond to a stressful situation, take a few deep breaths. Identify what's causing your reactions and feelings and direct your energy to constructive thoughts and actions. Establish one or two clear goals and support yourself with positive self-talk (refer to Chapter 3 for more on self-talk). Manage stress through exercise, meditation or whatever techniques appeal to you and support yourself with healthy food. That way, you can maintain your leadership integrity and professionalism, even in the most challenging situations.

Index

• M •

• T •

Notes

Notes

FOR DUMMIES®

Business

Small Business FOR DUMMIES

1-74031-109-4
$39.95

Share Investing FOR DUMMIES

1-74031-146-9
$39.95

Investing in Real Estate FOR DUMMIES

0-73140-724-5
$39.95

Charting FOR DUMMIES

1-74031-124-8
$39.95

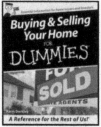

Buying & Selling Your Home FOR DUMMIES

1-74031-166-3
$39.95

MYOB Software FOR DUMMIES

1-7314-0541-2
$39.95

Sorting Out Your Finances FOR DUMMIES

0-7314-0746-6
$29.95

Superannuation FOR DUMMIES

0-73140-715-6
$39.95

Reference

Work / Life Balance FOR DUMMIES

0-73140-723-7
$34.95

Sustainable Living FOR DUMMIES

1-74031-157-4
$39.95

Wedding Planning FOR DUMMIES

0-73140-721-0
$34.95

Australia's Dangerous Creatures FOR DUMMIES

0-73140-722-9
$29.95

Technology

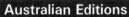

0-7314-0759-8
$39.95

1-74031-160-4
$39.95

1-7403-1159-0
$39.95

1-74031-123-X
$39.95

Cooking   Pets

1-74031-010-1
$39.95

1-74031-008-X
$39.95

1-74031-040-3
$39.95

1-74031-028-4
$39.95

Parenting   Health & Fitness

1-74031-103-5
$39.95

1-74031-042-X
$39.95

1-74031-143-4
$39.95

1-74031-140-X
$39.95

Health & Fitness Cont.

Football
1-74031-122-1
$39.95

Basketball
1-74031-135-3
$39.95

Asthma and Allergies
1-74031-054-3
$39.95

Fitness
1-74031-009-8
$39.95

Golf
1-74031-011-X
$39.95

Cricket
1-74031-173-6
$39.95

Aussie Rules
0-73140-595-1
$34.95

Sailing
1-74031-146-5
$39.95

Yoga
1-74031-059-4
$39.95

Pilates
1-74031-074-8
$39.95

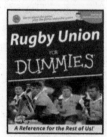

Rugby Union
1-74031-073-X
$39.95

Diabetes
1-74031-094-2
$39.95